RICHARD B. MORRIS is Gouverneur Morris Professor
of History Emeritus at Columbia University, editor
of *The Papers of John Jay*, and author of numerous
books on American history, including the prize-winning
The Peacemakers. He is also editor of the bestselling
Encyclopedia of American History. Professor Morris was
co-chairman, with James MacGregor Burns, of Project
'87, sponsored by the American Historical Association
and the American Political Science Association to
stimulate understanding of the Constitution.

WITNESSES
AT THE
CREATION
HAMILTON, MADISON,
JAY, AND
THE CONSTITUTION

Richard B. Morris

A MENTOR BOOK
NEW AMERICAN LIBRARY
NEW YORK
PUBLISHED IN CANADA BY
PENGUIN BOOKS CANADA LIMITED, MARKHAM, ONTARIO

Library of Congress Catalog Card Number: 88-62436

This is an authorized reprint of a hardcover edition published by
Henry Holt and Company, Inc. A Lou Reda Book. The hardcover
edition was distributed in Canada by Fitzhenry & Whiteside Limited.

Witnesses at the Creation is also available in a Plume edition
published by New American Library.

Design and drawings by A. Christopher Simon

ⓜ

MENTOR TRADEMARK REG. U.S. PAT. OFF. AND FOREIGN COUNTRIES
REGISTERED TRADEMARK—MARCA REGISTRADA
HECHO EN CHICAGO, U.S.A.

SIGNET, SIGNET CLASSIC, MENTOR, ONYX, PLUME, MERIDIAN
and NAL BOOKS are published *in the United States* by
NAL PENGUIN INC., 1633 Broadway, New York, New York 10019,
in Canada by Penguin Books Canada Limited,
2801 John Street, Markham, Ontario L34 1B4.

First Mentor Printing, January, 1989

1 2 3 4 5 6 7 8 9

PRINTED IN THE UNITED STATES OF AMERICA

To
Ellen Jay and Lloyd K. Garrison

Contents

THE
FEDERALIST:

A COLLECTION

OF

ESSAYS,

WRITTEN IN FAVOUR OF THE

NEW CONSTITUTION,

AS AGREED UPON BY THE FEDERAL CONVENTION,
SEPTEMBER 17, 1787.

IN TWO VOLUMES.

VOL. I.

NEW-YORK:

PRINTED AND SOLD BY J. AND A. M'LEAN,
No. 41, HANOVER-SQUARE.
M,DCC,LXXXVIII.

Title page of THE FEDERALIST, first edition, 1788.

BY WAY OF PREAMBLE

Alexander Hamilton

The American Constitution has functioned and endured longer than any other written constitution of the modern era. It imbues the nation with energy to act, at the same time restraining its agents from acting out of line. It safeguards our liberties and establishes a government of laws, not of men and women. It is a living, functioning reality touching every person's life, and the one surviving symbol of that exceptionalism that sets off America from other nations. Above all, the Constitution is the mortar that binds the fifty-state edifice under the concept of federalism, the unifying symbol of a nation composed of many millions of people claiming different national origins, races, and religions.

As drafted, the Constitution required that it be ratified by nine of the original thirteen states. But though it took a bare four months for the Framers of the Constitution to adopt it, nobody at the time was sure just how the people would respond. Because their proceedings had been secret, what the Framers agreed upon was not known until after its formal adoption on September 17, 1787. Then thousands of words poured from the presses, and many of them were hostile.

The focus of this story concerns the careers and contributions of three witnesses to the creation and ratification of the Constitution. Two of them were delegates to the Constitutional Convention; the third was Secretary for Foreign Affairs. All three determined that the instrument of government crafted in Philadelphia would, in James Madison's words, "decide forever the fate of republican government." All three feared that the foes of the Constitution would hold up its ratification or kill what might have been the last chance for the creation of a durable Union. Developing events revealed that this altogether new structure of government would, in the phrasing of John Quincy Adams, have to be "extorted" from "the grinding necessity of a reluctant nation." But if it was to be extorted, the feat was to be accomplished by reasoned argument.

What made these three statesmen join forces in New York City to plan and contribute a series of newspaper letters called *The Federalist*, aptly hailed by Joseph Story as "an incomparable commentary of three of the greatest statesmen of their age," and to this day considered the most profound collection of political essays written in this country? How the skillful interpretation of the Constitution by the trio of contributors, how their reasoned arguments for its necessary adoption, and how their reassurances to a bankrupt nation won friends for the Constitution in the great battles that lay ahead form the theme of this book.

When, on October 27, 1787, *The Federalist* first appeared—there were to be eighty-five letters in all—not a single state had ratified the Constitution and its outcome was in grave doubt.

The pseudonymous collaborators on *The Federalist*, writers who kept their authorship secret and only signed their letters "Publius," were Alexander Hamilton, James Madison, and John Jay, aged thirty-three, thirty-seven, and forty-two respectively. Out of a total of eighty-five letters, it is now accepted that Hamilton wrote fifty-one, Madison twenty-nine, and Jay five.

These three ranked among the principal nationalists in the country. No abbreviated sketches can capture the individual distinction of their minds, their contrasting personalities, their ambitions, or that sense of dedication to the national welfare which bound them together in this great literary undertaking.

Yet contemporaries could not be stopped from trying

to give thumbnail characterizations. The French chargé to Versailles wrote of Hamilton that he was "a great orator, intrepid in public debate, zealous and even extremist partisan of the Constitution and declared enemy of Governor George Clinton of New York." Hamilton, the Frenchman acutely observed, "is one of those rare men who has distinguished himself equally on the field of battle as at the bar, and owes everything to his talents," but, he cautioned, "he has a bit too much affectation and too little prudence." A minor figure at the Philadelphia Convention, William Pierce of Georgia, recognized that with Hamilton "there is no skimming over the surface of a subject. He must sink to the bottom to see what foundation it rests on."

Of James Madison, Pierce had this to say: "He blends together the profound politician and the scholar. In the management of every great creation, he took the lead in the Convention, and though he cannot be called an orator, he is a most agreeable, eloquent, and convincing speaker, a gentleman of great modesty, with a remarkable sweet temper."

And as for the senior member of the trio and the most prestigious at that time, John Jay, lawyer and diplomat, John Adams regarded him as more important in bringing about the adoption of the Constitution than "any of the rest, indeed of almost as much weight as all the rest. This gentleman," Adams insisted, "had as much influence in the preparatory measures in digesting the Constitution, and in obtaining its adoption, as any man in the nation."

All three writers were paper-hoarders, saving almost every scrap of their correspondence—even, in most cases, taking pains to make copies of their own letters and other writings. Indeed, it was John Jay, upon taking over the office of Secretary for Foreign Affairs, who realized as he wrote John Adams that "it is to papers in this office that historians must recur to accurate accounts" of the inside story of "the late Revolution," who brought system into the diplomatic files hitherto in extreme disarray. It is to James Madison most of all that we owe a careful, minute-by-minute accounting of what transpired at the Federal Convention. This meticulous obsession with paper-keeping did not prevent him in his old age from tinkering with his prose to soften aspersions applied to prominent individuals, or from tampering even with his own texts when earlier versions might later prove embarrassing. Alexander Hamilton, in turn, preserved his voluminous correspondence and legal papers substantially unaltered, and, as Secretary of the Treasury, kept careful and illuminating accounts of the finances of the federal government.

Yet, to this day, except for drafts of Jay's five *Federalist* letters, neither originals nor drafts of the eighty remaining letters have been seen save by their authors and the original printers. Whether Madison and Hamilton deliberately destroyed their drafts or copies because they wished to maintain anonymity and thus cloak their arguments in objectivity, or because they soon radically diverged in their interpretation of constitutional issues and as political archrivals would thereby have been embarrassed by the later appearance of these commentaries in their own handwriting, are speculative questions to this very day. All of Jay's were known to be extant in 1860, but Number 2 had disappeared by 1890, according to an editor of Jay's correspondence at that time. (The four remaining drafts are being published in this writer's forthcoming edition of "John Jay: Confederation and Union, 1784–1789; State Papers and Private Correspondence.")

Since the trio of witnesses all wrote their respective *Federalist* letters in New York City, they did not need to correspond with each other about the plan or composition of the letters; other personal correspondence between them during these months is devoid of clues.

To tell the story of the three "witnesses" and the events in their lives that helped shape their nationalist convictions and brought together three such diverse personalities to collaborate in championing the new Federal Constitution, the writer has examined the correspondence, notes, and memoranda of the principals, along with papers of their correspondents and their chief adversaries. Contemporary diaries, pamphlets, newspapers, broadsides, family recollections, and other relevant records have been submitted to scrutiny. Fortunately, all the significant Hamilton, Madison, and Jay papers for the years covered by our story have been edited and published or are in the course of publication. Many are so scrupulously detailed that direct conversations can be reconstructed covering the incidents they report. We can draw upon the journals of the Continental Congress, on which all three served with distinction, buttressed by the microfilm edition of its supplementary papers. We can find their respective roles in at least nine contemporary reports of the Federal Convention, including the best of them, prepared by James Madison himself, as well as a variety of reports and memoranda of the New York ratifying convention, a stenographic record of the Virginia ratifying convention, and the continuing publication of the multivolume *Documentary History of the Ratification of the Constitution*. Available as well are a respectable number of well-edited editions of *The Federalist*. The Antifederalist arguments have been collected in Herbert J. Storing's *The Complete Anti-Federalist*. In short, we have virtually all the facts, and they amount to high drama.

To paraphrase Arthur Koestler—but in a happier connection—the witnesses are gone, but the testimony still stands.

—RICHARD B. MORRIS
Columbia University
December 1984

1

The Plan Unfolds

The opening salvo was fired on October 27, 1787. The war of words was initiated by a combative youngish man in his early thirties, in height middling short, but somewhat stockier than the slender youth who had come to New York some fourteen years earlier to seek his fortune. Alexander Hamilton boasted a crop of reddish brown hair, violet blue eyes, an aquiline nose, and high coloring. He had managed to acquire the distinctive touch of a man-about-town, cocksure and debonair. Brilliant if impudent, a facile writer with a polemical style, Hamilton chose for his target none other than his state's governor, George Clinton.

On French leave from the Constitutional Convention in Philadelphia, Hamilton had taken on a formidable opponent. Known affectionately by his admirers as the "old Irishman," a tribute to his forebears, Clinton, both physically and politically, was a redoubtable personage. A massive figure of a man, he had served the state for a decade as its first and, until then, only governor. Now he had assumed the backstairs leadership of the state's Antifederalist forces opposed to creating a stronger central government, one with more effective powers than the one that was currently operative under the Articles of Confederation.

Hamilton, in an unsigned letter appearing in the New York *Daily Advertiser* on July 21, 1787, had let loose a string of accusations. He had accused Clinton of opposing the calling of the Constitutional Convention on the grounds that it was "calculated to impress the people with an idea of evils which do not exist."

George Clinton, New York's perennial governor and the state's foremost Antifederalist, by T. B. de Valdenuit (*Oneida Historical Society*).

Hamilton asserted that the government of the Confederation was fundamentally defective, a fact that everybody acknowledged. Hence, Clinton's efforts to turn public opinion against a document still in the course of being drafted in Philadelphia were, in Hamilton's words, "unwarrantable" and "culpable in any man," especially one in high office who was more attached "to his *own Power* than to the *Public good*."

Hamilton's literary assault on "His Excellency" touched off a running war of words with New York's powerful Antifederalist faction. Organized statewide by Clinton, its chief operatives were contemptuously denigrated by their opponents, the Federalists, as the "Custom House gang." They included General John Lamb, erstwhile radical leader of the Sons of Liberty on the eve of the American Revolution, his son-in-law Charles Tillinghast, and James Hughes, also an old

"Liberty Boy." Hamilton, no friend of mobs and mobbism, might have added that their numbers included even less savory riffraff.

If Clinton held his fire, his confederates took up his defense. The more immoderate members of the Clinton faction replied to Hamilton in kind. Men like Abraham Yates, Jr., exclaimed that "rather than adopt the Constitution I would risk a government of Jew, Turk, or Infidel." Such extremists, with their demagogic appeals, might well incite the less thoughtful body of the public to an irrational hostility toward that blueprint of government that thoughtful men had labored over in Philadelphia to achieve "a more perfect union." "A Republican" used the pages of the *New-York Journal* to "unmask the motives which prompted the attack on the governor." Adapting lines from an eighteenth-century English poet, Charles Churchill, in verse deemed applicable to the anonymous author, he declared:

> Fool reckons fool, and dunce awakens dunce,
> To Hamilton's too ready lies repair.

Obviously, even before Hamilton had signed his name to the new Constitution, his style gave him away, and he chose to flaunt his authorship of the original newspaper attack. In a newspaper letter of September 15, he defended his attribution to "the first Magistrate" (Governor Clinton) of such anti-Constitutional sentiments. If they are untrue, let him deny them, Hamilton challenged. Instead of assuming an overt role, Hamilton charged the governor with "improperly" using his influence "by undermining measures of a body, to which the general voice of the Union had delegated the important trust of concerting and proposing a plan for reforming the national constitution." Hamilton went further. Clinton's action was not only censurable, but should subject him "to impeachment."

Hamilton's imprudent acknowledgment of his authorship of the initial attack opened a floodgate of vitriolic personal attacks upon him. "Inspector," in the *Journal* of September 20, referred to Hamilton as "an upstart attorney" who was known to "palm himself upon a great and good man, for a youth of extraordinary genius, and under shadow of such patronage, make himself at once known and respected; but being sifted and bolted to the bran,[1] he was at length found to be a superficial, self-conceited coxcomb, and was, of course, turned off, and disregarded by his patron."

An enraged Hamilton cried foul. The denigration of his relationship with General Washington had touched a sensitive chord. Washington had indeed had a major impact on his young protégé's spectacular career. Hamilton's temporary break with the General a half-dozen years earlier was still an event he would like to forget. Quickly he dashed off an appeal to Washington to repudiate the charge that he had "palmed" himself upon the General and that "you *dismissed* me from the family." The round-trip correspondence took some two weeks. Washington, who on other occasions had had to cover up for Hamilton's rash behavior, sent back a cool reply. "I have no cause to believe that you took a single step to accomplish, or had the most distant idea of receiving an appointment in my family 'till you were invited thereto," the General replied. "And with respect to the second, that your quitting it was altogether the effect of your own choice," he added. Still, the General had no intention of being dragged into a personal feud between Clinton and Hamilton, for both of whom he expressed "the highest esteem and regard." He took occasion to caution his combative correspondent that the situation "calls loudly for unanimity," adding that he lamented that "Gentlemen of talent and character should disagree in their sentiment for promoting the public good."

Hamilton, a quick learner, got the message. It was clear that his literary polemics were converting a de-

---

[1] A process that separated the desired flour from the darkish, lumpy by-product, then considered less desirable.

bate over the merits of the new Constitution into a
personal fight, from which Hamilton might emerge
second best, while at the very same time he might well
be damaging the cause of the Constitution to which he
now claimed to be so ardently attached. For the time
being, and until New York ratified the Constitution,
Hamilton desisted in deference to Washington. Thereafter he would resume his feud with the governor.

Indeed, Hamilton never forgot and never forgave.
Neither did Clinton. Once the federal government was
established, Hamilton renewed his attacks. He accused
Clinton of secretly opposing the Union, charging him
with profiting personally from his long tenure in the
governorship. He poured vitriol on the image of Clinton as the "war-worn veteran," as "a Marius in courage, a Caesar in skill." To Hamilton, this was "mere
rant and romance." Writing a series of letters to the
press in March–April 1789 under the pseudonym
"H.B.," Hamilton excoriated Clinton's post-Revolu-
tionary career and denominated him "an enemy of the
AMERICAN UNION," one who condemned the new
Constitution even "before it was framed."

Clinton bided his time and took his revenge, even
though the opportunity did not arise until his adversary had been dead some seven years. As Vice-President
of the United States under James Madison, Clinton
broke the tie in the Senate and cast the deciding vote
in 1811 against renewing the charter of the First Bank
of the United States, Hamilton's pet project, the cen-
terpiece of his financial program as Secretary of the
Treasury, and an institution whose constitutionality he
had upheld in a brilliant opinion supporting a broad
construction of the Constitution. George Clinton had
the last word.

Happily, the Constitution would survive personal
feuds, but in the meantime it had to be ratified. Hamilton, recognizing Washington's letter as an implied
rebuke, changed his tune. Gone was the attribution of
improper motives to Antifederalist adversaries. In its
place he conceived the need to marshal all the arts of

advocacy that he had mastered as an attorney to persuade the voters by a scrupulously detailed exposition of the Constitution that its ratification was in the national interest as well as their own.

To this day, the planning and conversations that led to the co-authorship of *The Federalist* remain shrouded in mystery. One may surmise that the project was touched off by the publication, beginning on September 27, of a series of "Cato" letters, then attributed to Clinton but more probably the handiwork of one of his Antifederalist associates, in which the author promised to submit the Constitution to critical analysis, point by point. A response was exigent, and Hamilton was resourceful in seeking collaborators close at hand. Hamilton's home and law office next door were located at 57 and 58 Wall Street, some three blocks east of Broadway. John Jay, fearful of a recurrence of the two fires that had swept the lower part of New York City during the late war, had recently built for his growing family a stone dwelling with a metal roof standing foursquare on the corner of Broadway and the present Exchange Place (then named Verlettenbergh Hill). James Madison, in New York as a delegate from Virginia to the Continental Congress, was living nearby, at Mrs. Dorothy Elsworth's boardinghouse at 19 Maiden Lane. All three had over the years been in close consultation on crucial political, constitutional, and diplomatic issues. Hamilton, an old friend of both the Jays and the William Livingstons, Jay's in-laws, was a familiar figure at the Jay household. Madison and Hamilton had been allies in Congress in proposing nationalist measures, and had joined forces at the Annapolis Convention, the 1786 prelude to Philadelphia. Serving from time to time on the Congressional Committee on Foreign Affairs, Madison had, in the interest of his region, kept Jay under close surveillance, when the latter served in Madrid and Paris, and now in New York as Secretary for Foreign Affairs.

All three contributors to *The Federalist* shared a continental vision, but in appearance and temperament they were improbable partners. Jay, tall and spare, was eloquent in public address, but his words and actions usually evidenced lawyerlike caution. Inclined to be secretive, Jay, despite his widely recognized bump of self-esteem, was known as a man of probity. He towered a half-dozen inches over the dashing and combative Hamilton, and another inch or so more over the diminutive Madison. Of the three participants in the literary project, Madison, the introspective scholar, was perhaps the most reclusive, one who sedulously avoided confrontation and would choose others to advance his program. Madison's diffidence as a public speaker contrasted sharply with the eloquence of both Hamilton and Jay, and with his sprightly conversation within his own circle of intimates.

The systematic organization of *The Federalist*, and the extraordinarily rapid pace that its writers managed to maintain, suggest that its content and scope had been planned before the initial letter was written. Hamilton may have conceived of a less extensive series when he discussed plans with the McLeans, New York printers, to collect the newspaper letters in book form. *The Federalist* soon burst its original bounds, and Hamilton discovered after the first seventy-seven letters that the judiciary had been neglected, as well as the issue of trial by jury, and the absence in the Constitution of a bill of rights. Accordingly he sat down and wrote eight more letters, which he included in the two-volume edition that the McLeans published on May 28, 1788. The additional letters appeared in the New York newspapers in June and July of that year, a few while the New York ratifying convention was still sitting in Poughkeepsie, and the final two some days or even weeks after the New York ratifiers had concluded their deliberations.

Either a meeting of Hamilton, Jay, and Madison took place prior to Hamilton's departure for Albany in early October to attend the fall session of the State Supreme Court, or Hamilton must have consulted them individually but in quick succession around this time.

Madison would shortly leave on personal business for a fortnight's stay in Philadelphia, while Jay, thoroughly convinced of the critical importance of the plan, was prepared to do what he could for a start, but proved physically incapable of working for any length of time under sustained pressure. He had been suffering on and off from a debilitating illness, first diagnosed as tuberculosis and later as a painful attack of rheumatism, and was forced to confess that his vitality was fast ebbing. Still, with the clock ticking away, it is clear that he agreed to write four letters on the weakness of the Confederation and, when called upon, such others as his physical condition would permit, falling within his special sphere of competence. That illness explains the long pause between Jay's first four *Federalist* letters and the sixty-fourth, which did not appear until March 5, 1788.

Hamilton had made careful notes of Madison's penetrating observations at the Philadelphia Convention in June. Therein he depicted society as being divided into factions and interests, with debtor arrayed against creditor, party or faction further segmenting the public, and he advanced the necessity for a larger republic to protect minorities from oppression by the majority. Thus it was obvious that Madison could quickly enter the series with a treatment of a seminal topic that he had already prepared in draft form: his initial letter, the celebrated Number 10, first appearing in the press on November 22, 1787, after Madison's return to New York. It was to initiate a series of luminous contributions by Madison defining the bounds of federalism, asserting the need for a system of checks and balances, and the separation of powers.

It needed little of Hamilton's vaunted eloquence to persuade Jay and Madison to join him in this venture. In the first place, all three recognized that, to a people only slowly emerging from a deep depression, it would be essential to establish the prospect of a proposed union as being essential to a revival of prosperity. Second, it was necessary to demonstrate wherein the

Articles of Confederation had failed the nation. It was essential to disavow the repeated rumors of monarchical plots—the notion of importing one or another foreign prince to head the new government—and to show that the proposed Constitution was as consistent with true republican principles as had the separate states been under their own constitutions. At a time of depreciating paper money, moratory legislation, and even recent regional rebellion aimed at blocking the courts from enforcing the claims of creditors, the readers had to be reassured that the Constitution would provide security for both liberty *and* property.

Nor did Hamilton need to persuade men so well informed as Jay and Madison that the Constitution would fail to be adopted unless speedy affirmative action was taken in key states like Virginia and New York. All three were familiar with Washington's characterization of the country as limping along under the Articles of Confederation, "always moving upon crutches and tottering at every step." The three collaborators recognized their magnificent opportunity. Three of the best-informed political personages of the day could combine their experience, knowledge, and talents to disseminate the constructive argument that state attachments need not be sacrificed in the interests of a strengthened Union.

John Jay, who had for several years struggled to negotiate a treaty of commerce with Spain that the North favored and the South opposed, recognized the depth of sectional discontent. He had heard soundings of secession and even treason emanating from the Western country. From Jay's point of view, a Congress that had revealed its incapacity to rise above sectional differences and settle the outstanding issue with Spain over the free navigation of the Mississippi, a Congress that lacked the power to retaliate against British trade measures hurtful to so many branches of business and contributing to widespread unemployment, and a Congress that was too weak to prevent the Barbary pirates from seizing American ships and holding American seamen for ransom, was incapable of cementing the Union.

All three sensed the tension between North and South over the continuation of slavery and the slave trade—a tension reflected in the storm at the Philadelphia Convention when slavery and the slave trade were mentioned. Madison had failed to persuade the Convention to count all the slaves for purposes of representation, an idea repugnant to Northerners like Hamilton and Jay, who felt that Madison's proposal would have given the Southern states a big political advantage over the North, thus further fanning the flames of sectionalism.

Hamilton, pressed with a large law practice and unsure of how much time Madison and Jay could give to the project, was known to have attempted to recruit some others—for example, Gouverneur Morris, the stylist of the Constitution, who begged off, and James Duane, who obliged with a few letters, under the pseudonym of "Philo-Publius," which Hamilton felt were below the standards set for the series.

From the start of the project there was a consensus on some key points. First, they agreed to entitle the series *The Federalist*, a title that every one of the eighty-five letters carried. Thereby they stole a march on their opponents, who considered themselves the bona fide federalists and regarded Hamilton and his ilk as nationalists, centralists, or even monarchists.

It is apparent, too, that there was a consensus on the necessity of employing a single pseudonym for the whole series of letters. Quite probably Hamilton chose the pseudonym "Publius," the pen name he had used in 1778 when, as an army officer, he had blasted venal congressmen like Samuel Chase, the notorious war profiteer. For classicists like Jay and Madison, this pseudonym called to mind Publius Valerius Publicola, the great defender of the Roman Republic, a man extolled by Plutarch, with whom educated men of that day were almost as familiar as they were with the Bible. The three collaborators were steeped in the classics, in Cicero, Vergil, Horace, Suetonius, Seneca, and whatever else their earnest schoolmasters had made them parse. They were also steeped in John Locke, in Montesquieu, in English radical literature emanating from the days of Cromwell. They admired the great essayists Addison and Steele, and were knowledgeable about the enlightened Scottish philosophers, men like Hume and Robertson, as well as with international jurists of the stature of Grotius and Pufendorf. They were grounded in ancient history, thoroughly at home in European politics, and knowledgeable about European politicians, and could discourse learnedly upon the structure of confederacies and republics, both ancient and modern, their strengths and weaknesses, and their dissimilarities to the Union that was now being forged.

Any reader of *The Federalist*, especially Madison's thirty-eighth *Federalist* letter, would see how the writers professed to review every relevant case in ancient history. Therein Madison would show the difference between the lessons of classical history and those of the Philadelphia Convention, for in the former the basic laws were invariably drawn up by a single individual "of pre-eminent wisdom and approved integrity," whereas the Americans had improved on that experience by entrusting the task to an elected convention rather than to one man.

Standing in the forefront of the movement to scrap the Articles of Confederation and substitute a more centralized plan of government, the three authors of *The Federalist* could hardly have written under their own names without seriously detracting from the objective tone the letters sought to convey and that exhaustive analysis of the charter of government which they hoped to persuade the readers to assimilate.

Clearly, too, their acknowledged authorship would have raised serious doubts about the sincerity of their professions. Each of the three was known to have sought to secure a more centralized system than the Articles embraced. Considering the views they had professed in their earlier writings and in their speeches and actions at the Philadelphia Convention (although the records of the last would not then have been available for inspection), readers might have concluded that they were an illogical trio to essay the onerous task at hand.

Thomas Jefferson recognized *The Federalist* for what it really was—a superb work of advocacy. Writing to Madison from Paris in November 1788, he praised *The Federalist* as "the best commentary on the principles of government which ever was written," but, under the assumption that most of it was written by a single person, concluded that "in some parts it is discoverable that the author means only to say what may be best said in defense of opinions in which he did not concur."

Jefferson may have been thinking of Madison rather than Hamilton, but the latter was particularly fallible on the score of objectivity. Even though the sessions of the Convention were conducted under rules of the strictest secrecy, there were quite a few leaks. One could hardly expect otherwise when some of the delegates rotated between New York and Philadelphia, between City Hall, where they were in attendance at the Congress of the Confederation, and the State House, where they participated as delegates to the Constitutional Convention. It was bruited about that Hamilton, after weeks of relative silence, reacted forcefully to the proposals of New Jersey's delegates to substitute a modified version of the Articles of Confederation for the centralized Virginia Plan originally presented, which was to be the basis for the final draft. On June 18 he held the floor for a six-hour speech at the Convention in which he confessed that he wanted a higher tone in the Constitution if he could get it—a life presidency and a life Senate. If he sounded like an advocate of an elective monarchy, Hamilton's association with monarchy did not bother him, since he confessed to unalloyed admiration for the British Constitution and doubted that an effective executive

could be established on republican principles. But it
did cause a shaking of heads. He attributed opposition
on the part of state officials to the fact that "men love
power," and accused the state "demagogues" of fearing that their power would be curbed by a central
government. One could hardly label a man a Federalist who so recently had proclaimed that "two sovereignties cannot coexist within the same limits" and had
urged the dismantling of "the vast and expansive ap-
paratus" now erected by the states. One version of his
remarks has him criticizing popular governments as
"but pork still with a little change of sauce."

Hamilton needed a part of the next day to complete
his remarks. Therein he sought to define the parame-
ters of state-federal relations, coming out openly for
the abolition of the states as then constituted, and
proposing to confine them to "subordinate jurisdiction."

In *The Federalist*, Hamilton would find it necessary
to back away from this extreme plan of consolidation.
In *Federalist* Number 9, he warns against "splitting
ourselves into an infinity of little jealous, clashing,
tumultuous commonwealths, the wretched nurseries of
unceasing discord and the miserable objects of universal pity and contempt," while still seeking to reassure
his readers that the states had a role to play and that
the Constitution accepts them as "constituent parts of
the national sovereignty by allowing them a direct
representation in the Senate and leaves in their possession certain exclusive and very important portions of
sovereign power." This distinction between the external sovereignty exercised by the national government
and the internal sovereignty residing in the states had
been stressed by a variety of speakers at the Philadelphia Convention, but remained to be spelled out in
detail in Madison's own contribution to *The Federalist*.

Indeed, Hamilton, even after his return to the Convention in August, never left any doubt about his
dissatisfaction with the limited moves toward central-
ization that body was prepared to accept, but his contributions were now to prove more constructive and

his demeanor much more conciliatory. Still, who among those present at the final day, when the Constitution was signed, was likely to forget Hamilton's admission that he would sign, although no man's ideas were "more remote" from the final draft than his own were known to be? Having so recently placed himself on record as being in basic disaccord with the Constitution, Hamilton, by signing his *Federalist* letters under his own name, would be unlikely to persuade critical readers of the sincerity of his advocacy of ratification.

James Madison, generally accorded the tribute of being "the father of the Constitution" because the initial plan attributed to him provided the basic blueprint for the final document, found himself overruled time after time during the Convention. He had vigorously opposed the concession to the small states of equality in the Senate, and some of his own doubts were revealed in his admission in *Federalist* Number 37 that "a faultless plan was not to be expected." He had never accepted the veto provision set forth in the Constitution, and in *Federalist* Number 51 he inferentially favored amending the Constitution to substitute a joint veto by the President and the Senate to control the actions of the lower house—in other words, he preferred an absolute veto and placed himself in direct contradiction to Hamilton's exposition of presidential powers in *Federalist* Number 69, wherein the qualified veto provided by the Constitution is defended. Both prior to the Constitutional Convention and not long after its ratification, Madison was found to interpret Constitutional issues inconsistently with his exposition in *The Federalist.* As a Congressional delegate in the Confederation years, he had no doubts about Congress's supreme power in treating with the Indians, but in *Federalist* Number 42 he suggested that the issue under the Articles of Confederation was ambiguous and that it remained for the Constitution to confer on the national government exclusive powers in that area. His interpretation of the "necessary and proper" clause in *Federalist* Number 44 was far more expansive than the views he and Jefferson were to expound once the federal government was in operation.

Off the record, John Jay, like Hamilton, had advocated a more consolidated government than the Framers constructed. In a private letter written in 1785 and addressed to James Lowell, a Massachusetts commissioner in that state's boundary dispute with New York, after Jay had assumed his duties as Secretary for Foreign Affairs, he asserted:

> It is my first wish to see the United States assume and merit the character of one great nation, whose territory was divided into counties and townships for the like purpose. Until this be done the chain that binds us together will be too feeble to bear much opposition or exertion and we shall be deeply mortified by seeing the links of it giving way and calling for repair one after another.

Had this letter been publicized, Jay's credentials as an objective champion of federalism would have been critically undermined. The fact is that Jay, the most eminent nationalist among New Yorkers, had been deliberately excluded at Governor Clinton's behest from being a delegate to the Constitutional Convention. Instead, the governor was to see to it that, out of three delegates, only one Federalist would be chosen by the state legislature. Despite his personal animosity toward Hamilton, Clinton could hardly exclude him. The central role that Hamilton had played at the Annapolis Convention and in the summoning of the Philadelphia sessions could not be ignored. Any damage Hamilton might cause, Clinton figured, would in effect be offset by two Antifederalist companions, Robert Yates, a respected Albany lawyer from a family of lesser gentry, and John Lansing, an Albany lawyer who had shrewdly purchased with depreciated securities some forty thousand acres of confiscated Tory property. When Yates and Lansing left the Convention because of their disaccord with its nationalizing trend, New York State now lacked a quorum, and Hamilton's signature on the Constitution really had no binding value. Of the three *Federalist* collaborators, however, Jay proved to be the most conciliatory, the readiest to meet his opponents halfway, to admit imperfections in the Constitution, and even make the kind of concessions to secure ratification which dismayed his collaborator James Madison.

In sum, it should be borne in mind that *The Federalist* constituted a masterly effort of advocacy, written to persuade the people of New York, and the other twelve states as well, to accept what Hamilton, in *Federalist* Number 85, conceded to be "a compromise of as many dissimilar interests and inclinations." It by no means perfectly mirrored the positions of its authors. Nor was it written exclusively with a view to the contemporary situation, but as Hamilton remarked in *Federalist* Number 34, it looked forward "to remote futurity." If the authors could not account for all future contingencies—for the unwritten Constitution, the Cabinet, the party system, the imperial presidency, judicial activism, and much else not envisioned by the Framers—they did provide their contemporaries with an exposition of the Constitution that has remained profound, searching, challenging, and, as subsequent commentators have attested, everlastingly controversial.

The collaborators on *The Federalist* agreed at once upon one matter. With popular elections for delegates to New York's ratifying convention in purview, speedy production and publication of their letters were exigent. Fortunately for New York City's readers, they had the benefit of what almost amounted to a newspaper, available at least every other day. There was, first of all, *The Independent Journal*, published by Thomas Greenleaf, a man of known Antifederalist views, but punctual in producing his Saturday and Wednesday issues. Then the *Packet*, edited by Samuel and John Loudon, came off the press on Tuesdays, while John Jay's protégé, Francis Childs, put out the *Advertiser* on Thursdays. One way or another, every reader in town could be reached promptly, and whether they subscribed to the newspapers or read them at the popular taverns or coffeehouses, everybody seemed to know what was in them. To meet press deadlines, the three collaborators wrote under pressure, with little opportunity for full consultation with their fellow contributors. Madison, after retiring from the presidency, recalled "that, while the printer was putting into type parts of the number, the following part was under the pen and to be finished in time for the press."

According to family tradition, Hamilton initiated *The Federalist* aboard one of his father-in-law's three sloops regularly deployed to ship lumber products from Philip Schuyler's mills near Saratoga to the New York market. Hamilton, his litigation in Albany behind him, seated himself in a cabin, took pen and ink, and by candlelight began drafting:

TO THE PEOPLE OF THE STATE OF NEW YORK

After an unequivocal experience of the inefficacy of the subsisting Federal Convention you are called upon to deliberate on a new Constitution for the United States of America. The subject speaks of its importance, comprehending in its consequences nothing less than the existence of the Union, the safety and welfare of the parts of which it is composed, the fate of an empire, in many respects the most interesting in the world.

He continued writing as night dropped a curtain over the majestic river. The important question, as Hamilton put it to his readers, was "whether societies of men are really capable or not, of establishing good government from reflection and choice." He alerted his readers to expect opposition to these ideas from state officeholders and from others consumed by "perverted ambition" and hoping to profit from "the confusions of the country" or its "subdivisions" into "several partial confederacies." Warning his readers against "a torrent of angry and malignant passions" that would be let loose, he reminded them that "the vigour of government is essential to the security of liberty."

Hamilton then spelled out the plan of the series. It would seek to consider the following, and the printer, obviously at his direction, italicized the items:

> *The utility of the* Union *to your Political prosperity—The insufficiency of the Present Confederation to preserve that* Union— *The necessity of a government at least equally energetic with the one proposed to the attainment of this object—The conformity of the proposed Constitution to the true principles of republican government—The analogy to your own state constitution—and lastly, The additional security, which its adoption will afford to the preservation of that species of government, to liberty and to property.*

Promising that his "next address" would treat the subject of the advantages of Union and the dangers to which every state "will be exposed from its dissolution," the author affixed his signature, "PUBLIUS." A different "Publius" would address this theme in *Federalist* Number 2, and within a few days. John Jay, the senior collaborator, assumed responsibility for the four ensuing letters.

Greenleaf's printer's devil was waiting at Hamilton's residence following his disembarking from the Albany journey. Hamilton pulled the handwritten sheets of *Federalist* Number 1 from his portfolio, tossed them to him, while Greenleaf held open his type sticks and presses. The following day, October 27, 1787, Hamilton had the satisfaction of seeing it spread out in *The Independent Journal*. Exhausted from his efforts, he might well have nodded over his printed copy, and justifiably reflected on the distance he had put between his obscure origins and his present prominence. To do so would have recalled remote memories—the journey from St. Croix to America in 1772, and even more remote and distasteful recollections going back more than a quarter of a century.

2

Alexander Hamilton and the Quest for Fame

Toward the latter period of his involvement in *The Federalist*, Hamilton provides a clue to that volcanic drive which would bring him close to the top. In his seventy-second *Federalist* letter he alludes to "the love of fame" as "the ruling passion of the noblest minds." In these few phrases Hamilton, in autobiographical vein, reveals his own powerful drive to achieve renown and thereby bury shameful memories reaching back to his earliest days.

Not that Hamilton's remote past could easily be buried. John Adams, in a typically uncharitable moment, called Hamilton "the bastard brat of a Scot's pedlar." Adams's characterization was aimed right at the jugular, for Hamilton's illegitimacy was not a matter of spurious conjecture; its ugly truth was embalmed in the court record. Childhood and early poverty left galling memories—memories effaced only by romanticizing the past, establishing respectable credentials in the present, and feeding one's cyclonic ambitions for the future.

His mother, Rachel Faucett, a young, willful, and reputedly comely redhead beauty from the British West Indian island of Nevis, was married at sixteen, on the Danish island of St. Croix, to John Michael Levine or Lavien, a Dane or German, reputed by Hamilton's family to be a Jew, if not an observant one. Finding every moment of their life together intolerable, Rachel ran away from her husband, replicating the exam-

Alexander Hamilton, miniature attributed to Charles Willson Peale, painted at the time of Hamilton's marriage in 1780 (*Columbiana Collection, Columbia University*).

ple set by her mother, who had won a legal separation from her physician husband, Dr. John Faucett. Mother and daughter, a restless if liberated pair, moved around the West Indian islands. When they returned to St. Croix, the vindictive Levine charged his wife with whoring. Under the sex-biased laws obtaining in that island, he had her arrested and thrown into jail. Her incarceration, instead of making Rachel subservient to her husband's wishes, only sparked her rebellious spirit. After serving out her term, Rachel deserted her husband and her son by him, Peter, and moved on to St. Kitts with her mother, who by now was reduced to poverty.

Never reconciled to Levine, she took up with a Scot named James Hamilton, scion of a prominent Scottish family, and something of a charming drifter and ne'er-do-well himself. This illicit if romantic union produced two sons, James junior and Alexander, the latter born on the island of Nevis in 1755 or 1757 (according to the record or tradition one prefers).

Determined to end the travesty of formal wedlock, Levine in 1759 sued for divorce in the matrimonial court of Christiansted, St. Croix's main town, charging Rachel with begetting two illegitimate children, of abandoning their child, Peter, and of giving "herself to whoring with everyone." The court granted Levine an uncontested divorce on the grounds of adultery, and Rachel, the guilty party, was barred from remarrying. Both the mother and two children by Hamilton were cut off from inheriting anything of Levine's small estate.

Rachel and Hamilton made the circuit of the islands, finally settling at St. Croix, where the scandal of Rachel's imprisonment fifteen years earlier and Levine's divorce, brought after an interval of nine years, had still not died down. Whether the bankrupt Hamilton shoved off and abandoned his brood or whether the restless Rachel threw him out is not clear. Neither boy ever saw his father again. What we do know is that Hamilton's mother resumed her maiden name of Faucett on the tax rolls, and that of Levine for other dealings. There is little doubt that the tight and tiny West Indian islands, English or Danish, buzzed with gossip about the "Hamilton woman."

An early account of Alexander, even at eight years of age a child prodigy unlike his more plodding older brother James, describes him as somewhat diminutive for his years, slender, but with well-proportioned and attractive features, ruddy complexion, dark blue deepset eyes, and a thatch of reddish brown hair. The genes of both parents were clearly visible even at first glance.

Years later Alexander would relate to his own family one of his earliest memories of Nevis, a green-jeweled casket of an island. He recalled how, as a four-year-old, he stood on a stool in a tiny schoolroom. A Jewish woman teacher listened at his side as he recited the Decalogue in Hebrew. He could still remember urchins on the island uncharitably calling out "little bastard" and "Jew lover" as he made his way back to his mother's home at the very end of the town where the main street ceased and the road around the island began. Little as he was, young Hamilton was prideful and sensitive, and he would not suffer slights, as some of his playmates would ruefully remember.

Then followed a jumble of memories of a fatherless boy at Christiansted, where his mother had taken up residence at 34 Compagnienst stade, and set both James and Alexander to work running a provision shop, assisted by a couple of slaves.

A later and, to Hamilton, an unforgettable scene occurred in 1768: Rachel Faucett Levine was sick abed, suffering from a racking fever, which her youngest son caught. She died. He survived. The vindictive Levine reappeared and had Rachel's two sons by Hamilton declared illegitimate, cutting them off from her paltry estate, all of which, except for two slaves, went to the eldest and legitimate son, Peter, long since removed to South Carolina. With their mother's relatives bankrupt, Rachel's two younger children were thrown back on their own resources. James was apprenticed to a carpenter, while Alexander eked out a livelihood as a clerk for the export-import firm of Beekman and Cruger, both of prominent New York merchant families. During Hamilton's employment the partnership was dissolved and Nicholas Cruger managed the firm himself or occasionally in joint operations with Cornelius Kortright.

Though he possessed a marvelous head for figures and surprising business acumen for one so young, Alexander was still the soul of discontent. In a letter written in November 1769 he poured out his restless ambition to a boyhood friend and schoolmate, Edward Stevens, then studying at King's College (now Columbia) in New York City. "Ned," he wrote, "my ambition is prevalent that I contemn the groveling and condition of a Clerk or the like, to which my Fortune, etc. condemns me and would willingly risk my life, though not my Character, to exalt my station. I'm confident, Ned, that my Youth excludes me from any hopes of immediate Preferment, nor do I desire it, but

I mean to prepare the way for futurity. I'm no philosopher, you see, and may just be said to Build Castles in the Air. My Folly makes me ashamd and beg you'll Conceal it, yet Neddy we have seen such Schemes successfull when the Projector is Constant. I shall conclude saying, I wish there was a war."

The war was coming, and Hamilton would be a part of it.

Before his deliverance from the drudgery of clerking, Hamilton, in the three years after writing Ned Stevens, threw himself into his job with his characteristic élan, even operating Cruger's business in the latter's absence for a considerable period in 1771–72. Hamilton took risks, made decisions, disposed of wormeaten flour and a cargo of waterlogged mahogany, fattened up a shipment of mules that had arrived as skeletons, and stood for no nonsense in ordering about Cruger's employees, even those who were senior in years—ship captains and supercargoes—but who lacked Hamilton's indefatigable enterprise. Hamilton did little "groveling" himself while keeping Cruger's firm afloat. As he informed his employer about going after bad debts, "Believe me, Sir, I dun as hard as is proper."

It took an act of God and a good friend and patron to get Alexander Hamilton off St. Croix and onto the continent where he would get his war. The friend was the Reverend Hugh Knox, an Irish Presbyterian clergyman who had come to the West Indies by way of the very Presbyterian and very Whiggish College of New Jersey (Princeton). A stout Whig himself, Knox, perhaps the first to recognize Hamilton's intellectual capacity, gave him access to his library and encouraged the teenager's bookish instincts and literary efforts.

Beginning in early 1771, when Hamilton described himself as "a youth about seventeen," he began sending some rather tasteless poetry to the *Royal Danish American Gazette*, of which the following is a typical verse:

Celia's an artful little slut;
Be fond, she'll kiss et cetera—but
She must have all her will:
For, do but rub her 'gainst the grain
Behold a storm, blows wind and rain,
Go bid the waves be still.

Whether drawn from personal experience or not, Hamilton's poetry stressed the carnal, predatory, and feline character of the fair sex.

Soon he had a greater theme. On the night of August 31, 1772, a hurricane leveled a large part of St. Croix, with several fatalities and huge property damage. Hamilton seized the occasion, doubtless with prodding from Knox, to describe the catastrophe by way of a letter to his father, James Hamilton, a letter with strong religious overtones: A vindictive Deity is teaching the islanders a lesson in humility, "an incensed master, executing vengeance on the crimes of his servants." Then the Lord relents; "the lightning ceases, the winds are appeased." But before we rejoice at our deliverance, the author warns us, let us remember those who did not survive, the injured, and the penniless, victims of the disastrous storm. "Succor the miserable and lay up a treasure in Heaven."

Did Hamilton "get religion," or was he playing up to the religiosity of his patron and the islanders generally? Certainly that expression of deeply felt piety wore off rather quickly after his coming to America. He never shared the lifelong religiosity of his New York friend and political associate John Jay. During the Constitutional Convention in Philadelphia, the deistic-minded Benjamin Franklin, to cool the intensity of the debate as well as rising tempers, proposed that henceforth clergymen be invited to begin each session with a prayer. Hamilton opposed the motion as likely "to bring on some disagreeable animadversions"; or, according to a later version, he expressed confidence that the Convention could transact the business entrusted to its care without "the necessity of calling in foreign aid."

What roused Hamilton to the formal piety of his youth was the threat posed by the radical ideology of the French Revolutionary years, with its deistic and even antireligious overtones. Then, taking a leaf from Jefferson's Democratic-Republican societies of the 1790s, he proposed to counter their influence by establishing a Christian Constitutional society to support the Christian religion and the Constitution.

His religiosity toward the end of his career was best exemplified in the circumstances surrounding his fatal duel with Aaron Burr, whose challenge Hamilton felt honor-bound to accept. The night before he met Burr, Hamilton wrote his wife, Elizabeth: "The scruples of a Christian have determined me to expose my life to any extent rather than subject myself to the guilt of taking the life of another. This must increase my hazards, and undoubtedly my pangs for you." Dying from the fatal encounter with Burr on a shelf partway up the Palisades at Weehawken, Hamilton asked to receive the last rites. Episcopal Bishop Moore heard the repentance of the dying man and administered the sacrament. Hamilton died on July 12, 1804.

It was his deliverance to America that the mature Hamilton could never forget. His "hurricane letter" established his reputation for precosity, and with Knox's help, bolstered by a little group of influential admirers, including Nicholas Cruger, Hamilton sailed in the early fall of 1772 for New York via Boston. He was never again to leave the continent. In fact, of the *Federalist* trio, John Jay was to be the only one with direct knowledge of the European world.

All of Hamilton's sponsors were dedicated Whigs to whose cause Hamilton became a quick convert. Hamilton settled down briefly in New York. He later conceded that he had come to America with a broad bias toward monarchy, a bias that eroded under the spell of powerful republican ideologists but was never completely eradicated. The Whig republicans took him up at once and gave him both hospitality and tutelage. The partner of the mercantile firm of Kortright and Company, which would handle a trading account set up for young Hamilton's support, was Hugh Mulligan, who turned Hamilton over to his bachelor brother Hercules. An Irish radical activist and Liberty Boy, Mulligan found Whig sponsors among the clergymen of the town. Their joint plan was to provide Hamilton with the essential preparatory background for admission to college. Their choice was the republican-minded, Princeton-born Francis Barber, who headed a preparatory school in Elizabethtown, New Jersey.

Hamilton's studies with Barber and his close association with two leading Whig Presbyterian intellectuals, William Livingston, soon to be Revolutionary governor of New Jersey, and Elias Boudinot, a war activist and later President of the Continental Congress, could only reinforce his Whig proclivities. William Livingston, a powerful writer whose prose and conversation were sprinkled with sardonic wit, had an abiding affection for his brood of children, including four eligible daughters. He welcomed Hamilton at his home during the latter's stay at Barber's Academy. It is doubtful whether Hamilton had ever spent a night in as grand a place as "Liberty Hall" at Elizabethtown, a uniquely designed octagonal and spacious mansion with an unrivaled rose garden, whose bushes in season delight visitors to this day. Hamilton, a born flirt, paid assiduous court to the Livingston girls.

It was at Liberty Hall that he first met John Jay, the rising New York lawyer, whose courtship of the beauteous Sarah Livingston was not only assiduous but serious. Hamilton attended the wedding ceremony of the couple at the bride's home in April 1774, and at the start of his political career, Jay was first among Hamilton's correspondents.

By that time Hamilton had moved back to New York, to the disappointment of his New Jersey friends and sponsors, who felt that the College of New Jersey was the proper place for a sound education in stout

Whig principles. Never one to underestimate his own abilities, in an interview with the Reverend John Witherspoon, Princeton's president and a Whig enthusiast, Hamilton insisted on being admitted with advanced standing in view of his accomplishments to date. The academically conservative trustees refused, while King's College, under Loyalist and Episcopalian auspices (though nondenominational), proved more flexible. Hamilton entered as a special student in 1773, being tutored privately by the college faculty in the subjects he felt he needed. The following year found him regularly assigned to the sophomore class.

When Hamilton in later life contemplated his college days, he must have had a series of kaleidoscopic impressions. Working with his customary assiduity in mastering a curriculum that was more liberal than most colonial colleges offered, he took private tutoring in mathematics with one of the Whig professors, Robert Harpur, and the latter's accounts show that Hamilton gave Harpur a present at the close of the war of more than five guineas. The mathematics lessons would soon prove the most immediately useful activity that a future artillery officer could undertake. In addition, Hamilton drew heavily on the college's library, familiarizing himself with the writers on international law, with Locke and Montesquieu, and imbibing heavy drafts of David Hume, from whose essays he was to draw so conspicuously throughout his life.

King's College, a Loyalist stronghold, where the president, the Reverend Myles Cooper, denounced "these rebellious Americans" as "harebrained fanaticks," could not shelter its students from the political hurricane that swept the town. The college was only a stone's throw from "the Fields" (now City Hall Park), where a Liberty Pole had been erected by rebellious mobs and where mass meetings opposing British rule provided a source of continuous agitation. Hamilton was quickly drawn to this hub of protest. Earlier he had caused a sensation at his first public appearance in July of '74, when he addressed one such meeting at the Fields to denounce the act of Parliament closing the port of Boston in reprisal for their tea-dumping.

Almost at once he was sending off to the newspapers a series of letters and various broadsides in which the King's College student helped stir the agitation to fever pitch. By the time the first Continental Congress met in Philadelphia in the fall of '74, he had enunciated the doctrine that Parliament had no constitutional authority over the colonies. Already he had advanced to the far left position to which more mature and better-known Patriots such as Thomas Jefferson, James Wilson, and John Adams were also laying claim. His pen was moving fast and furiously now. Goaded into action by a series of four "Westchester Farmer" pamphlets, in which an Anglican Tory clergyman, Samuel Seabury, attacked the Congress, Hamilton responded by appealing to natural rights, the more extreme radical line that Whigs were soon to adopt. "The sacred rights of mankind are not to be rummaged for among old parchments or musty records," Hamilton declaimed. "They are written, as with a sunbeam, in the whole volume of human nature by the hand of the Divinity itself, and can never be erased or obscured by mortal power." Again, in his analysis of the trade laws that Parliament had passed, young Hamilton demonstrated that brilliant grasp of economic problems which both astonished and confounded his contemporaries.

A gifted agitator and eloquent writer, Hamilton would bestir his compatriots, while recognizing at the same time that there were limits to which agitation might be carried. He advocated moderation in dealing with Tories, opposed mobbism, and stood fast for civil rights. When a mob broke down the gates at King's College and threatened to tar and feather the detested Myles Cooper, Hamilton, to give his president a chance to escape, harangued the mob long enough for Cooper to exit by a back gate, soon to take refuge on a British warship in the Hudson, sail for England, and publicly acknowledge young Hamilton's role in saving his hide.

Again, when Connecticut militiamen invaded New

York and attacked the shop of the detested Tory printer James Rivington, destroying his type, Hamilton protested to John Jay that such violence would lead to "contempt and disregard of all authority." Jay, a man of moderation, who consistently distinguished between Tories who acted out of conscience and those who took overt steps to damage the Patriot cause, was in complete agreement. Hamilton, often a target himself for the passions of mobs, was, as we shall see, thoroughly consistent. In the postwar period he preached the virtue of moderation and discrimination in the treatment of former Loyalists, many of whom were numbered among his most valued clients.

A born activist, Hamilton was not content to talk and write about the cause. Every morning now found him drilling in St. George's churchyard with a volunteer company known as the Corsicans, in admiration of the hero of the moment, Pasqual Paoli, and his fellow Corsicans, who put up a fight initially against the city-state of Genoa and then against France. Hamilton first came under fire during a successful engagement to remove a score of cannon from the fort at the Battery, right under the guns of British warships. His aspirations for command could not be denied, and his cramming in mathematics apparently qualified him for a commission as captain in command of the New York Provincial Company of Artillery, a post secured for him by John Jay. He recruited his own company of sixty-eight officers and men, and used his own personal credit to clothe and equip them.

Although Hamilton and his company, assigned to the main Manhattan defense works on Bayard's Hill, fortunately missed the rout of Washington's forces in the Battle of Long Island, he was forced, with the rest of the defending troops, to pull back to the defenses on Harlem Heights. In the retreat of the main American army across the Hudson to New Jersey, Hamilton first caught Washington's eye by playing a key role at New Brunswick. Stationing his battery on the high west bank a few hundred yards from the Raritan River, he covered Washington's crossing to the west side of that river and held up Cornwallis's pursuit while Washington struck out for Princeton. Someone reported seeing Hamilton in action and was struck by the appearance of "a youth, a mere stripling, small, slender, almost delicate in frame," marching, his "cocked hat pulled down over his eyes, apparently lost in thought, with his hand resting on a cannon, and every now and then patting it, as if it were a favorite horse or a pet plaything." Alas for Hamilton, his plaything was soon to be taken away from him! His role in the brilliantly successful attack upon the Hessians at Trenton, and his spectacular action in the battle of Princeton in firing a ball that entered the college chapel and, according to tradition, pierced the portrait of George II, commanded Washington's attention. The General now chose him as an aide-de-camp. His intellectual gifts, his fluency in French, and his bearing, manners, and socially impeccable sponsorship among the Patriots all proved to be assets to him.

March 1, 1777, the date of Hamilton's appointment, marked a turning point in his career. Now he was rocketed to the center of decision-making but, until the last moment at Yorktown, was never permitted to command troops in battle again during the American Revolution. Buried under a mountain of paperwork, he still had time to imbibe much of Washington's recognition of the need for national unity and an American national character. He had time, too, during the years from 1778 to 1782, to clarify his own thoughts on constitutional and fiscal reform.

These were first given brilliant exposition in his famous "Liberty Pole" letter of September 3, 1780, to James Duane, in which he expounded his ideas on national sovereignty and set forth at length a devastating critique of the Articles of Confederation. He proposed the early assembling of a convention "vested with plenipotentiary authority" to establish "a solid coercive union," granting Congress complete sovereignty, reserving for the states internal police power relating to the rights of property and life, and the levying of internal taxes. Congress, under the Hamilton plan, would have complete sovereignty to act in all matters relating to war, peace, trade, finance, and foreign affairs. He went on to recommend a system of executive departments to be set up by Congress, along with a national bank.

Most delegates felt, however, that this plan was premature and that completing the ratification of the Articles should have priority, after which remedies to strengthen the powers of Congress might be considered. Even earlier, Hamilton had enunciated in an undated letter to a "Member of Congress" what was to form the basic maxim of the Hamiltonian system: "The only plan that can preserve the currency is one that will make it the *immediate* interest of the monied men to cooperate with government in its support." These thoughts he hammered home in a letter to Robert Morris of April 30, 1781, and in his published "Continentalist" letters of 1781 and 1782. In his sixth and final "Continentalist" letter, appearing in the *New-York Packet* on July 4, 1782, Hamilton declared:

> There is something noble and magnificent in the perspective of a great Federal Republic, closely linked in the pursuit of a common interest, tranquil and prosperous at home, respectable abroad; but there is something proportionably diminutive and contemptible in the prospect of a number of petty states, with the appearance only of union, jarring, jealous and perverse, without any determined direction, fluctuating and unhappy at home, weak and insignificant by their dissensions in the eyes of other nations. Happy America, if those to whom thou has intrusted the guardianship of thy infancy know how to provide for thy future repose, but miserable and undone, if their negligence or ignorance permits the spirit of discord to erect her banner on the ruins of thy tranquillity!

In some respects Hamilton behaved during the war as though the medieval code of chivalry were still in existence. It was Hamilton, en route with Washington to West Point, who was handed the packet of papers that had been found in the boot of Major John André by "three simple peasants," documents intercepted at Tarrytown, New York. With all doubts about Benedict Arnold's treasonable plans to turn West Point over to the British removed, Hamilton lost his composure when he confronted Arnold's Tory-minded wife, Peggy Shippen Arnold. Always impressionable where good-looking women were concerned, Hamilton was taken in by her hysterical professions of noninvolvement, underscored by swoons and copious tears, and was wrongly convinced of her innocence.

Not only the forlorn female in distress, but the fate of the aristocratic André, a spy by every rule of international law, appealed to his sense of chivalry. He wrote an anonymous letter to British General Clinton proposing that Benedict Arnold be exchanged for André. When that unauthorized intermeddling failed, Hamilton appealed to Washington to have the British spy executed as a gentleman by being shot, rather than suffering the death of a varlet by dangling from the gallows. Washington flatly turned down Hamilton's plea. He was fighting an all-out war and, unlike Hamilton, did not believe that exceptions should be made when the adversary happened to be a gentleman.

The forbearing Washington put up with Hamilton's indiscretions and his incessant itch to defend his personal honor. It was bruited about that Hamilton in turn was becoming increasingly disapproving of the irascible moods and manners of his commander. Chained to a desk job that he had come to loathe, he deliberately picked a quarrel with the General. An insufferably touchy young man, Hamilton seemed to go around with a chip on his shoulder and incessantly seek out controversy. Hamilton quit his post, but Washington in the end yielded to Hamilton's importunities and gave him his chance for glory at Yorktown. In the

Elizabeth Schuyler Hamilton, portrait by Ralph Earl (*Museum of the City of New York*).

assault on the Number 10 redoubt in that ultimate battle, Hamilton led the main attacking force. First over the parapet into the redoubt, he directed a bayonet attack that was over in minutes.

By now, friends and foes alike recognized that Hamilton was bitten by ambition. Washington, Hamilton's friend and patron over the years, conceded that Hamilton was ambitious, but considered that his ambition was "of that laudable kind, which prompts a man to excel in whatever he takes in hand." Others recognized his audacious enterprise and quick perception. Hamilton knew that, for him, more than sheer ability was required to reach the heights. What would help was the backing of a powerful and wealthy family. In short, he needed a wife to quicken his quest for fame. Writing to his dear friend, the South Carolinian John Laurens, in the spring of 1779, he made clear what he was seeking. His wife would have to be a paragon: young, beautiful, shapely, "sensible (a little learning will do), well bred, chaste, and tender." Getting down to money, Hamilton added, "as to fortune, the larger stock of that the better," for, as he confessed, "money is an essential ingredient to happiness in this world." The young lady he would marry a year later possessed some if not all of his exacting specifications. She was Elizabeth Schuyler, the daughter of General Philip Schuyler, a commanding figure among the Albany Dutch gentry, a holder of thousands of acres in the Mohawk Valley, along the Hudson, and in the Saratoga region, and continuously prominent in upstate politics. That one stroke attached Hamilton to an influential and socially impeccable family. The parvenu had now completed the process of gentrification.

By the standards of the time, theirs was a love match, to which Hamilton's effusive letters to "my beloved Betsey" and "my angel" would attest. "Love me," he wrote her from the army. "Let your happiness always consist of loving," he enjoins in another missive. Indubitably, Hamilton loved Betsey after his fashion, and there were eight children of the marriage. Moments of connubial bliss were not permitted to interfere, however, with a long-term flirtation with his sister-in-law, Angelica Schuyler Church, nor to inhibit other extralegal entanglements.

Worldly, witty, frivolous, and possessive, Angelica had a girlhood crush on dashing Alexander which she never lost, and the behavior of the two was a topic of gossip among family and close friends. In a spoofing letter written shortly before his marriage, Hamilton suggested to Angelica that his wife-to-be would be "much less dangerous when she has a rival equal in charms to dispute the place with her. I solicit your aid." To Angelica, the supreme coquette, this was a challenge and thereafter she never withheld her affection and admiration from her "petit fripon."

There may have been times when gallantry passed the bounds of flirtation, and Hamilton's adoring wife was sorely tried. One such occasion might have occurred in November of 1789, when Hamilton was al-

Angelica Schuyler Church, Hamilton's sister-in-law, who cherished a lifelong affection for her "petit fripon" (*contemporary miniature reproduced in* CENTURY MAGAZINE).

ready immersed in his duties as Secretary of the Treasury. Angelica, long married to John Barker Church, a speculator and gambler, had spent most of her postwar years with her spouse in England, filling her idle hours with affectionate letters to Hamilton. Her opportunity to see him again occurred in 1789. Church was now occupied with his duties as a newly elected Member of Parliament, and Angelica sailed to New York without him. Hamilton kept two separate accounts covering the cash he advanced to Angelica during her stay. One he headed "Monies paid to Yourself," and another simply, "For You." Angelica seems to have made a fleeting visit to her upstate family and then chose to occupy rooms at Mrs. Cuyler's from May to October instead of staying with Betsey and Alexander. In November she removed to an unnamed boardinghouse, and Hamilton laid out £23/0/3 for the account, as he put it "of your last landlady." Apparently he assumed the costs of this last move, as a bill for Angelica's "music master." One may pardonably speculate that a consuming passion covered these cryptic entries. It was all very furtive, but not uncharacteristic of the way Hamilton arranged his extramarital affairs.

Hamilton, along with his son Philip and General von Steuben, a house guest of the Hamiltons, took Angelica to a departing packet. Betsey's pregnancy at this time prevented her from accompanying them. As the farewell party walked to the Battery and saw the ship in full sail, Hamilton wrote Angelica: "We gazed, we sighed, we *wept.*" In turn, Angelica wrote Alexander from shipboard that very evening, preferring French to express how grief-stricken she was at having to leave him behind. "I have almost vowed not to stay three weeks in England," she continued, adding now in English: "How can I be content when I leave my best and most invaluable friends."

Some years later, Hamilton, as Secretary of the Treasury, was accused by political foes of using intermediaries to purchase Revolutionary War veterans' certificates secretly, at a huge discount. His defense was that he was being blackmailed for sleeping with the wife of one of the speculators. "My real crime is an amorous connection with his [James Reynolds's] wife," he would one day publicly admit. It is evident from this sordid incident that, whether it was true or fictional, Hamilton was prepared to go the limit to protect his public honor even at the sacrifice of his private life.

Thus, from the beginning almost to the end of his career, Hamilton held pessimistic views about women as well as the rest of mankind. That pessimism had early roots, and may fairly be traced to the humiliations he unjustly attributed to his mother (not his irresponsible father, whom he extolled). Rachel Faucett Levine Hamilton was the first "loose woman" he had ever known, and judging from his teenage poetry, he appears to have had some experiences with a few tropical trollops on the islands. When John Jay finished his fifth *Federalist* letter, Hamilton in the one that followed made the point of blaming three loose women for leading their countries astray: the "prostitute" Aspasia, who induced Pericles to attack the Samnians, and Mesdames Maintenon and de Pompadour, mistresses of Louis XIV and XV respectively, whose political intrigues led to religious persecution or foreign adventurism. Sex, to Hamilton, was the great corrupter.

The busy life into which Hamilton plunged after Yorktown reflected his conviction that the country needed a government that could act, that was imbued with energy, and that was supreme. Quickly admitted to the New York bar even before the formal ending of the war under special regulations waiving the customary long-term clerkship in the case of war veterans, Hamilton soon rose to the top of his profession. His incisive mind and massive legal erudition, assimilated with phenomenal rapidity, were quickly recognized, and as attorney and counselor-at-law he was *primus inter pares.*

Absorbed though he was in a large practice, Hamilton did not turn away from his political obligations. As a delegate to Congress he vainly sought to secure adequate and permanent funds for the Confederation government. Then, as a member of the New York Assembly, he was further frustrated in his efforts to enlarge Congressional power. Finally, his post as Receiver of Taxes for New York proved a disillusioning experience. He was soon forced to announce in the press that he had "received nothing on account of the quotas of this State for the present year." The lesson was clear. The taxing power of the Confederation would have to be beefed up, and Hamilton urged the New York legislature to pass a resolution for a general convention of the states to amend the Articles of Confederation. He was to press this point again and again in the years ahead, but his rebuffs augmented his pessimism, if they did not lessen his determination. As he wrote to John Jay in July of 1783, on the news of the coming of peace, "Every day proves the inefficacy of the present confederation; yet the common danger being removed, we are receding rather than advancing in a disposition to amend its deficits." In sum, Hamilton declared, "We at this moment experience all the mischiefs of a bankrupt and ruined creditor."

In turn, only a few months later Jay wrote Hamilton from Passy to express his concern at the newspaper accounts coming to him from America. "Violence and associations against the Tories pay an ill compliment to the Government and impeach our good Faith in the opinions of some, and our magnanimity in the opinions of many." Developing this theme, Jay continued: "The Tories are almost as much pitied in these Countries as they are execrated in ours. An undue Degree of Severity towards them would therefore be impolitic as well as unjustifiable." Deploring "indiscriminate punishment" for "that whole class of men," Jay urged a policy of "clemency, moderation, and benevolence. . . . [Let us not] sully the Glory of the Revolution by licentiousness and cruelty. . . . These are my sentiments," Jay concluded, "and however unpopular they may be, I have not the least desire to conceal or disguise them."

Jay's letter struck a responsive chord in the law offices at 58 Wall Street. Hamilton fully shared Jay's views about the need to discriminate between inoffensive Loyalists who had taken their stand from conscience and violent partisans who had committed overt acts against the Patriot cause. Among Hamilton's very first clients were former Tories, for the evacuation of New York City in the late fall of 1783, Hamilton confessed, brought "so plentiful a harvest to us lawyers that we have scarcely a moment to spare." Affluent or, in some cases, recently impoverished Loyalists were being hounded by a vindictive New York State legislature (and by the legislatures of most other states as well). Confiscation of Tory properties continued despite the provision in the Treaty of Peace. In New

York, for example, the legislature enacted the Trespass Act after its members had knowledge that a Preliminary Peace with Great Britain had been signed and announced by the King in Parliament. That state statute provided a remedy in law by an action of trespass permitting Patriots whose property had been occupied by Loyalists or British subjects during the late war to recover damages and prohibited the pleading of British military orders by way of justification. Enacted in March of 1783 and reenacted over a veto by the state's Council of Revision, it opened the floodgates to Patriot claimants.

Among the numerous cases arising under the Trespass Act was the controversial litigation of *Rutgers* v. *Waddington*, really a test case of the validity of the statute. Elizabeth Rutgers, by that time an aged widow, had been one of the thousands who fled New York City when it was captured by the British in the summer of '76. On her departure she vacated a brewhouse and malthouse situated on Maiden Lane. This property was assigned by the British commissary general to two British merchants, Benjamin Waddington and Evelyn Pierrepont, whose agent was Joshua Waddington. Apparently they had occupied the premises rent-free until May 1780, when the British military commander ordered them to pay rent to the Vestry for the Poor, with which order they complied for the next three years.

The case was litigated in the Mayor's Court, beginning in February 1784. Attorney General Benson and John Lawrence brought suit for back rent due the widow Rutgers. At a time when anti-Tory feeling was at its peak, it took considerable courage for Hamilton to undertake the case of the defendants. Although he was associated in this litigation with Jay's brother-in-law, Brockholst Livingston, as well as with Morgan Lewis, Hamilton carried the burden of the defendant's case.

When, in June of 1784, Mayor James Duane, presiding over the Mayor's Court, heard the opening argument, one of those attending the trial happened to be James Kent, later chancellor of the state, who at that time was clerking in the office of Attorney General Benson. Hamilton, of all the attorneys participating, left the strongest impression on Kent's memory. Writing many years later, Kent praised Hamilton's "fine melodious voice and dignified deportment, his reasoning powers, and persuasive address." To Kent, Hamilton "soared far above all competition. His preeminence was at once universally conceded," and his "impassioned eloquence" carried conviction even with a hostile audience.

John Adams had once described Mayor Duane as having "a sly, surveying eye, a little squirrel-eyed," and though he conceded that Duane was "very sensible," Adams averred that he was also "very artful." On this occasion Duane might well have earned the reputation of an artful dodger. Hamilton set forth a full-dress argument that a state law in violation of a treaty made by Congress was unconstitutional, and exhorted the court to exercise judicial review. He also cited a large corpus of authority from the law of nations and urged that the statute be construed in a manner that would not violate either the treaty or international law.

Duane, in his decision, straddled the major question: Was an act of the state legislature in derogation of a national treaty invalid? Essaying Solomonic distinctions, the court held that the British commissary general, being a civilian, acted beyond his authority. Hence the court found that in the period occupied under the commissary general's license the brewery was not used "for the carrying on of the war," according to the terms of the statute. This, of course, was a technicality, but it allowed the court to assess damages in favor of the widow Rutgers for the period from 1778 to 1780, while refusing damages for the subsequent period to 1783, when the defendants had occupied the premises under license from the British commander-in-chief. Thus Duane straddled, and even today it is hard to reconcile some of the statements of the court issued by way of dicta, notably that (1) statutes contrary to the law of nations as embodied in treaties are void, while (2) the court cannot override the *express, specific* wishes of the legislature, but (3) in the course of clarifying dubious texts, it may assume that it was the intent of the legislature to conform to international law.

Moderate and ambiguous though the decision was, it evoked a storm of protest among hard-line anti-Tories. Committees were formed and a resolve of the assembly denounced the decision as "subversive of law and order" and even censured the court. Hamilton was singled out for special denunciation. The faction behind Governor Clinton made as much political capital out of the case as it could. Anti-Tory denunciations filled the columns of New York's newspapers. Isaac Ledyard, writing as "Mentor," denied the validity of Hamilton's arguments in *Rutgers* and insisted on the unrestricted sovereignty of the State of New York. Some of Hamilton's hotheaded opponents were so infuriated by his stand that they actually concocted a plot to challenge him successively to a series of duels until the champion of Tory rights was finally liquidated. Fortunately for all parties concerned, Hamilton's adversaries never followed up their threats. Instead, good solid businessmen rushed to Hamilton's office with their cases

Of all the cases Hamilton was ever to handle—and they were manifold, ranging from libel to murder—*Rutgers* v. *Waddington* seems to have left the most indelible impression upon him. Using the pseudonym "Phocion," Hamilton wrote two pamphlets, the first in January 1784, the second in April of that year. In them he urged moderation for ex-Tories and strict observance of the terms of the Treaty of Peace. Hamilton denounced his critics as pretending "to appeal to the spirit of Whiggism; while they endeavor to put in motion all the furious and dark passions of the human mind." He reminded them that the spirit of Whiggism was "generous, humane, beneficent, and just" (almost in Jay's earlier language to him), whereas his opponents were inculcating "revenge, cruelty, persecution, and perfidy." He had concluded his first letter on a note that recurs through much of Hamilton's writings: "The safest reliance of every government is on men's interests. This is a principle of human nature, on which all political speculation, to be just, must be founded. Make it the interest of those citizens who, during the Revolution, were opposed to us, to be friends to the new government, by affording them not only protection, but a participation in its privileges, and they will undoubtedly become its friends." Hamilton's prediction was borne out by time. The Loyalists who remained in America became good, stout Federalists.

In his second "Phocion" letter, Hamilton attacked "bigotry in politics" and zealots on both sides, and urged toleration. "[Let us] set out with justice, moderation, liberality, and a scrupulous regard for the Constitution." If we do not, Hamilton warned, "the rights of the subjects will be the sport of every party vicissitude." And Hamilton, like Jay and Madison, loathed parties.

Hamilton, when stirred to eloquence, as he was in writing this pamphlet, set *Rutgers* on the world stage in one of his concluding passages:

> The world has its eyes upon America. The noble struggle we have made in the cause of liberty has occasioned a kind of revolution in human sentiment. The influence of our example has penetrated the gloomy regions of despotism, and has pointed the way to inquiries, which may shake it to its deepest foundations. Men begin to ask every where, who is this tyrant, that dares to build his greatness on our misery and degradation? What commission has he to sacrifice millions to the wanton appetites of himself and the few minions that surround his throne?
>
> To ripen inquiry into action, it remains for us to justify the revolution by its fruits.

We have the chance, Hamilton concluded, to advance "the cause of human happiness," and if we succeed, "the world will bless and imitate!" If we fail, he warned, and confirm the long-taught lessons "of the enemies of liberty, that the bulk of mankind are not fit to govern themselves, that they must have a master, and were only made for the rein and the spur, we shall then see the final triumph of despotism over liberty." Should that occur, "we shall have betrayed the cause of human nature."

A few years later Hamilton maneuvered through the legislature a bill repealing the Trespass Act.

Rutgers stands out as a marker on the long road that led to judicial review, a doctrine so carefully sculpted by Hamilton himself. Judicial review, which Hamilton championed in *Rutgers* and the "Phocion" letters, proved to be a doctrine to which Hamilton firmly adhered, although he would take care to couch his arguments in language less calculated to repel those who feared an overpowering national judiciary. Echoes of *Rutgers* are heard in *Federalist* Number 22, in which Hamilton laid bare the Confederacy's defects, of which the crowning one, he noted, was its want of a judiciary. Therein he maintained that treaties of the United States must be considered the law of the land and not exposed to the hazards of thirteen different legislatures and thirteen courts of final jurisdiction.

Hamilton wrote all the "Publius" letters on the judiciary, beginning with his celebrated seventy-eighth. Therein he argued that no legislative act "contrary to the Constitution can be valid." Hence, when the "will of the legislature stands in opposition to that of the people declared in the Constitution," the judge ought to be governed by the latter rather than the former. At the same time, Hamilton, still wary about arousing among the people a sense of panic about a super-judiciary, insisted that the judicial branch would "always be *the least dangerous* to the political rights of the Constitution" because it would be the least in a position to annoy or injure them. The executive, he pointed out, held the sword; the legislature commanded the purse; but the judiciary, he contended, had no influence over sword *or* purse.

As Hamilton saw it, the judiciary's complete independence was essential in a limited constitution, nor would he concede that the legislature was the constitutional judge of its own powers. Instead, he visualized the courts as the intermediate bodies standing between the people and the legislature to keep the latter within bounds. Denying that this role rendered the judiciary superior to the legislature, Hamilton argued that these arrangements only guaranteed the superiority of the people to both branches.

To maintain judicial independence, Hamilton defended the prohibition under the new Constitution against reducing the salary of federal judges and singled out impeachment as the only provision for their removal consistent with such independence. In Number 80, Hamilton supported the grant of authority to the federal courts to override state statutes in contravention of the Constitution, and in the following letter he upheld the doctrine of separation of powers, opposing legislative oversight of the federal judiciary and supporting the appellate authority of the federal courts to examine the trial record and pronounce the law arising upon it, along with the facts, thereby disposing of critics who objected to the court's overriding the finding of facts in a jury trial in an inferior court.

In sum, Hamilton seized upon the opportunity in his concluding *Federalist* letters not only to enlarge upon his arguments in "Phocion," but to dispose of the savage attacks on Article III of the Constitution (the judiciary branch) that were launched by the Antifederalists after the Constitution had been framed and submitted to the people for ratification.

Rutgers v. *Waddington* and his two "Phocion" letters set Hamilton's thinking on the need for a supremacy clause in a revised constitutional structure, one buttressed by an independent judiciary, while setting him up as a target for Tory-haters, Antifederalists, and popular demagogues who distrusted him for his current and continued association with creditors rather than debtors, with banks and bankers rather than mortgagors, and for his conspicuous effort to ally the affluent and the public creditors on the side of a strengthened central government.

Hamilton, despite "Phocion"'s concern for the world's "millions," never doubted the notion of prosperity filtering down from the rich to the masses. His most intemperate moments in the *Federalist* occurred when he defended the rich and powerful. It may have been tasteless for Hamilton in his concluding *Federalist* letter to confess that "the perpetual charges which have been rung upon the wealthy, the well-born, and the great have been such as to inspire the disgust of all sensible men." Hamilton's imprudent disclosure reflects his own life and early struggles for recognition. The poor waif who was not well-born owed his advancement in equal parts to talent and influence. He accepted unquestioningly the deferential society that he had found in America, and understood how to tap the springs of money and power for ends that were not ignoble.

3

John Jay:
Aristocrat as Nationalist

Working at feverish speed in response to Hamilton's challenge, Jay took just ten days to write his first four *Federalist* letters. Four days after Hamilton's initial *Federalist* appeared, the *Independent Journal* printed *Federalist* Number 2, authored by Jay. Therein he raised the central question: Do the American people wish to be "one nation, under one federal government," or "do they prefer to divide themselves into separate confederacies?" A united nation, he pointed out, seemed so natural to a country composed not of detached and distant territories, but of "one connected, fertile, wide-spreading" land, which was "the portion of our western sons of liberty." Providence, he argued, had blessed the people with great and varied natural resources and means of communication. It was Providence, as he had so often reminded his fellow Americans, that had "been pleased to give this one connected country to one united people, a people descended from the same ancestors, speaking the same language, professing the same religion, attached to the same principles of government, very similar in their manners and customs, and who, by their joint counsels, arms and efforts, fighting side by side throughout a long and bloody war, have nobly established their general Liberty and Independence."

In so eloquent a plea, Jay might be pardoned for stretching the facts. The American people in 1787, native American Indians excluded, of course, did not

John Jay, mixed stipple and line engraving by artist "B.B.E." London 1783.

all claim England as their mother country, as Jay himself well knew. While predominantly Protestant, their allegiance was to many different religious sects, and they were divided by deep sectional loyalties and interests. His own initial partner in this literary venture was of foreign birth, and he himself boasted non-English origin. National union, however, was Jay's great passion, and he warned his countrymen that should America reject union, then with a bow to Shakespeare's *Henry VIII*, he ended this letter with the lament: "FAREWELL, A LONG FAREWELL, TO ALL MY GREATNESS."

Jay's next letter, the third *Federalist*, dealt with an analysis of "just" wars. A nationalist rather than a chauvinist, Jay reminded his countrymen that individual states had provoked hostilities with the Indians and that such unjust and counterproductive actions were less likely to be committed by the Union. He doubtless had in mind the ruthless behavior of Governor Clinton. Despite a treaty with the Iroquois made by Congress in 1784, one that protected them in their lands, the governor ignored Congress and, by two illegal treaties, in effect ousted the Iroquois from the state. Contrariwise, Jay asserted, "not a single Indian war has yet been occasioned by the aggression of the present Federal government." Thus, Jay took an early stand against injustice to native Americans, unpopular though that position might be even in his home state, a stand consistent with what he had already taken and would continue to take against injustice to blacks. In both views he outdistanced most of the Founding Fathers.

"Just" wars, Jay argued, arose from violations of treaties or "direct violence." Hence, the Philadelphia Framers demonstrated wisdom in committing the interpretation of treaties "to the jurisdiction and judgment of the courts appointed by, and responsible only to one national government." A careful workman even under pressure, Jay had labored over all his drafts, and in *Federalist* Number 3 he deleted the phrase "national courts," preferring the statement he sent to press. This change reflected his sensitivity to the fear shared by the Antifederalists of a large federal judiciary administering a body of federal common law and in the process undermining the authority of the state courts. The Federal Convention had sidestepped the issue in Article III, which vests the judicial power in a Supreme Court "and in such inferior Courts as the Congress may from time to time ordain and establish." A ticklish issue, and Jay handled it with circumspection.

In his draft of *Federalist* Number 4, Jay anticipated the treatment of parties and factions which was to be developed in Madison's celebrated initial contribution, the tenth *Federalist,* perhaps the most quoted of all his essays. Pursuing the theme of the importance of national union in averting conflicts with foreign powers, Jay begins his draft with a quotation attributed to

Addison on the effects of party conflicts. "The Parties and Divisions amongst us may in several Ways bring destruction upon our Country, at the same time that one united house would secure us against all the Attempts of a foreign Enemy." Then, in the final paragraph of the draft, Jay speculated that if foreign governments "find us either . . . destitute of an effectual Government . . . or split into Factions of three or four independent . . . Republics or Confederacies . . . what a poor pitiful Figure will America make." Jay therein acknowledged the weight of one of the most forceful contemporary arguments against party and faction, the likelihood that they would lead to foreign penetration and the establishment of outposts of alien influence in American public life. In these fleeting references, which he subsequently suppressed and refrained from publishing, Jay was obviously referring to the relationship between factions and geographic divisions. He must have concluded that the subject deserved more concentrated attention in a future installment, and it was Madison, not Jay, who would pick up the theme of "the spirit of party and faction." Instead, Jay confined himself to the argument that one nation would be better able to provide a strong defense and reestablish public credit than would thirteen disunited states or three or four confederacies.

Throughout, Jay reworked his drafts to cut down verbiage, use pithier language, and avoid offending the sensibilities of the opponents of the Constitution. For example, the draft of *Federalist* Number 5 strikes this discordant note: "Wicked Men of great Talents and ambition are the growth of every Soil, and seldom hesitate to precipitate the Country into any Wars and Connections which may promote their Designs." Surely there was enough history to substantiate the assertion, with its prophetic cast, but sober second thoughts prompted its omission.

Instead, Jay in Number 5 uses a calmer tone to alert the reader to the dangers of sectionalism and division into several confederacies. Far from the likelihood

The Federalist Number 5, John Jay's original draft of the opening page, with his corrections and interlineations (*John Jay Papers, Rare Book and Manuscript Collection, Columbia University Libraries*).

that such confederacies would form alliances among themselves, Jay warned that they would probably end up on opposing sides. Like the excellent jury lawyer that he was, he uses the concluding paragraph of *Federalist* Number 5 to sum up his side's case:

> Let candid men judge then whether the division of America into any given number of independent sovereignties would tend to secure us against the hostilities and improper interference of foreign nations.

Jay's poor health, and the urgent orders of his old-time Loyalist friend, Dr. Samuel Bard, conspired to force him to withdraw at this time from collaborating on *The Federalist*. He still had a heavy load of troublesome government business to handle as Secretary for Foreign Affairs, and it would be months before his strength would permit him to tackle another essay under the pseudonym of "Publius." He could retire temporarily from the fray, knowing that Madison would shortly return from Philadelphia and could be counted on to share responsibilities with Hamilton.

One would have difficulty in all of the thirteen states in 1787 in matching two collaborators so different in physical appearance and temperament as were Hamilton and Jay. Gilbert Stuart had painted Jay in London four years earlier, capturing on canvas the sensitive, proud face, the high forehead, the penetrating eyes, the conspicuously aquiline nose, and the lips that formed an almost straight line. A colorless complexion, accentuated by highly powdered hair, set off his customary black jacket and matching vest, above which white ruffles peered.

Divided in temperament as well as in their views of the most effective means to a shared end, Jay and Hamilton stood united in their determination to substitute for the weak Articles of Confederation a constitution that would give the central government the power to act as well as the wherewithal to do so, one that would protect the interests of the American people from division at home and intrigue abroad, and surmount the state and sectional rivalries that had foreclosed unified action since the coming of peace.

Save for Jay's protégé, Hamilton, none of the Founding Fathers bore the stamp of his origins more visibly than did John Jay. He could never forget that he was descended from French Huguenot refugees, nor would he let his family forget. In some spare moments borrowed from a crowded career, he wrote down an account of his ancestors' adventures. On occasions when he gathered with his children and grandchildren, he would read them the story of what his ancestors had endured, to make sure that they, too, would remember.

A great storyteller, Jay held his family spellbound as he told about his forebears, merchants settled at La Rochelle in France, and all Huguenots, for a time a tolerated minority in Catholic France. They prospered and felt perfectly secure. Had not the great Henry IV, at the close of the sixteenth century, granted the Huguenots equal rights with Catholics as well as religious toleration limited in character and to specific towns? Like so many of the Jews of Hitler's Germany who failed to recognize the portents when the *Führer* came to power, the Huguenots did not discern the shape of things to come when Louis XIV married his mistress, Madame de Maintenon, a devout Catholic, enemy of heretics, and special *bête noire* of Alexander Hamilton, who chose her as an example of the evil influence of women meddling in affairs of state. The shock came in 1685 with the revocation of the Edict of Toleration after an experiment of less than a hundred years. Now the practice of the Huguenot religion was forbidden, children were to be educated in the Catholic faith, and Huguenot emigration was prohibited.

The Huguenots' remaining delusions were speedily dissipated by a ruthless government, which disclosed its full hand. It leveled the Huguenot church at La Rochelle, and it dispatched troops into the city and quartered them among the Protestant residents. Dragoons moved into the home of Jay's great-grandfather Pierre Jay. Acting secretly, Pierre dispatched his family aboard ship for England. He himself stayed on to salvage what he could of the wreck of his fortune, but the suspicious absence of his family led to his own arrest and imprisonment. A series of improbable events saved Jay's forebears. Through the offices of friendly Catholics, Pierre was released and managed to escape on a vessel for Spain.

Meanwhile, Pierre's second son, Auguste, had been out of France on business. Not knowing that his family had been dispersed, he returned to La Rochelle, stepping into a trap. He managed to escape on a ship bound for Charleston, South Carolina, whence he removed to New York. There he shipped out as a super-cargo for Hamburg, only to be captured by a French privateer and imprisoned in a fortress near St.-Malo. Taking advantage of dark and stormy weather, he eluded the guards, climbed the fortress wall, dropped into a ditch, and eventually managed to get out of France and find safe haven in America.

In the new land, Auguste's fortunes were advanced when he married Anna Maria Bayard. Of Dutch and Huguenot ancestry, Anna Bayard's father was the nephew of Governor Peter Stuyvesant and the descendant of French Protestants who had taken refuge in the Netherlands in the late sixteenth century, and her mother was the daughter of Govert Loockermans, reputed to be the richest man in the colony. Auguste took his son Peter into a business partnership, and Peter in turn advanced his social and business fortunes by marrying Mary Van Cortlandt, while Peter's sister Frances had previously married Frederick Van Cortlandt, Mary's brother. The Van Cortlandts ranked among the most prominent Dutch political families in New York, their wealth in no small part derived from valuable land patents acquired by their forebears, and like the Van Rensselaers and Schuylers, they were among the limited number of large landowners who took the Whig side of the Revolution.

Unlike his collaborators on *The Federalist*, Hamilton and Madison—and most of the Founding Fathers, for that matter—Jay could and did assert in later years: "Not being of British descent, I cannot be influenced by that delicacy toward their national character, nor that partiality for it, which might otherwise be supposed not to be unnatural." Jay never forgot his background and never forgot that he was a descendant of a persecuted French religious sect. His origins provide a clue to his inordinate suspicions toward Catholic Spain and France, suspicions that experience only helped to reaffirm his doubts about their intentions. However, like Hamilton—both were born under the Empire and both were devoted to the English common law—Jay

Sarah Livingston Jay, steel engraving of painting by
Lorenzo Chappell (*Columbiana Collection, Columbia
University*).

would in time develop a considerable measure of tolerance toward things British.

Jay's marriage to Sarah Van Brugh Livingston had
an extraordinary impact on his personal and professional life. Both as to family connections and personal
charms, "Sally" seemed a prize worth winning. Her
father, William Livingston, had kept the New York
kettle aboil by his opposition to Crown measures. In
1771 he had removed his family to Elizabethtown,
New Jersey, and when the Revolution came he had
been elected the war governor of the state, holding
that post for some dozen years. A great wit, with a
cutting sense of humor rare even among politicians of
his generation, Livingston also boasted the dubious
distinction of being perhaps the homeliest of the Founding Fathers. Fortunately his four handsome daughters
did not inherit his looks, but did share his abiding
interest in politics. On her mother's side, Sally was
also well connected. Susannah French Livingston was
the daughter of Philip French, a wealthy landowner of

William Livingston, John Jay's Whig intellectual father-in-law, long-time governor of New Jersey, and a delegate to the Constitutional Convention; portrait by John Wollaston the Younger (*Courtesy of Fraunces Tavern Museum, New York City*).

New Brunswick. Thus by marital connections Jay was related to some of the leading and most affluent among the Whig families in New York and New Jersey.

More important, however, Sally's beauty, charm, gaiety, high spirits, and even her roles as a style-setter in women's fashion and as a popular hostess, perfectly complemented Jay's sedate and reserved personality, his obstinacy, and his well-known self-esteem. One could not remain stuffy with Sally around. Eleven years his junior, she held her rather formidable husband in respect bordering on veneration. To Jay, his beloved wife was always "Sally," but to her he was almost always "Mr. Jay." In the intimate circle of the Jays, everyone recognized the lifelong attachment and abiding affection of the pair, unusual even for those times.

Indeed, to their relatives and friends the pair seemed inseparable. In a marriage lasting more than thirty years they never were apart save where wartime exigencies, health, or government business intervened. Thus, during the British invasion of New York, Jay felt that Sally was safer at her father's Liberty Hall residence at Elizabethtown. Of all the diplomats' wives, she was the only one to accompany her husband abroad on a diplomatic mission during wartime. Abigail Adams did not join her husband until war's end. Overseas, separations of the pair lasted the bare few months when Jay, after the strenuous peace negotiations, went to Bath for his health and to settle a family estate. As Supreme Court Chief Justice, beginning in 1789, Jay had to undertake the arduous circuit-riding duties imposed on the members of his bench by federal law. These journeys kept Jay apart from his family for many months between 1790 and early 1794, and the following twelve months saw him in England negotiating the treaty that bears his name—another painful separation. During each of these absences John and Sally systematically wrote each other three times a week, carefully numbering their letters in case any of them went astray (and some, of course, did). Away from home on a military mission in the summer of '76, Jay wrote Sally that if she had received half the letters he had written, "I dare say you will at least set me down an attentive husband and (what is not always the case in Matrimony) a constant Lover." Constancy was indeed the key word in this marriage.

The light touch that Sally lent to the marriage counterbalanced Jay's deadly earnestness and strong sense of responsibility. He was a parent not only to his own children, but acted in a parental role toward the least capable members of his own large family—his elderly father and mother, who invariably looked to John to bring stability to the family, of whom four of John's brothers and sisters suffered mental or physical handicaps. Eve, the eldest, was, judging from her record in childhood and her strife-torn marriage, the most neurotic. When her Tory preacher husband abandoned her, John assumed the responsibility and cost of bringing up her son Peter Jay Munro, whom he always regarded as one of his own. Then there was Augustus, the second-born, who was mentally retarded and could neither read nor write. Peter and Anna, the third son and second daughter, were blinded by smallpox in the epidemic of 1739. James, who picked up a knighthood in the course of his controversial efforts to raise money in England for King's College, manifested a lifelong sibling rivalry with John and took few pains to conceal his envy and even hostility toward his successful younger brother, while Frederick or "Fady," the youngest, assumed his father's role of merchant and auctioneer, but was never distinguished for business acumen. Indeed, John Jay shouldered heavy family burdens and did so uncomplainingly and with generosity and compassion.

Jay's conspicuous stand favoring moderation toward Loyalists may well have been rooted in his early associations with them. He was graduated from a Loyalist citadel, King's College, class of '64, clerked under a Loyalist attorney, Benjamin Kissam, was distantly related to the Loyalist De Lancey family (two of whose daughters he unsuccessfully courted, according to malicious Tory gossip), argued legal issues in a debating society and the Moot (a mock court for the training of law students) with associates, at least half of whom would choose the King's side, and was a prominent member of the Social Club, which held its entertainments on Saturday evenings in wintertime at Fraunces Tavern, on the corner of Broad and Dock streets, and in summer at Kip's Bay, where they had built a clubhouse. Since more than half of its members espoused the Loyalist cause, they held their final gathering in December 1775. Thereafter, Whig and Tory families went their separate ways.

Normally regarded as cautious and prudent, Jay also

had a combative streak and did not suffer affronts lightly. Almost a quarter-century had passed since the incident, but his own family had not forgotten it, least of all Jay himself, who recalled the incident with a certain relish. It happened at King's College in Jay's senior year. Some of Jay's fellow students engaged in a disorderly prank and broke the dining room table. Doctor Myles Cooper, the High Tory president, came storming in, lined up all the students, and proceeded to interrogate them one by one. Each student denied breaking the table or knowing the culprit who had done so.

In turn, Jay, as his son William later related the interrogation, denied breaking the table. Then the next question from President Cooper:

"Do you know who did break the table?"

Jay's answer: "Yes, sir."

"Who is it?"

"I do not choose to tell you, sir."

Warning that he would hear from him further, the irate president made his exit while trying to preserve his dignity.

That was not the end of it. Jay was summoned before the faculty, but before making his appearance he looked up a set of the college statutes that he had been obliged to copy in his own hand, and that bore his signature as well as Myles Cooper's. There was nothing in the statutes requiring one student to inform against another, although students were enjoined against "contumacious" behavior. Jay pleaded the statutes in his defense before the committee. Feeling no sympathy with lawyerlike undergraduates, the faculty promptly suspended him.

Jay's suspension must have been a shock to his family, particularly to his father, who had been so intimate a friend of the first president, Samuel Johnson, Cooper's predecessor, too sensible a fellow to have ever gotten himself into such an impasse. Fortunately for all concerned, an indulgent faculty allowed Jay to return to college in time for commencement, and three years later even conferred a master's degree upon him.

That combative and self-righteous streak of Jay's seemed always ready to surface in his youthful days. Only admitted to the bar a few years, he ventured to take on the prestigious attorney general of the province, John Tabor Kempe. The latter was considered an *arriviste* by socially secure young men like Jay, and between the two there seems to have been bad blood for some years. When Kempe, acting for the governor, interposed in a case in which Jay was engaged and did so without consulting Jay, the latter charged Kempe with rudeness in ignoring the ordinary "rules of politeness." He demanded an explanation, but Kempe's response only roused Jay to the boiling point. "This is the first instance I ever met with of such an Address," Kempe replied, and he considered the charge entirely without foundation. In rejoinder, Jay criticized Kempe's failure to offer an explanation. "A rupture with you, sir, would be very disagreeable to me," he added. "But I had rather reject the friendship of the world than purchase it by patience under indignities offered by any man in it." Jay's overreaction to the incident speaks volumes for his concern about his reputation and his readiness to court the permanent enmity of a powerful royal official rather than suffer a slight to his self-esteem.

There were times when Jay allowed his contentious nature to take an extreme course. By 1773 Jay had become one of the three managers of the city's Dancing Assembly, regularly held every fortnight during the fall and winter, and patronized by New York's most fashionable residents. Applying rigid social standards, Jay turned down an application from one Robert Randall. The latter charged Jay with giving "a stab to his honor." Jay admitted that Randall had "a right to satisfaction." "I will either ask your pardon or fight you." The result will never be known. Jay proposed a time and place for a meeting, but no duel seems to have occurred, and both parties survived the literary confrontation.

Jay's obstinate and combative streak was perhaps never more evident than in his conduct as clerk to a boundary commission appointed in 1769 to settle a territorial dispute between New York and New Jersey. Jay expended considerable time and money without being reimbursed. Both colonies at length accepted the commission's report. The only barrier to the settlement was the presentation of the commission's records for review by the Board of Trade in England. Here Jay balked and refused to release a copy until he was requested to do so by an Order in Council or an act of the New York Assembly. The Assembly so ordered. To all parties concerned, except John Jay, the young lawyer's obstinate course seemed incomprehensible. The fact remains, however, that had he turned over the product of his labors before his own claims for back pay and other outlays were settled, he probably would have forfeited his chance of getting so much as a penny. Thus early did Jay reveal that tenacity with regard to observing established procedures which was to stamp his entire career.

Some ungenerous spirits, mostly of Loyalist persuasion, laid Jay's gradual espousal of the Patriot cause to his disappointment at not securing a land patent in Vermont (then claimed under a royal grant to New York) that he had solicited of the governor. Some put it to the governor's denial to him and his college friend and law partner, Robert R. Livingston, Jr., of appointments to a pair of judgeships they had solicited. His critics were not prepared to ascribe motives other than self-interest to their opponents, and could not imagine that those who differed from them might be acting out of principle. John Jay was, above all, a principled man. In espousing the Whig cause he would abandon his law practice permanently, and thereby cut himself off from what was proving to be a substantial source of income.

If principles were important to Jay, so too were

family connections and the momentum of events in which he was caught up. Jay's father and brothers had espoused the Whig cause early on, but no clue to Jay's political preference can be found among his clients, a mixed bag of Tories and Whigs. In some thousand cases that he litigated during the seven years of his active practice, he had shown equal diligence in pleading the cause of Tory and Whig clients. Finally, one can hardly ignore his marriage, which attached him to one of the foremost Whig families in the colonies, headed by his father-in-law, soon to become the first Patriot governor of New Jersey, succeeding his royal predecessor William Franklin, Benjamin Franklin's illegitimate son.

Still, no one could have guessed the direction Jay would take when he first entered politics in 1774. The events that would seriously disrupt his law practice transpired when news reached New York of the closing of the port of Boston by the British government in retaliation for the Boston Tea Party. That repressive action triggered a response throughout America. New York City elected a Committee of Fifty-one, in which conservatives had a slight majority. Among the latter was John Jay, along with some nineteen future Tories. Jay quickly assumed leadership, calling for the assembly of a general congress "without delay." Elected to the First Continental Congress, which convened in Philadelphia in September 1774, Jay found that battle lines were quickly drawn between radicals and conservatives, with which latter bloc Jay was quickly identified.

The radicals captured the momentum from the start. Congress endorsed the Suffolk Resolves, declaring the Intolerable Acts passed by Parliament unconstitutional, advised the people to arm and form their own militia, and recommended economic sanctions against Great Britain. By the margin of a single vote the radical bloc managed to defeat the plan proposed by conservative-minded and later Tory, Joseph Galloway of Pennsylvania. Levying heavily on Franklin's old Albany Plan of Union, Galloway's losing plan had been backed by fellow conservatives, including John Jay and James Duane of New York and Edward Rutledge of South Carolina.

Jay himself had gained attention almost from the very start of the sessions. The prestigious orator from Virginia, Patrick Henry, argued for the setting up of a new constitutional structure, in a Congress in which votes would be proportioned to population. Jay took the floor to rejoin that Henry's plan was premature, since arbitrary government "must run over, before we undertake to form a new constitution." As for the present Congress, Jay proposed a rule giving each represented province an equal vote. Jay's motion prevailed, and the precedent established at the First Congress served for its successor throughout the Confederation years.

John Jay's eloquence had left a mixed impression on the delegates. Patrick Henry expressed "a horrid opinion" of the New Yorker, while John Adams, who shared Henry's radical stance, generously characterized Jay as "a Man of Wit, well-informed, a good Speaker, and an elegant writer." "Negociation, suspension of commerce, and war," in that order, were the three courses Adams ascribed to Jay. War must be waived for the present, Jay argued, while negotiation and the suspension of commerce must be given their chance.

Having faced down the conservatives, the radicals now sought to win over to their side some of the least intransigent and most promising talents among their opponents. John Jay, who had perhaps grudgingly signed the Continental Association—the nonimportation and nonexportation agreement—was drafted to prepare an eloquent "Address to the People of Great Britain." When it was read, as Jefferson reported, "there was but one sentiment of admiration." In this direct appeal over the heads of King and Parliament, Jay charged the British government with establishing "a system of slavery," claimed for the colonists the rights of Englishmen, and denounced as "heresies" the contention that Parliament had unlimited sovereignty over the colonies. For a certainty, Jay insisted that that body had no right to dispose of their property without their consent. That action "no power on earth" had the right to do, he contended. Finally, Jay warned: "We will never consent to be hewers of wood or drawers of water." Strong language indeed from the moderate-minded John Jay, and his stunned Tory friends accused him of abandoning his "old principles" to court popularity.

Still, even after Lexington and Concord, Jay did not rush headlong into the fray. On his return to Philadelphia in May of 1775 to attend the Second Continental Congress, which the First Congress had summoned, he still nurtured the hope that the British government—the King, if not Parliament—would yield to America's demands for self-rule. Although his moderate views had not abated, he agreed to prepare a "Letter to the Oppressed Inhabitants of Canada," wherein he reminded the people of that land that "the fate of the Protestant and Catholick Colonies" was "strongly linked together," and invited their support in breaking "the fetters of slavery." This literary effusion must have been a real chore for a man of Jay's Huguenot background, for one who professed little tolerance for the dispensation of the Church of Rome.

In the spring of '75, Congress heard nothing but bleak news. Parliament had ignored the petition of the First Continental Congress, the Ministry was planning to dispatch troops, and a shooting war had broken out at Lexington and Concord. In response, Congress resolved to place the colonies in a position to repel force by force.

It was at this critical juncture that the moderate party, including Jay and John Dickinson of Delaware, decided to take a last stand against war. Jay now moved for a second petition to the King, which Dickinson seconded. Jay seems to have written an initial draft, but Dickinson rewrote it, a prudent move indeed. Jay's was much too conciliatory for the temper of Congress, and he made too many concessions to the British government. He asked that "every irritating measure be *suspended*," while Dickinson proposed the *outright repeal* of objectionable statutes. Jay explicitly disavowed independence as an end, a pledge that Dickinson shrewdly sidestepped. Jay proposed that, should the royal government prefer not to deal with Congress, negotiations might be conducted with the colonial assemblies. Dickinson, who understood that Congress could not be expected to adopt a self-denying ordinance when it had in fact assumed jurisdiction over war and peace and foreign affairs, avoided including this proposal, at the same time arranging that the petition be signed by individuals to offset the fact that it was adopted by a general Congress, a body so unpalatable to George III. In scrupulously keeping from ruffling the sensibilities of Congress, Dickinson had avoided making the injudicious and even unnecessary concessions that Jay's draft contained. Jay's draft clearly would never have been adopted; Dickinson's was, but over strenuous objections.

Thus, what John Adams commented upon as that "strange oscillation between love and hatred, between war and peace—preparations for war and negotiations for peace" occupied Congress at a time when George Washington was already at his command post in Cambridge. Ticonderoga and Crown Point, not to speak of Bunker Hill, had developed a momentum of their own. To offset the conciliatory note struck by the Olive Branch Petition, Congress adopted the more defiant "Declaration of Taking up Arms," a joint product of Jefferson and Dickinson.

Perhaps more patient than others in Congress, Jay found his hopes shattered when news came on November 9, 1775, that the King had refused even to receive the Olive Branch Petition. The King's affront struck Jay to the quick. By temperament an activist and a believer, like Hamilton, that government must be infused with energy, Jay was readier than before to adopt a continental approach to the distribution of war power, an approach that would not long thereafter stamp him as a nationalist. When New Jersey proposed to dispatch its own petition to the King, Congress named John Dickinson, George Wythe of Virginia, and John Jay to talk the New Jersey assembly out of their plan. Jay told the Jerseymen that "we had nothing to expect from *the Mercy* or *Justice* of Britain," that petitions were no longer the appropriate means, but rather vigor and unanimity were "the only Means." Only the "Petition of *United America* presented by Congress" could be justified, Jay insisted; all else was "unnecessary."

Thus, whether he willed it or no, Jay was propelled into the war against Great Britain. He served on various crucial Congressional committees, including the Committee of Secret Correspondence to secure aid from abroad. Carrying on an active correspondence with the American agent to France, Silas Deane, he used an invisible ink, according to a formula provided by his elder brother Sir James. He urged New York Patriots to bar all of the state's inhabitants who voted against sending deputies to the provincial convention from enjoying "the protection of the United Colonies," inhibiting their movements, publishing their names, and disarming them. He prodded Patriots back home to assume the powers of government, including taxation. Taxation, not more paper money, was the answer, he urged. As the groundswell for independence seemed to be carrying all before it, Jay inched toward overt resistance. He applied for and was duly given the colonelcy of the Second Regiment, New York City militia.

Owing to the pressures of Congressional duties, Jay missed the birth of his firstborn, Peter Augustus Jay, in January 1776, but his wife's recovery from childbirth was slow and both his parents were seriously ill, sufficient reasons in Jay's mind to quit Philadelphia toward the end of April and choose instead to serve as a delegate to the third New York Provincial Congress, to which he had been elected that spring. In the meantime he was besieged by his fellow moderates in the Continental Congress to return and help check the rising tide of independence. On June 7, Richard Henry Lee introduced a motion declaring the "United Colonies" independent. New England, Virginia, and Georgia pressed for action; Edward Rutledge, supported by Robert R. Livingston, James Wilson, and John Dickinson, urged delay. On June 28 Rutledge pleaded with Jay to return to Congress and stop the triple-mounted threat—independence, the adoption of the Articles of Confederation, and an agreement on a plan for treaties with foreign powers.

Jay chose instead to stay in New York, but not because he did not share the views of his fellow moderates. On the one hand, he played a leading role in putting his own province in a state of defense against an anticipated British attack. On the other, he was blocking action by the New York delegates at the Continental Congress to vote for independence. Thus, Jay readily assented to serve on provincial committees— one to draft a law relating to the perils to which the colony was exposed by "its intestine enemies," and the other to act on the Congressional mandate of May 15, 1776, requesting them to establish their own state governments. Still, he was not ready for overt independence, and on June 11, four days after Richard Henry Lee's resolution had been offered in the Continental Congress affirming independence, Jay moved in the New York Congress "that the good people of this Colony have not, in the opinion of this Congress, authorized this Congress, or the Delegates of this Colony, in the Continental Congress, to declare this Colony to be and continue independent of the Crown of Great Britain."

Jay's presence in New York spared him the embarrassment of having to cast a vote on independence when it came up in Philadelphia on July 2. His explanation to Edward Rutledge may have seemed a lame one to its recipient, who was not fully cognizant of the immediate perils that New York faced. He was engaged in "plots, conspiracies, and chimeras dire," Jay explained, adding, "We have a government, you know, to form, and God knows what it will resemble."

The transformation of John Jay from circumspect legislator to forthright Patriot was determined by two events coming in quick succession: the passage of the Declaration of Independence and the invasion of his own state by the British fleet and British and Hessian armed forces. By the time the Fourth Congress of the state had made a quorum at White Plains on July 9, Congress had already acted on independence. Jay responded at once, drafting the committee report on the Declaration, which the New York Congress adopted that afternoon. "While we lament the cruel necessity which has rendered that measure unavoidable," his resolve declared, "we approve the same, and will, at the risk of our lives and fortunes, join with the other colonies in supporting it." The next day the Provincial Congress changed its name to "the Convention of the representatives of the State of New York."

Even before the passage of his resolution on independence, Jay had for some months exercised a leadership role in the de facto war that the Patriot party was fighting. Inside New York City, Jay saw abundant evidence of treachery. At the insistence of the Provincial Congress he had been requested to confer with General Washington and take measures to cope with subversive elements. Jay served on a three-man committee to round up suspects, and they picked up quite a bag. The leading malefactor proved to be no less a personage than David Matthews, the city's mayor. Jay's committee, after examining him, dispatched him to a jail in Litchfield, a quiet spot in Connecticut that they expected would be safe from British invasion. Along with Matthews, sixteen others were sentenced or jailed for treasonous practices, disaffection, counterfeiting, or aiding the enemy.

Jay's searching investigation brought to light a plot involving Thomas Hickey, a Continental soldier, up to his ears in a conspiracy to capture General Washington. Jay's committee turned this case over to the army. Hickey's house in Flatbush was surrounded; he was court-martialed and hanged, even though it was by no means clear that before independence had been declared a person aiding the British cause could actually be guilty of "treason," which technically, under English law, involved an attack on the person of the King. Feeling that the question demanded clarification, Jay saw to it that the New York Convention enacted a law prescribing the death penalty for treason.

Meanwhile, the British fleet was threatening the city, hopeful of dividing the state by sending ships and troops up the Hudson. For some days late in July, John Jay mysteriously disappeared. He felt he owed his wife some explanation, and he wrote her from Poughkeepsie on July 21 that "in defiance of the God of Sleep whom the bugs and fleas banished from my pillow last night, am I set down to write a few lines to my good little wife. On leaving Rye [his family's home] I informed you of my intended journey," adding: "We have paid a visit to the forts in the Highlands, and after a jaunt of three days which afforded us pleasure as well as exercise, I arrived here about an hour ago in perfect health. Should I continue this kind of life for three weeks or a month my cloaths would be too narrow for me."

Only at a later time did Jay show Sally the brief diary entries he had made recording the extraordinary "jaunt of three days." First, he and his committeemen traveled to Salisbury Furnace in Connecticut, some sixty-odd miles northwest of Hartford, to secure cannon for Washington's army. Technicalities, he was told by the officials at the furnace, required them to receive an order from Governor Trumbull. Jay set out for Lebanon, where he talked the governor into giving him the order, but not before Trumbull consulted his Council. Jay then rushed back to Salisbury Furnace, where they agreed to make the cannon, but referred him to Livingston Manor for securing the shot and trucks. His visits accomplished, Jay hired teams to carry four twelve-pounders, together with fifty rounds of shot for each cannon, to Hoffman's Landing on the Hudson. On his return journey he overtook the cannon and shot, and arranged for their transfer across the river to Fort Montgomery aboard a sloop that was about ready to sail.

This journey, breathless and dangerous, provides us with another dimension of Jay, the cautious and prudent man who could be galvanized into incredible action. Jay himself was dissatisfied with the measures of defense that were being taken, including the construction of a boom across the Hudson, presumably to stop the northward thrust of the British fleet. Writing several months later to Robert Morris, the Pennsylvania merchant-financier, Jay declared: "Had I been vested with absolute power in this State, I have often said and still think that *I would last spring have desolated all Long Island, Staten-Island, the City and County of New York, and that part of the County of Westchester which lies below the mountains.* I would have stationed the main body of the army in the mountains on the east, and eight or ten thousand men in the highlands on the west side of the river," thereby preventing the British army and naval forces from using New York and its magnificent harbor for the better part of seven years. A timid Congress was not prepared for a scorched-earth policy, and negatived Jay's bold proposal.

In addition to his military duties, Jay headed a committee to round up Tories engaged in conspiratorial activities against the Patriot armed forces. Among the first victims of Jay's vigilance was his long-time friend, schoolmate at King's College, and fellow attorney, Peter Van Schaack. A man of conscience, Van Schaack refused to take an oath of allegiance to the Patriot cause, and in what was perhaps Jay's bitterest decision, he banished Van Schaack to Kinderhook and later had him expelled from American lines. At war's end, Jay and Van Schaack had a cordial reunion in London. As Jay put it in a frank and amicable letter, he had acted against his friend as a matter of principle.

"Your judgment, and consequently, your Conscience differed from mine on a very important Question. But though as an independent American, I considered all who were not for us, and You among the Rest, as against us, yet be assured that John Jay did not cease to be a friend to Peter Van Schaack." Jay arranged for his friend's return to America, was the first on shipboard to greet him when he arrived in New York, and followed with admiration Van Schaack's career as an innovative teacher of law students at Kinderhook.

To Jay, the Patriots had crossed the Rubicon and there was no turning back. When his old friends Beverly Robinson and Oliver De Lancey failed the loyalty test, their defiance could not be overlooked. Robinson, it was later disclosed, was thick in Benedict Arnold's treason plot, and Oliver De Lancey had organized a Tory force to fight against the Patriot cause. To Jay, their departure was good riddance.

Jay ran a secret life as well as a public one. He organized and operated a spy ring. He never mentioned names, even in later years, when he told the story to his family friend, James Fenimore Cooper. Jay picked out a resident of Carmel who served in the ranks of the militia. He then arranged to have him appear to be attempting to desert. According to prearranged plan, he was caught and jailed. Then Jay arranged to facilitate his escape. Bearing all the credentials of an imprisoned deserter, the spy had no difficulty in being accepted as a Tory, infiltrating the British and Tory lines, and collecting intelligence about their planned military forays, information that led to the breaking up of several Tory recruiting rings. The spy, it was later established beyond a doubt, was Enoch Crosby, but Cooper, in *The Spy*, called him Harvey Birch and denied that Crosby's name had ever been revealed to him by Jay—a denial consistent with Jay's lifelong discretion. Enoch Crosby's identification is confirmed by entries in the now-published minutes of the Committee for Detecting Conspiracies, which Jay headed, along with Crosby's application for a federal pension.

Jay was now confronted with a more creative challenge. He was picked by the New York Convention to draft a constitution for the state, and in that chore he performed a neat trick, balancing the radical weight exerted by Robert Yates of Albany and Henry Wisner and Charles De Witt of Ulster against the more moderate ideas of James Duane, Gouverneur Morris, Robert R. Livingston, and himself. Jay drew heavily on some of the constitutional ideas that John Adams had circulated, proposing a constitution that combined monarchical, aristocratic, and democratic notions.

Jay was picked to write the draft, and the resulting constitution was surprisingly innovative. It limited the power of the governor by placing appointments in the hands of a Council of Appointment and making him share a veto power with a Council of Revision. The clause on religious toleration was too sweeping for Jay's own taste, as he would have preferred the inclusion of a restrictive clause barring persons who would not disavow any superior allegiance to a foreign power. This proposed restraint on Roman Catholics was defeated in committee, and the state constitution ended up with the broadest statement of religious toleration of any of the state charters adopted during this period. Jay did, however, have a cautionary clause included, preventing "liberty of conscience" from being construed so as to encourage licentiousness, and he managed to persuade the Convention to make provision at war's end for voting by secret ballot. Retrospectively, Jay recognized how delicately balanced the constitution was between opposing groups. "Another turn of the winch would have cracked the cord," he later told his younger son, William.

The new state refused to release Jay from its tenacious grip. Named Chief Justice of the state's Supreme Court, he presided over the bench at Kingston, where he had his fill of war crimes—murder, assault, rape, counterfeiting, and grand larceny. If that was not enough, the Supreme Court justices were required to preside at courts of oyer and terminer to hear cases before the next sitting of the Supreme Court circuit. He sentenced ten men to the gallows, no light-hearted chore for a man of conscience.

At long last, and after an absence of more than three years, Jay returned to Philadelphia in December of 1778, this time as a delegate from New York, ostensibly to settle its controversy with the Vermonters, who were claiming status as citizens of a separate state and threatening to confederate with the Canadians if they were turned down by Congress. The issues into which Jay plunged were so large, however, that the narrow purpose of his representation was quickly ignored.

Congress, in December of 1778, was the scene of almost unprecedented infighting. On one side were arrayed the Adamses of Massachusetts and the Lees of Virginia; on the other, the friends of Silas Deane, the first agent to be sent by Congress to France. Deane, despite the useful services he had performed abroad in securing material aid from the French, was charged with crooked bookkeeping. The charge could never be established one way or the other, as Deane failed to bring his books along with him. His enemies denounced him for having corrupt dealings with French agents, particularly during the years when the American rebels were getting secret aid and funds from the French before they openly joined the United States in a formal alliance.

When Jay arrived on the scene, he found that the Deane issue had embroiled Yankees against New Yorkers. Henry Laurens of South Carolina, never known for patience or tact, was presiding over the Congress and adding fuel to the fires by standing out as one of Deane's chief critics. Deane's friends in Congress managed to force Laurens to resign. The resignation was really a victory for Conrad Gérard, the French minister to the United States, who played a big role in Congress's decision-making. He wanted Congress to pick as Laurens's successor a person who could be counted on to be a friend of France. The compliant delegates quickly turned to Jay and elected him president. Jay would soon disclose, however, that he was no man's tool, nor any foreign nation's. Aside from the mistaken view of Jay's partiality toward France, his reputation as an able public servant was an important factor in his election. "The weight of his personal Character," Gouverneur Morris wrote to George Clinton on the day of the election, "contributed as much to his Election as the Respect for the State which hath done and suffered so much or the Regard for its Delegates which is not inconsiderable."

Problems piled up on Jay from the start. Thomas Paine was then serving as paid secretary of the Committee for Foreign Affairs. With characteristic indiscretion, Paine plunged into the Deane controversy by publishing in the newspapers an account in which he insisted that the supplies with which France had provided the United States before the formal French alliance were a gift to the United States and not a loan, as Caron de Beaumarchais, one of France's chief agents, would always contend. Even Alexander Hamilton, after a scrupulous examination of the books when he became Secretary of the Treasury, was puzzled. Paine's inexcusable indiscretion affronted the honor of the King of France by revealing that the French had been for some years secretly engaged in funding the American rebellion behind the backs of the British and before making a formal alliance with America. Like so many intelligence "secrets," the British had known about it all along, but merely lacked proof.

When Paine refused to retract his statement, an angry Gérard demanded that he publicly repudiate his charge. At the prompting of Congress, President Jay called Paine to the bar and sharply interrogated him. Congress then voted to remove him from his post, but Paine anticipated his ouster by resigning. Who let the cat out of the bag and disclosed the confidential journals of Congress to Paine? Congress first pointed the finger at Charles Thomson, the incorruptible perma-

Thomas Paine, whose indiscretions on France's secret aids to America led to his rebuke by Congress's president, John Jay; portrait by John Wesley Jarvis (*National Gallery of Art*).

nent secretary, but then Henry Laurens admitted that he had taken the journals home with him and let Paine have a look. What may have seemed to outsiders like a tempest in a teapot was considered a serious issue in the world of diplomacy, where appearances were often more important than reality—and still are—and what one writes down for the record is often very different from what one actually says and does.

During the period of somewhat more than nine months in which Jay served as president of the Continental Congress, a host of critical problems confronted that body for resolution—constitutional, fiscal, military, and diplomatic. While lacking the executive powers exercised by the President of the United States under the Federal Constitution, the president of the Continental Congress not only presided over Congress but exercised his vote as a delegate, received and replied to correspondence addressed to him in his formal capacity, signed Congressional resolutions and drafted a number of them himself, and, in Jay's case, played a not inconsiderable role behind the scenes in the continuing and always delicate negotiations with Gérard in settling on peace terms.

To start with, Jay had a constitutional crisis on his hands. On January 6, 1779, Maryland formally refused to join the Confederation unless all states with western lands ceded their claims to Congress. It so happened that the final draft of the Articles of Confederation omitted any provision requiring the approval of all the state legislaturcs, and it was Jay's publicly expressed contention that since twelve of the thirteen states had already ratified, "for every purpose essential to the defense of these States in the progress of the present war, and necessary to the attainment of the objects of it, these States now are as fully, legally, and absolutely confederated as it is possible for them to be."

John Jay had now openly espoused the cause of national supremacy, with which he would henceforth be identified. When Pennsylvania defied a decree of the Congressional Committee on Appeals in cases of prize and capture, Jay saw to it that a condemnatory resolution was adopted. Congress resolved "that no act of any one State can or ought to destroy the rights of appeals to Congress." In Jay's handwriting and in words assertive of the fundamantal tenets of national sovereignty, Congress went on to resolve:

> That Congress is by these United States invested with the supreme sovereign power of war and peace;
> That the power of executing the law of nations is essential to the sovereign supreme power of war and peace;
> That the legality of all captures on the high seas must be determined by the law of nations.

Two years later, in a resolution drafted by James Madison, Congress reasserted its authority to seize prizes of the enemy.

From his position as president of Congress, Jay saw Continental money depreciating at an alarming rate, prices soaring, inflation rampant. America's credit was vanishing fast, both at home and abroad. In an impassioned state paper issued near the end of his presidency, Jay felt obliged to remind the American people that they were honor-bound to pay off the national debt within a reasonable period after war's end, called upon the states to pay their taxes ("requisitions" was the polite term), advocated reducing the amount of currency in circulation, and advised them to rely henceforth on loans and taxes. Reassuring the people that "independence was now fixed as fate," he predicted that the nation had sufficient assets to pay off the national debt in eighteen to twenty years after war's end. He counted on burgeoning assets from a natural increase in population and a flood tide of immigration. As Secretary of the Treasury, Alexander Hamilton later proved that Jay's optimism was abundantly justified.

In an eloquent passage, Jay declared: "Let it never be said that America had no sooner become independent than she became insolvent or that her infant glories and growing fame were obscured and tarnished by broken contracts and violated faith, in the very hour when all the nations of the earth were admiring and almost adoring the splendor of her rising."

This exhortation presaged a recurrent theme found in *The Federalist*, a theme that Jay's two collaborators would underscore in scorching prose.

4

Triumph at Paris:
The Winning of Independence

Throughout the long summer of '79, Jay presided over the feverish debates in Congress defining America's peace objectives. This was not his first foray into the arcane world of diplomacy. Back in the fall of '75, as a member of a secret committee to correspond "with our friends in Great Britain, in Ireland, and other parts of the world," he and his colleagues had had several cloak-and-dagger meetings with an unofficial emissary of the French government named Archard de Bonvouloir. The meetings, shrouded in secrecy, took place on the outskirts of Philadelphia, with each committee member approaching the appointed rendezvous by a different road. The Frenchman made it clear that he had no authority to make any formal offers, but he encouraged talk of exchanging American produce for French munitions and engineers. While these talks were going forward, Silas Deane was already carrying out his pseudo-secret mission in Paris on behalf of Congress.

Now four years had passed; France had been America's overt ally for a year and a half, and Congress felt that the time had come to settle upon its war and peace aims and to select commissioners to go abroad and effectuate them. Sectional interests and personal rivalries determined the votes of the delegates on such seminal points as boundaries, fisheries, navigation of the Mississippi, and much else. Complicating frank discussions were the pressures exerted by the ever-watchful French minister, Conrad Alexandre Gérard, chatting interminably with those Congressional delegates who appeared more concerned about France's goals in the war than America's, and seemed uninhibited by the Congressional rules of secrecy.

Jay was sickened by the pressures exerted by special interests and by the chicanery that too often kept sensible men from agreeing on sensible peace ends. "There is as much intrigue in this State House as in the Vatican," Jay observed to Washington, "but as little secrecy as in a boarding school." The General, who shared Jay's tight-lipped approach to commenting on sensitive matters, and who had suffered more than one affront from Congress about his conduct of the war, saw the point and commiserated with his friend.

The eight months of 1779 during which Jay had presided over the Congress were consumed by quarrels over war aims. In settling upon these objectives, the delegates were obliged to keep in mind both the treaties of alliance and of commerce with France and the secret treaty that France had made with Spain the following year. In the first place, diplomatic actions had been taken in Europe which Congress had not fully appreciated. In 1778 France had made two treaties with America, a treaty of alliance and a treaty of amity and commerce. In the former, Louis XVI had pledged to continue in the war against Great Britain until the independence of the United States was attained, with the proviso that neither party should conclude peace with Great Britain without the formal consent of the other having first been obtained. Then the following year France broke the spirit if not the letter of its treaties with America through a secret alliance with Spain. These diverse treaties posed all sorts of difficulties to the American negotiators abroad. The treaty of commerce between France and the United States bound each party not to interfere with the fishing rights enjoyed by the other, but by the secret pact with Spain of 1779, France agreed with Spain that if she could drive the British from Newfoundland, the fishery should be shared *only* with Spain—this provision clearly in conflict with fishing rights in the area, which Congress claimed as having been traditionally enjoyed by New Englanders from time immemorial.

But even more seriously, the Franco-Spanish treaty bound both parties to continue the war until Spain recovered Gibraltar. If then the Americans needed the consent of France to get out of the war, they would be fighting until the present day, as Britain still maintains a tenacious hold over the Rock.

To Congress, though, the news that Spain had come into the war, the text of her arrangements with France withheld, was joyfully regarded as an opportunity to set up a tripartite alliance. Little did Congress realize the degree of horror with which the King of Spain, Carlos III, and his principal minister, the Conde de Floridablanca, regarded revolutions and particularly the American one. To their minds, a successful war by the American colonies would spread like a contagious disease throughout their vast Spanish-American empire in the New World.

The Deane imbroglio had two constructive effects on the peacemaking that lay ahead. The quarrel convinced the delegates in Congress that it was necessary to be represented abroad by men who could be counted on to put the public good ahead of private gain or personal rancor, and impelled Congress to spell out its peace aims. Of the three commissioners whom Congress had appointed to represent America at Versailles, only Benjamin Franklin survived the purge. Congress sacked both Deane and his archenemy, Arthur Lee. John Adams was elected commissioner to make peace with Great Britain, and John Jay, in deference to the Deane faction, was elected minister plenipotentiary to Spain. Helped by his own vote in the New York delegation, Jay "squeezed in," as Laurens ungenerously put it. "The choice of Jay leaves nothing to be desired," Gérard wrote to the Comte de Vergennes, France's prestigious foreign minister. "To much intelligence and the best intentions he joins an amiable and conciliatory temper." If Gérard meant to suggest that Jay was "pliable," he soon would be undeceived. A third minister, ex-President Henry Laurens, was assigned to the United Provinces, as the Netherlands was then known.

The peace terms that Congress finally agreed upon (subject to later modifications) included a northern boundary for the United States that would include what was later known as the Northwest Territory, an area that Parliament had assigned to Canada under the notorious Quebec Act of 1774. The Mississippi was set as the western boundary, Florida as the southern. Perhaps most controversial, Congress claimed for Americans the free navigation of the Mississippi to the sea. Rather vague instructions were voted regarding the fisheries in the North Atlantic, which New Englanders had traditionally exploited. The fishing rights were not to be yielded at the peace, Congress instructed, while failing to put this claim forward in the form of an ultimatum. With these charges from Congress, the three commissioners were dispatched overseas on different voyages, but it is a matter of legitimate speculation whether they would have accepted their respective assignments, had they known what lay in store for them.

Ignorant of the feelings of the Spanish court, Congress counted on John Jay to make Carlos III recognize American independence, to bring Spain into the war on America's side, to induce that proud nation to concede America's rights to the navigation of the Mississippi River, the mouth of which was then controlled by Spain, and to secure other aids to support the American cause.

When, in late October of 1779, the Continental frigate *Confederacy* weighed anchor and stood out into the Delaware Bay for the long voyage across the North Atlantic to Spain, it carried quite a civilian company in addition to its sailors and fighting men. John Jay took his wife with him, leaving his young son, Peter Augustus, in the joint care of the Livingstons at Liberty Hall and his own family, who had removed to the relative safety of Fishkill in New York during the years of the British occupation of the lower part of the state. Accompanying the Jays were Peter Jay Munro, Jay's twelve-year-old nephew, Brockholst Livingston, Jay's brother-in-law and personal secretary, and William Carmichael, the official secretary of the Jay mission. Gérard, who was retiring as French minister, seized the opportunity to take passage as well.

The members of the party were showered with gifts and cordial good wishes, but the most precious of all came from West Point:

> General Washington presents his most respectful compliments to Mrs. Jay. Honoured in her request by General St. Clair he takes pleasure in presenting the inclosed with thanks for so polite a testimony of her approbation and esteem. He wishes most fervently that prosperous gales, unruffled seas, and every thing pleasing and desirable may smooth the path she is about to walk in.

Sally treasured the note, adding at the bottom in her own hand: "A lock of the General's hair."

Alas for Washington's good wishes, instead of unruffled seas, the *Confederacy* was pounded by heavy gales, causing the mainmast to crash to the deck, followed almost immediately by mizzenmast, foremast, and even bowsprit. With an improvised small mast and sails, the ship struggled through strong winds and heavy seas. Jay, backing up the frigate's captain against an irate Gérard, voted to terminate the passage at the French island of Martinique. How a seasick John Jay was able to make this rational stand in backing the captain's navigational decisions we will never know, for, as Sally wrote home of their voyage, "My dear Mr. Jay suffered exceedingly at least five weeks and was surprisingly reduced."

Martinique's gaiety and volcanic grandeur delighted the Jays, but also shocked them. Jay, whose aversion to slavery would one day turn him into an antislavery leader in New York, was sickened at the sight of slaves going about their duties weighted down by iron collars around their necks, dragging fifty-pound chains, and bearing on their backs marks of the lash. These sights of cruelty and degradation he would always remember. Switching ships, the Jays reached Cádiz, Spain, in January 1780.

The Jays would never forget Spain and the unexpectedly frosty reception they experienced before being authorized by the Spanish government to proceed to Madrid. John, Sally, and company traveled the tedious journey to the capital over dusty, flea-plagued roads, with overnight stays in filthy lodgings for which they were bilked by extortionate innkeepers. Traversing La Mancha, but by a less circuitous route than that taken by Don Quixote, they finally reached Madrid in April 1780.

For two years the Jays occupied a residence in San Mateo Street, and it was a lonesome spot at best. While, as he knew, the royal court was engaged in diplomatic flirtation with spies and unofficial envoys from Great Britain, with whom it was at war, Jay was left to cool his heels in Madrid or else to follow the court in its various perambulations to *palacios* built by the kings and their courtiers to pursue their hunting and other royal pleasures as the seasons dictated.

Never accorded an audience with King Carlos III, Jay had minimal satisfaction in dealing with the Conde de Floridablanca, a man whose temper tantrums were legendary. Jay secured such pitifully small sums of money for his country from France's ally that he was at one moment forced to declare a default of funds that Congress had secured abroad using his name as guarantor. If money advanced amounted to a pittance, recognition of an independent United States was abhorrent to a monarchy that considered the American revolutionaries a threat to their own adjacent colonies in the New World.

Nevertheless, Jay's dealings with the Spanish ministry proved both prudent and canny. When Congress, under pressure from France, withdrew the instruction to Jay that set the free navigation of the Mississippi to the sea as an ultimatum, Jay realized that his official mail from Congress had been intercepted and that Floridablanca had already seen this new vital concession and could afford to stall. In a confrontation with Floridablanca, Jay warned the Principal Minister that although Congress had dropped its insistence on the navigation of that mighty river, he considered this and any other revised instructions as conditional on Spain's prompt concessions to America's other demands. When Spain stalled once more, Congress, at length realizing that Spain had no intention of making any concessions, backed Jay's interpretation of the instruction and applauded his refusal to abandon the Mississippi.

In sum, Jay and Floridablanca were mutually sick of the sight of each other. As Spain's Principal Minister put it, Jay's "two chief points were: 'Recognize our independence; Spain, give us more money.' " With this stinging commentary on the Jay mission, the Spaniard paid grudging tribute to an opponent who was not only consistently right, but consistently righteous. Gratified by the approval of his conduct by Congress, Jay admitted that in Spain he had experienced "one continued series of painful perplexities and embarrassments."

Meanwhile, events moved ahead of the snail's pace of negotiations. Yorktown had sealed the fate of the Lord North ministry that ran the war with America from the British end but had refused to end it or come to terms with the rebellious subjects. A new administration under the Earl of Rockingham took over, and peace negotiations would begin in earnest. Originally, John Adams had been named a sole commissioner to make peace with Great Britain, but since the French violently objected to him, he was superseded by a commission that included not only Adams himself, but also Benjamin Franklin, our prestigious minister to France; John Jay, our unacknowledged minister to

Benjamin Franklin, Peace Commissioner and friend of
John Jay, portrait by J.S. Duplessis (*National Archives,
Washington, D.C.*).

Spain; Henry Laurens of South Carolina, Jay's predecessor as president of Congress, who would have been
a minister to Holland had he not been captured by the
British on the high seas and thrust into the Tower of
London; and Thomas Jefferson, who could not get a
boat from America to get to the peace talks in time
and never did participate.

Since the other negotiators had not yet made their
way to Paris, Franklin, who had befriended Jay throughout the latter's stay in Spain, now pressed him: "Come
hither as soon as possible." The Jays could hardly wait
to shake the dust of the Spanish plains from their
traveling bags. Jay had had it. "The object of my
coming to Spain was to make *propositions*, not suppli-
cations," he declared, and was soon crossing the
Pyrenees to what would prove his greatest diplomatic
triumph.

In the absence of the other two American commissioners, Franklin and Jay took turns negotiating with the British. Paris, swept by an epidemic of influenza, found Jay an early victim. So Franklin proceeded with preliminary talks with Richard Oswald, the British negotiator designated by Lord Shelburne, now the head of the new British government. On July 10, 1782, the Old Doctor, as his intimates called the learned Benjamin Franklin, sat down with Oswald and read him a memorandum, which he called "a few hints." He did so without any advance notice to the Comte de Vergennes, France's minister of foreign affairs. Franklin divided his proposals into "necessary" and "advisable." The former pretty well conformed to instructions that Congress had laid down. They were: (1) "full and complete independence of the Thirteen States, with all troops withdrawn"; (2) "a settlement of the boundaries of *their* colonies and the loyal colonies"; (3) the boundaries of Canada to be moved back before the Quebec Act of 1774, which carried Canada south to the Ohio River; (4) freedom of fishing on the banks and elsewhere for both fish and whales.

Then, as a friend, Franklin recommended certain "advisable" articles. These included an indemnity of persons whose homes were destroyed by the British or Indians; an admission by the British government of their "error" in starting the war; reciprocal trade privileges; and lastly, "giving up every part of Canada."

Now, Franklin was a well-meaning negotiator, but he could be both untidy and imprecise in his handling of affairs. For years a chief British spy, New England-born Dr. Edward Bancroft, had been serving as secretary in Franklin's official residence at Passy, and revealed many secrets to the enemy. In his early dealings with Oswald it is clear that Franklin exceeded his instructions while at the same time the peace terms he laid down lacked precision. Why recognize the "Thirteen States"—why not the United States of America, quite a different matter? Where do we find any insistence that the boundaries of the United States run to the Mississippi, in accordance with Congress's instructions? What about drying rights on the shore for New England fishermen? And if Franklin really meant the part about Canada seriously, why did he include it among the "advisable" and not the "necessary" articles? One may surmise at least two reasons for his devious conduct: first, because the French court was adamantly opposed to our acquisition of Canada, and second, because Congress made no demand for an area that American arms had failed to conquer and had actually, at Washington's request, disavowed any military plans for a Canadian invasion.

It is clear that what Franklin needed at this point was a tough-minded lawyer to plead his case and define his terms more precisely. Jay was clearly the right man at the right place. He had now recovered from his attack of influenza and thereafter played a central role in the negotiations. Unlike Franklin, Jay wanted everything spelled out. Most of all, he demanded preliminary recognition by Great Britain of the independence of the United States before proceeding with peace talks. Jay had good reasons for his insistence. The commission given Richard Oswald by the British government authorized him to conduct peace talks with the thirteen colonies; it implied no recognition of an independent United States. His chief, Lord Shelburne, had declared in Parliament that he still regarded "the independence of America to be a dreadful blow to the greatness of the country," and that should independence be established, "the sun might be said to have set." Such a leader, despite his amicable views toward America generally, could hardly be regarded as a solid bet for independence by the Americans in Paris. Jay was aware that the American army was moving toward dissolution, wracked as it was by mutiny and discontent over the failure of Congress to pay its troops. He knew, too, that virtually every American ship-of-war had been swept from the seas or was in badly damaged shape, while the British still kept an army of almost ten thousand men in New York and other forces in interior forts, where they could be counted on to stir up trouble with the Indians and prevent American westward settlement. Jay demanded not only recognition but the evacuation of British troops *before* the treaty was concluded, not after. And how right he would be, as the British took another fourteen years to pull out their garrisons stationed on American soil, contrary to the treaty that was finally negotiated!

Jay's talks with the Spaniards and the French only bolstered his suspicions that the American commissioners could not count on either nation backing him or his colleagues. After a long conversation with the Spanish ambassador to Paris, the Conde de Aranda, Jay reported his unsatisfactory meeting to Franklin. Based on Aranda's diary, his dispatches to his own court, and Jay's and Franklin's detailed accounts of their negotiations, which they transmitted to Secretary Livingston, it is possible to reconstruct the dialogue between the principals.

"When the Conde asked me what territory the United States expected," Jay informed the Old Doctor, "he sat down at a table with a French edition of Mitchell's great map of North America [erroneous, as we now know, but the best available then]. I drew my line along the Mississippi from its source south to 31° NL, the old northern boundary of West Florida, which, as you know, the British held after 1763 and the Spaniards recaptured. My finger moved east along that degree to the Chattahoochee, and then followed the undisputed northern boundary of East Florida to the sea."

"Then what happened?" asked Franklin.

"Here is the map I just received from Aranda, with a red line, which would confine us to within inches west of the Appalachians. You know Congress won't accept that, and you also know that Spain will not grant us the free navigation of the Mississippi."

"What did you answer?"

"A clear no," replied Jay, and Franklin applauded.

"What's our next best course?" continued Jay.

"We must seek the help of our good friend the

Comte de Vergennes. The French court has never failed us in the past," Franklin replied. Jay looked skeptical.

Thereafter the two journeyed to Versailles to visit Vergennes at his apartments, where Franklin and Jay raised two points: first, America's insistence that England recognize the independence of the United States *before* entering into a detailed treaty of peace; second, that France exert its influence to satisfy America's demand for concessions by the Spaniards of territory west to the Mississippi.

The date wa August 10, 1782. The Americans showed the Comte de Vergennes the commission that the British government gave to Richard Oswald. As Vergennes read over the commission, Jay pointed out that it did not recognize the independence of the United States.

"What difference does that make," Vergennes replied, "so long as there is an implied commitment in the commission, as I see it, to make independence an article of the treaty itself?"

"Not good enough," Jay replied. "If the British do not recognize our independence, they can stall the negotiations and our war could go on forever."

"I do not agree with you, M. Jay, even though the commission does authorize Oswald to treat with you as commissioners of the 'Colonies or Plantations,' they will come around in the final treaty."

Franklin seemed to nod in half agreement with the French foreign minister, muttering, "It will do."

Jay was obdurate, as he recognized that behind Vergennes' conciliatory position lurked a fear that the United States would quit the war once it had gained its chief aim—recognition of its independence.

Then, turning to the Spanish claims, Vergennes called in his undersecretary, Gérard de Rayneval. Both Frenchmen looked over the map and Aranda's line as well as Jay's and informed the Americans: "You claim more than you have a right to."

Jay and Franklin, a heavy-hearted pair, rode back in the carriage together to Passy, Franklin's residence.

An agitated Jay denounced the French position. "Don't you see, Dr. Franklin," he urged, "that Vergennes favored independence for America not out of any attachment to the principles of the Declaration of Independence, but because he regarded such an event as the blow he could administer to England, France's hated rival?" And then, without stopping for an answer, "Can't you see that the French are trying to coop us up between the mountains and the Atlantic and divide the rest between the Indians and the Spaniards?" Moving ahead like a prosecuting attorney, Jay charged, "Can't you see that France wants America to remain under her direction until their and our objects are attained, and until Spain is satisfied that everybody else is excluded from the Gulf and the Mississippi?"

Franklin responded, "Yes, I do concede that Spain is planning to coop us up within the Allegheny Mountains and the Atlantic, but so far as the French court and Vergennes are concerned, I think they are operating from friendly motives and are not trying to slow down the peace negotiations."

"I respectfully disagree, Dr. Franklin," Jay rejoined. "Vergennes fears that once America makes peace with the British, we might drop out of the war. You and I know that France and Spain together will never take Gibraltar, the prize that Spain is really fighting for."

"Since I see that the coach has returned us to Passy," Franklin proposed, "let's have dinner and talk about this afterwards."

After dinner, Franklin, ever loyal to the French court and mindful of its immense help to America in the war, refused to concede that France was playing the Spanish game. "Forget about technicalities," he snapped at Jay. "Let us be mindful of France's generosity to us in the past. Remember, too, that we have been instructed by Congress to make no peace without the advice of the French Court."

"We also have another instruction," Jay rejoined,

"which sets independence as a precondition to entering into any treaty."

"Have we any reason to doubt the good faith of the King of France?" asked Franklin.

"We can depend upon the French," Jay countered, "only to see that we are separated from England, but it is not in their interest that we should become a great and formidable people, and they will not help us become so."

"If we cannot count upon France, upon whom else may we depend?" Franklin inquired.

"We have no rational dependence except on God and ourselves," Jay replied.

"Would you deliberately break Congress's instructions?" Franklin pressed.

Jay did not hesitate. "Unless we violate these instructions, the dignity of Congress will be in the dust," he asserted. "I do not mean to imply that we should deviate in the least from our treaty with France," Jay added. "Our honor and our interests are concerned in inviolably adhering to it, but if we lean on her love of liberty, her affection for Americans, or her disinterested magnanimity, we shall lean on a broken reed that will sooner or later pierce our hands."

"Then you are prepared to break our instructions from Congress," Franklin pressed, "if you intend to take an independent course now?"

Jay had made up his mind. "*If* the instructions conflict with America's honor and dignity, I would break them—like this." As Jay later told the story to his family, he stood up and hurled his long clay pipe into the fireplace, where it shattered into a dozen fragments.

The crucial decision was to be Jay's alone, for Franklin, in the third week of August, was suddenly stricken with an acute attack of kidney stones, intensified by the Old Doctor's chronic gout. Jay still failed to get any territorial concessions from the Conde de Aranda, while Vergennes' undersecretary, Rayneval, urged on Jay a compromise line that denied the legitimacy of the claims of the American states to territory west of the Appalachians, or America's claims to the free navigation of the Mississippi to the sea.

As Jay sat poring over the Spanish and French maps in his living quarters at the Hôtel de la Chine in Paris, a servant brought in a letter from Rayneval. The letter urged Jay to compromise his territorial claims against Spain, denied that the Americans had any right to territory west of the Appalachians, and proposed his own compromise line, a little more liberal than Spain's, but still far removed from the Mississippi. Rayneval would have put the Indians west of the line under Spanish protection; for those east of the line, arrangements would have to be worked out by the Americans with the natives. Then the real shocker: Rayneval denied America's right to the free navigation of the Mississippi!

An angered Jay was tempted to tear the letter up, but prudence suggested that he place it in a pigeon-hole of his desk and save it for the record. A few minutes later there was a knock on Jay's door, and gaining admittance was Matthew Ridley, a fellow American from Maryland who managed to get around in the best circles of Paris. He informed Jay that Rayneval had left Versailles on some secret mission. Now thoroughly aroused, Jay acted immediately. First he broke off further talks with Aranda, writing a confidant in Spain: "There is a tide in human affairs which waits for nobody, and political mariners ought to watch it and avail themselves of its advantages."

Rayneval, as Jay guessed, had gone secretly to England, where he held talks with Lord Shelburne at the latter's handsome country estate, Bowood in Wiltshire. Although Rayneval's mission as described in his *written* instructions was to be prompted first by Vergennes' concern that the war should be ended and not held up further by Spain's inflexible and recalcitrant insistence on regaining Gibraltar, Vergennes' emissary, doubtless at his superior's *oral* prompting, let Shelburne know that France opposed America's territorial claims, particularly to lands lying north of the

Ohio (the old Northwest) as well as her claims to the fisheries off the North Atlantic coast. On the latter point he was explicit: "We do not want the Americans to share in the fisheries"—a point he repeated at a meeting with Shelburne the following day. He made no secret of his anti-American views, which he reported dutifully to his chief, and the substance of which Shelburne in turn informed the British Cabinet.

Not knowing what was going on, but suspecting the worst, Jay adopted a second course of action. He picked an Anglo-American, Benjamin Vaughan, who happened to be both friend and former private secretary to Lord Shelburne and a close friend of Franklin's, and dispatched him secretly to England. "Tell Lord Shelburne," Jay instructed, "that we will not modify our stand on the west, the Mississippi, or the fisheries, but that a peace agreement at this time would open up a rich commerce between England and America and lead to ending the war."

Jay did not apprise Vergennes or Franklin, fearing that to do so would jeopardize the secrecy of the project. He now proposed a commission that, in effect, recognized the United States. Shelburne and the Cabinet, seeing an opportunity to exploit a potential split between the allies, pounced upon it. Once that commission was issued to Oswald, negotiations moved ahead quickly. The United States was recognized not only by commission, but also in the first article of the treaty. Generous boundaries—the line-of-the-lakes to Florida, the Atlantic Ocean to the Mississippi—were granted to the Americans, virtually all of the fishery rights (the word somehow was turned into "liberties" when John Adams made his appearance at the negotiations) were conceded, and, significantly, *not* on a reciprocal basis. The United States offered no inshore fishing rights to English subjects. Some compromises were necessary if so liberal a treaty was ever to be ratified by Parliament. The treaty pledged to have the states revise legislation confiscating Tory property and honoring legitimate debts due to British merchants before the war. Both pledges were largely ignored by the states, who acted in a vindictive spirit, their obduracy on these issues involving Jay himself in many years of negotiations before something like a fair settlement on the debts was obtained.

Benjamin West, the famous American artist then living in London, painted the closing scenes when the Americans and the British signed the Preliminary Peace Treaty in Paris on November 30, 1782. The canvas portrays Adams, Franklin, Jay, Laurens, and William Temple Franklin, the American commission's secretary and grandson of the Old Doctor, but a large blank space was left on the right-hand side of the canvas for Richard Oswald, who negotiated the Preliminary Treaty for England, and his able secretary, Caleb Whitefoord, neither of whom posed for the painting. The treaty, so generous to America, was too unpopular in England for its British authors to want to claim permanent identification with it.

"Blessed are the peacemakers," Whitefoord remarked, "but those of modern date *on a changé tout cela*, and changed too with a vengeance."

That was not quite the end of it, however. The Americans had, by their alliance, agreed not to sign a separate peace without the consent of the King of France. So for almost nine more months the American peace commissioners futilely negotiated with a new British peace commissioner, the scientist and intellectual David Hartley, on the wording of the final terms and the inclusion of a treaty of commerce, which the Americans desperately needed, having put themselves outside the British Empire. The British, now under a different set of ministers, were adamant on all points, and the Definitive Treaty was signed on the morning of September 3, 1783, at the lodgings of David Hartley, at the Hotel d'York on the rue Jacob in Paris's Latin Quarter. The building is the present site of a publishing firm, and a plaque on its façade duly commemorates the event.

Alexander Hamilton, who had played so spectacular

Definitive Treaty Between the United States and Great Britain, September 3, 1783, closing page (*National Archives, Washington, D.C.*).

a role in the decisive victory at Yorktown, extolled the treaty that his friend John Jay and his fellow peace commissioners had negotiated in Paris. "The peace which exceeds in the goodness of its terms the expectations of the most sanguine," Hamilton wrote Jay, "does the highest honour to those who made it." He went on to cite "the articles of boundaries and fisheries" as exceeding "expectations."

If anything, Hamilton understated the exceptional importance of this durable treaty. Had not the United

States won its independence in 1783, there would have been no need for Hamilton and Madison to have consistently supported Jay in arguing the case for the supremacy of treaties, or for the three to have written *The Federalist.* The old Confederation would have died aborning, and one would be free to speculate on the political futures of Patriot leaders such as the three who did as much as any to create a nation out of a loose and ill-functioning amphictyony.

Even Hamilton could hardly have foreseen how durable this treaty proved to be, and what expansive possibilities it afforded his countrymen. By the terms of the Convention of 1818 with Great Britain, the northwest boundary between the United States and British North America was extended along the forty-ninth parallel from the Lake of the Woods to the crest of the Rockies, and that line was extended west of the mountains to the Pacific by the Oregon settlement of 1846. But the greatest tribute of all to the durable character of the Treaty of 1783 was the mutual disarmament of the United States–Canadian border, a move initiated in 1818, when the Great Lakes were disarmed, and concluded by the Treaty of Washington of 1871, which created the longest unfortified boundary in the world.

More immediately, however, the treaty enormously enhanced the reputation of John Jay. In July of 1784 he returned to New York to receive the freedom of the city and to learn that while en route home he had been elected by Congress the new Secretary for Foreign Affairs. He was to find that a united America had only moments to celebrate its independence. Soon there were signs of discord and a deep and widespread depression following an all-too-brief period of prosperity. A shaky Congress would prove impotent, while Jay, Hamilton, and Madison recognized the necessity of implementing a then popular figure of shape and of speech and of fastening the hoops to the barrel before the thirteen staves fell apart.

5

James Madison: Republican Champion of the Rights of Man

James Madison has frequently been called "the father of the Constitution," a judgment supported by his initial centralizing plan of government, the so-called Randolph Plan, which in essence, but with important compromises, was the one finally adopted. It is true that his comments during the debates at the federal convention were lengthy, learned, and incisive, and that, of all those present in Philadelphia during the summer of 1787, he kept the most careful record of what was said and done, even though he would not permit it to be published until after his death.

Historical mythology is content to bury the fact that he disagreed with his colleagues at the convention on crucial issues, and was frequently overruled. Nonetheless, he was universally recognized as an intellectual prodigy and the best informed American on issues of public law. His contributions to *The Federalist*, some twenty-nine letters in all, shed illumination on such complex issues as the role of factions and parties, federal-state relations, the necessity of a separation of powers, a system of checks and balances, and his concern with minority rights.

Some have discovered a "split personality" in *The Federalist*. They have found Madison's nationalist views of the "necessary and proper" clause and the "supremacy" clause less expansive than Hamilton's. Hence, what was federalist about *The Federalist* reflected more often the cast given it by Madison's than by Hamilton's contributions, which carried a more nationalistic and centralizing tone. Later, as politics eroded the relationship between these two contributors, both would find passages in *The Federalist*—passages that they themselves had written—a source of embarrassment. The time was not to be many years off when Hamilton would give the Constitution a broad construction and Madison, now a political opponent, would adopt a contrary stance.

James Madison's origins were as different from Jay's as the latter's were from Hamilton's. Jay's were mercantilist and French Huguenot, with some Dutch infusion; Hamilton's were Anglo-Scot West Indian; but Madison's ancestors, who originally spelled their name with two *d*'s, were among the early emigrants from England to the colony of Virginia and proved especially adept in the feverish land-grabbing that characterized pioneer days. James's father, James Madison, Sr., stood out in upcountry Virginia as a respectable planter and slaveholder, as well as a political personage to be reckoned with in his region. His eldest son, also named James, was born in 1751 of the senior Madison and his young bride, Nelly Conway. Young Madison was reared on the family estate of Montpelier, where he resided, except when in public service, for the eighty-five years of his long life.

Young Madison never had to earn a living and never did pursue a profession. Although a deep student of law, particularly international law and political theory, and richly read in the classics, in which his range was encyclopedic, he early on adopted an Addisonian literary style, which came from a careful reading of *The Spectator*. Madison stood out as the gentleman politician *par excellence*; he only occasionally succumbed to brief bouts of land speculation, and was most diffident about plantation management, where his talents never did shine.

The contrast between Madison and his collaborators

on *The Federalist* was even more marked in terms of physical characteristics than in their perceptions of how the nation should be shaped. With the bearing of a solemn country parson and the speech of a *philosophe*, Madison seemed to most people to be a cold fish. To a close circle of intimates, however, he proved a masterful conversationalist, his talk spiced with wit and learning. But he lacked human warmth. Typical was his comment to Edmund Randolph on the death in 1782 of the wife of his close friend Thomas Jefferson. "Perhaps this domestic catastrophe," he remarked, "may prove in its operation beneficial to the country by weaning him from those attachments which deprived us of his services." In short, isn't it about time for Jefferson to get back into politics, where he belongs?

Physically frail since childhood, his adult height a bare five and a half feet, Madison stood almost dwarf-like in a region where his close companions were all six-footers. His voice, even in maturity, was so feeble that some of his remarks at the Constitutional Convention were inaudible. His belief in his own physical disabilities, compounded by a lifetime as a hypochondriac, kept him from traveling extensively, and his own recognition of his lack of oratorical gifts dissuaded him from pursuing the ministry or the law, for both of which he had an affinity. Thus, when Congress met at Philadelphia, he would remain there after adjournment, staying through the hot, humid season rather than risk the trip home. How a man with so frail a constitution, so introspective, sedate, and prim, who preferred to be clad in black to fit an outwardly humorless disposition, could have withstood the rigors of campaigns on the hustings which were to be widely initiated within a few years of his death, or the one-on-one wooing of voters considered a necessity today, would be truly incomprehensible. Perhaps no better reflection can be found of the vast gulf separating the age of the Founding Fathers from our own.

Madison was fully cognizant of that shyness and fear of making himself ridiculous that cut him off from the run of politicians of his own day. As he told the tale himself, one day, while staying at a residence in Williamsburg, someone put a hand through the window and stole his hat. "It was about a mile to the palace, and I was kept from going to the latter for two days, by the impossibility of getting a hat of any kind. At last, however, I obtained one from a little Frenchman who sold snuff—very coarse—an extremely small crown and broad brim, and it was a subject of great merriment to my friends," he recalled. Madison does not tell us whether they found the new hat ridiculous or were amazed that he did not dare venture onto the streets of Williamsburg uncovered. Probably both elements entered into the hilarity.

Reared under the shadow of an overly protective grandmother—Frances Taylor Madison, who at the age of sixty ran a five-thousand-acre plantation—and a vigorous extrovert of a father, this eldest son for fifty years signed his name "James Madison Junr.," long after his father's death. Yet Madison, of all three *Federalist* authors, proved the most paradoxical. Always a very private person, even to those who knew him intimately, he could reveal a less inhibited side when operating in a small circle where he felt at ease and where his hidden depths of dry and ribald humor might be revealed. Despite his profound personality handicaps, Madison in fact proved the most successful politician of the three collaborators—the co-founder of the American party system (not a word about which appears in the Constitution), and the only one of the three *Federalist* contributors to reach the presidency.

Like many of the other Founding Fathers, Madison soon recognized that they were actors on a great stage of history and felt it incumbent upon himself to see that history properly recorded his and their deeds and words. No one of his generation was more assiduous in arranging for the publication of his public papers; no one was more careful to exclude private correspondence. Some writings of a private nature he destroyed; other personal items were scattered among kinfolk, friends, and ultimately autograph collectors. He made a point of going over letters written more than fifty years earlier and of excising embarrassing personal references to events he could not bear to recall. He went even beyond that, authorizing his wife, Dolley, to withhold letters likely to "injure the feelings of anyone or wrong in themselves." Regrettably, his stepson John Payne Todd rifled the collection of some of its choicest items to pay his gambling and liquor debts, although he was duty-bound to turn them over to the United States government.

To compound the problems of discovering such of the intimate Madison as revealed in his papers, his biographer, Senator Cabell Rives, persuaded the government to entrust the records to his custody. As a result they were located in the Confederacy during the Civil War, with only part being returned at war's end. It took another seventy-five years before an additional nine hundred items were recovered by the federal government.

The extant writings are particularly uninformative about Madison's early years. His earliest experiences left scars that were never obliterated, while other nearby contacts spurred him to a course of action and a display of energy that must have astonished his intimates. Madison clearly recalled the Indian raids of his childhood, when the frontier was a shambles as a result of Braddock's defeat. His home was virtually a garrison, to which various relatives living further West frequently sought relief. Stories of frontier atrocities left him with a permanent impression of the native American as nothing but a savage, a view that his friend and mentor, Thomas Jefferson, failed to share. Contrariwise, Madison spent his childhood at ease playing alongside the many black children who were quartered on the plantation, and toward blacks he would develop a humane but ambivalent position.

Could young Madison have recalled the time when, as a feeble child, he was ailing? Could he have remembered seeing his father opening a medicine chest and picking out a bottle marked "for an Epilepsy," which he administered by spoon to James junior?

"Am I an epileptic?" Madison, a notorious hypochondriac, often asked himself. "I certainly seem to have all the symptoms. I get sick when I travel. I get dizzy spells, and then there was my breakdown at college. I couldn't even carry a gun when I first lined up with the Minute Men of my own county." It must have irked Madison that, unlike Hamilton, he spent the whole war without fighting a lick.

Throughout his life Madison was convinced that the attacks he suffered could be interpreted as "epileptoid hysteria" rather than the disease itself. But since epileptoid hysteria is usually associated with the years immediately following puberty, and Madison seems to have suffered them at a much earlier age and continued to experience them, according to *his own* accounts— not those of eyewitnesses—throughout his long life, he seems to have suffered some temporarily debilitating nervous or physical disorder, which, without records of the symptoms or appropriate diagnosis, cannot be pinpointed at this distance from events.

What this disease, or conviction of Madison's that he suffered it, did was to plunge him into his studies and books with furious intensity, finding therein a substitute for competitive physical activities or experiences with the opposite sex. We know that by the time he was eleven years old he had devoured every book in his father's house, and that henceforward for some years he was tutored by the learned Donald Robertson (who taught him French with so broad a Scottish accent that no Frenchman could ever understand Madison), who drilled Madison in his Latin lessons, and started him on Greek. Robertson trained his young student in logic and crammed into his head the basic curriculum of the University of Edinburgh when Robertson studied there. So vastly broadened were Madison's intellectual horizons that it is understandable that in later years he is reported to have paid this generous tribute to his tutor: "All that I have been in life I owe largely to that man."

Exposure to the Scottish intellectual influence seemed inescapable, as Madison pressed ahead with college studies at the College of New Jersey at Princeton, then headed by the Reverend John Witherspoon, whose thinking was permeated by Scottish notions of "common sense" and by Whiggish ideas about resistance and liberty. A war hawk, Witherspoon attended the Second Continental Congress and signed the Declaration of Independence, whose ideas he eloquently championed. In those days Madison must have seemed like an aged freshman, as he had already reached his nineteenth year, when most entering students were several years younger. Anxious to make up the lost time, he compressed three years of college work into two, graduating in September 1771. It was a grind, but it seemed as though Madison might bear up under it, until without apparent warning he snapped during a brief bout of postgraduate studies.

What James Madison brought back to Virginia from his years of intensive study at Princeton were an aroused commitment to the cause of the Patriot party and a deep sympathy for the plight of religious dissenters. Presbyterian Princeton stood foursquare against the establishment of religion—that is, government support of a favored religion by taxation of persons regardless of their religious preferment. Contrariwise, the Princetonians' stated goal was to share "in the instruction of the Youth . . . to cherish the spirit of liberty and free enquiry; and not only to permit, but even to encourage their right of privatejudgment, without presuming to dictate with an air of infallibility, or demanding an implicit assent to the decisions of the preceptor." These were the college faculty talking, not the students, but it is understandable that Madison came back to Virginia with a fiery commitment to the persecuted dissenters of his colony and an indignation at the British measures that would lead to Revolution, with the latter burning on a lower flame.

To Witherspoon, Madison was the model of the very proper student, but he carefully withheld from his revered president a collection of ribald verses that revealed a different side to the introspective grind. Writing about a fellow Princetonian whom he held in low esteem, Madison scribbled:

> Great Allen founder of the crew
> If right I guess must keep a stew
> The lecherous rascal there will find
> A place just suited to his mind
> May whore and pimp and drink and swear
> Nor more the garb of Christian wear
> And free Nassau from such a pest
> A dunce, a fool, an ass at best.

A member of the radical Cliosophic Society, Madison wrote some wretched doggerel about his hated rivals, the Toryish Cliosophic members. In one piece he has the poet laureate of the latter society beaten up on a journey, struck about the eyes, ears, and nose with a chamber pot; Urania is brought from beneath her bed, and healed by Clio, who takes the victim to her private rooms, whence

> Straight an eunuch out I come
> My voice to render more melodious.

In another literary effort, unsigned, he attributed the venereal disease caught by one of the Clios to the less than platonic relations he had engaged in with the daughter of a stagecoachman. One of Madison's biographers credits this piece to the future President, but it could have been a creation of his classmate Hugh Henry Brackenridge, a man of greater literary talent.

All of this suggests depths hidden beneath a sedate, prim, and humorless exterior. Smiles always came hard with Madison, and these off-color literary outpourings may have been a way of sublimating sexual urges. Whether the poetic outbursts and the heavy study load he carried offer clues to Madison's inner conflicts, it is around this time that he suffered what seems to have been a breakdown, physical or nervous, traditionally attributed to overstudy and possibly triggered by extreme anxiety about his own health.

As a result, Madison was forced to discontinue his postgraduate studies and go back home. As the eldest son, he passed the time tutoring his brothers and sisters, of whom there were seven in all, ranging in age from one to nineteen years. How he coped with the infant and what he was able to impart is merest speculation. One thing is clear. At an age when Hamilton was hoping for a war, Madison was writing a friend: "I am too dull and infirm now to look out for extraordinary things in this world, but my sensations for many months have intimated to me not to expect a long or healthy life." How poor a prophet Madison proved! Not only did he live to the ripe age of eighty-five, but he was destined to participate prominently in some of the most crucial and contentious events in the history of his time.

Aside from a head brimming with new learning, Madison brought back from Princeton a burning concern about the plight of dissenters and strong Whiggish views critical of British measures toward the colonies. While other young men of his age were gaming, cockfighting, horseracing, or flirting with eligible young ladies of their neighborhood, Madison, after a tediously slow recovery of health, accompanied by a diminishing concern about himself, began to make inquiries about what was going on in adjacent counties. He was horrified at what he discovered. On a short trip to Culpeper County, adjacent to his own Orange, he visited the county jail. There he saw and talked to a group of Baptists imprisoned for voicing their religious sentiments. He was shocked by their plight and by the information they conveyed that they were held in close jail for voicing religious sentiments antipathetic to those of the established Church of England. "I shall not be silent," he reassured them upon leaving. And he kept his word.

Madison voiced his feelings without reservation to his intimate friend and fellow Princetonian, William Bradford of Pennsylvania. "It's a good thing that the Church of England was not established throughout the colonies," Madison remarked, for slavery and subjection would have resulted. Already he was beginning to feel stifled by the freedomless atmosphere of Virginia. "I want to breathe your free air," he confessed. "I expect it will mend my constitution and confirm my principles. I have indeed as good an atmosphere at home as the climate will allow, but have nothing to brag of as to the state and liberty of my country."

Then the climactic observation:

"Poverty and luxury prevail among all sorts; pride, ignorance, and knavery among the priesthood, and vice and wickedness among the laity. This is bad enough, but it is not the worst I have to tell you. That diabolical, hell-conceived principle of persecution rages among some and to their eternal infamy, the clergy can furnish their quota of imps for such business." Madison's language now began to convey an antireligious tone that made the orthodox suspicious of him and prompted him to go so far as to seek a wall of separation between church and state, a metaphor that it was left for his friend Jefferson to invent.

Referring to the inmates he had visited at the Culpeper jail, he lamented: "I have neither patience to hear, talk, or think of anything relative to this matter; for I have squabbled and scolded, abused and ridiculed so long about it to little purpose, that I am without common patience. So I must beg you to pity me, and pray for liberty of conscience."

The prayers Madison invoked were answered, but not through any collaboration from the Anglican clerics whom he had so forthrightly ridiculed. The persecution of religious dissidents he had witnessed in his own colony and the freer air he breathed on a brief trip to Pennsylvania and upstate New York in the summer of '74 shook him out of his long lethargy and prompted him to enter the political arena. His first move was to gain election to the Committee of Safety for Orange County, a part of a nationwide grassroots movement of protest against British rule. His second came in 1776 when he was elected to the Virginia Convention. There, despite his youth, he was named to the committee to frame a constitution and a declaration of rights, winning instant recognition from a leadership distinguished for maturity, experience, and eloquence, none of which qualities he had as yet exhibited.

The chief architect of Virginia's Declaration of Rights, a model for so many other states, was George Mason, an elder statesman, who began the Declaration with the revolutionary statement "that all men are born equally free and independent." Was this not an open invitation to a slave insurrection? Not so, the liberals responded. The slaves were not constituent members of the society and hence "could never pretend to any benefit from such a measure." Mason's ringing assertion was permitted to stand. Then came Mason's phrasing of the clause on religious toleration: "all men should enjoy the fullest toleration in the exercise of religion, according to the dictates of conscience, unpunished and unrestrained by the magistrate, unless, under colour of religion, any man disturb the peace, the happiness, or safety of society, or of individuals."

Mason did not go far enough for James Madison. That political neophyte had the presumption to propose an amendment establishing absolute religious freedom, rather than toleration within limits. Madison, who shrank from speaking in public, looked about in vain for a sponsor. Patrick Henry declined, recognizing that Madison's proposal amounted to the disestablishment of the Anglican Church in Virginia, now cut off by war from its parent, the Church of England. Forced to compromise, Madison persuaded the convention to replace Mason's words "fullest toleration in the exercise of religion" with "free exercise of religion," a more sweeping phrase, implying an inherent personal right rather than a limit upon state action. This was as much as Madison could get, but not as much as he wanted.

As a member of the Committee on Religion, Madison was now bolstered by a bushel of petitions (one circulated by the Baptists listing ten thousand names) from the dissenting areas. The petitioners demanded "equal liberty and freedom from the burden of church establishment." Madison now initiated a move to end "without delay all Church establishments" and the abolition of "every tax upon conscience and private judgment."

Battle lines were drawn. Thomas Jefferson, leader of the liberal wing of the convention and quickly to become Madison's close friend and lifelong associate, joined Madison in the fight to disestablish the Church. The pair were opposed by the prestigious Edmund Pendleton and ultimately by Patrick Henry, the greatest spellbinder of his day. This battle was part of a larger war over the revision of the laws, in the course of which the conservative Pendleton sought to block the more thoroughgoing reforms that Jefferson espoused. Together, Jefferson and Madison had to settle for a partial victory, exempting dissenters from having to pay taxes to the established Church, but merely suspending for a time payments for the salary of the clergy fixed by the state.

Out of the battle, however, emerged that close friendship and lifelong political association of Jefferson and Madison. Looking back on the tight bonds that the pair had then forged, Jefferson attested some thirty years later: "I can say conscientiously that I do not know in the world a man of purer integrity, more dispassionate, disinterested, and devoted to genuine Republicanism; nor would I in the whole scope of America and Europe point out an abler head." Except for Madison's greater sensitivity to property rights, Madison and Jefferson shared a common political philosophy and a more vigorous nationalist outlook.

For a brief moment it seemed that Madison's entry into the political arena would come to a premature end. When he ran for reelection in April 1777, he was badly beaten. Ever the man of conscience, ever prim, proper, and unbending, Madison, unlike his two opponents, refused to provide free whiskey or buy votes, both common practices of that day. His constituents attributed this to parsimony, but Madison's purity was probably unique among political candidates in Virginia.

Would this defeat return Madison to Montpelier and a career of plantation management for which he had minuscule talent? The fates determined otherwise. Within six months, and under the state's brand-new constitution, he was elected by house and senate to the Council of State, which shared with the governor executive and administrative responsibilities. It is testimony to Madison's statewide reputation that although he was repudiated by the whiskey-drinking voters of his own district, he was selected for the Council by the Virginia political establishment without campaigning and on the basis of recognized merit.

Persistent in his effort to achieve freedom of conscience in matters of religion, Madison did not seem to recognize any inconsistency in his denial of such freedom to political dissenters or in his ultracautious stand on freedom for the black slaves, despite his detestation of the system of slavery. For Tories, Madison gave due process the back of his hand. On one occasion he expressed the wish to get his hands on the notorious New York Tory printer James Rivington "for twenty-four hours in this place," where Virginians would guarantee that the royalist would be properly punished; on another, he was gleeful at the idea of administering "a coat of tar and surplice of feathers" to a local parson who refused to observe the fast designated by the Continental Congress for July 20, 1775, or preach on fast day on grounds of conscience. Madison objected when a hotheaded, obstreperous Tory who had the presumption to debate the issues of the war with a French officer in the Continental army was merely fined twelve shillings and imprisoned for one hour. With little evidence, Madison labeled the culprit "a dangerous enemy to the State" and thereby revealed himself as a more hotheaded persecutor of political heresy than most of his neighbors. That, of course, was the early Madison, not the author of the First Amendment of a later date.

Madison loathed slavery, and after the Declaration of Independence he privately favored enlisting and liberating the slaves, a project that his political colleagues rejected. He himself sold his personal black servant when he was in Philadelphia, explaining to his father that under the benign laws of that state, Billy would be free in seven years. Confronted with the political realities of his own state at war's end, he could go no further than to help defeat a resolution that would have outlawed manumission of slaves by their masters. Henceforth, he temporized and compromised. He backed the three-fifths compromise at the Federal Convention, according to which, for purposes of representation and direct taxes, to the total of all free persons and those bound to service for a term of years would be added "three fifths of all other Persons," meaning slaves. The Constitution was careful to avoid using the word "slave" or "slavery" in any portion of its text. In *The Federalist* Number 54, Madison defended the three-fifths clause as appropriate to the condition of slaves, possessing as they did a mixed character of both persons and property, while conceding that the slave was "a moral person, not a mere article of property." Although he vigorously opposed the attempt at the Constitutional Convention to extend beyond twenty years the prohibition of the *foreign* slave trade as "dishonorable to the American character," he became increasingly timid on repressing the *domestic* slave trade.

If slaves were not a part of the constituency, as his Southern colleagues argued, then Madison saw little space for freed slaves in the United States, and his original opposition to slavery became transmuted into avowed support for colonizing them in Africa or perhaps some remote American territory, even accepting the presidency of the Colonization Society at the age of eighty-two. Earlier, at the time of the Missouri Compromise, he asserted that under the Constitution the federal government was limited to regulating the importation of slaves *into* the United States, and insisted that once a state was admitted to the Union, Congress could not prevent it from permitting slavery.

Inconsistent and even timid on issues like slavery and the status of the freed blacks, which might bring him into conflict with a majority of his Virginia constituency, Madison was tenacious in support of religious liberty. What Jefferson was unable to achieve when in the state legislature or as wartime governor, Madison committed himself to carry through. He picked up the Jeffersonian spear when his older friend was abroad as minister to France. Henceforth his time was divided between sessions as delegate to the Continental Congress and brief terms in the state assembly. In the latter capacity he threw all his weight against a proposal of the Protestant Episcopal Church, the successor in Virginia of the Church of England, to have a general assessment levied for the support of religion and to incorporate the clergy of their denomination. Patrick Henry, a proponent of the measure, used every trick in the book to buy time to get votes by modifying the proposal to require the people to pay a tax for the "support of the Christian religion or of some Christian church," thus wooing some other sects over to his side.

In the great debate that ensued, Madison argued that religion was corrupted when established by law, and drew upon his broad scholarship to cite chapter and verse. Despite Madison's logic, Henry's emotional appeal gathered force. It looked for a time as though the Episcopal Church would be incorporated, for what Patrick Henry wanted he generally got. In desperation about Henry's tactics, Madison appealed to Jefferson in Paris. "What we have to do, I think, is devoutly to pray for his death," his friend responded. Since neither could count on the Lord to act quickly enough, Madison adroitly supported a move to elect Henry governor and remove his most dangerous opponent from the legislature. The tactics worked. Henry had insufficient time to get his measure through, and a new election sent back to the House of Delegates a majority opposed to incorporation. Now Madison brought his big guns up against the church tax measure.

Back in June of 1785 he had scored a great propaganda coup by drafting a "Memorial and Remonstrance against Religious Assessments," asserting the right of every man to exercise religion according to his own convictions and conscience. Madison's tract elicited so extraordinary a popular response that the assessment bill never came up for a vote. Madison had won, and he was to remember that victory on at least two later occasions.

Few state papers had so momentous an impact on American constitutional law as did Madison's "Memorial and Remonstrance," which may be said to have germinated the First Amendment that he later authored. The relevant portion of the First Amendment, which, with some alteration by others, was Madison's handiwork, reads: "Congress shall make no law respecting an establishment of religion, or prohibiting the free exercise thereof." Note that the amendment restricts *Congress*, not the states, because at the time the Bill of Rights was ratified, at least two states, Massachusetts and Connecticut, did have established religions, while in other states test oaths barred persons of some religious denominations from voting or holding office. In the sweeping constitutional revolution initiated in the 1940s by the Supreme Court, the Fourteenth Amendment was construed to extend this prohibition to the *states* as well as to *Congress*.

Thus, by amendment and judicial interpretation, was erected what Thomas Jefferson hailed as "the wall of separation," and during the past generation, especially in recent years, that figure of speech has generated fierce debate. While valiantly upholding the prohibition against the establishment of religion, the Supreme Court has been busy chipping away at its foundations. In 1947 a divided court upheld the reimbursement of parents with public funds for costs of busing their children to parochial schools. Subsequently, the Court upheld the use of public funds to provide parochial schools with textbooks, and as recently as 1984 the Court has seen fit to permit the display on municipal property of a crèche, a symbol sacred to Christianity. Hardly had the Court's decision been announced when one heard the renewed call for prayer in the schools, a call widely trumpeted by public figures and fundamental religionists alike. In the supercharged debate over school prayer, many people need be reminded of President John F. Kennedy's "easy remedy": "Pray a good deal more at home."

One point should be made, however, in probing the views of the Founding Fathers regarding the "wall of separation." Even Madison, in his "Memorial and Remonstrance," advanced as a ground for opposing tax support of any and all religious denominations his own conviction that the policy of the general assessment bill was "adverse to the diffusion of the light of Christianity" and amounted rather to an expression of "unchristian timidity."

In sum, the Founding Fathers held ambivalent views on the role of religion in government. Their ideas ran the gamut from the position of rationalists or deists like Thomas Paine and Benjamin Franklin to orthodox piety as exemplified by a John Adams or a John Jay. Some, like Dr. Benjamin Rush, the notable signer of the Declaration of Independence, advocated that education be conducted in the Christian way, and Alexander Hamilton, as has been remarked, proposed in his later years the creation of a Christian Constitution Society, which died aborning. Both of these notions would be utterly abhorrent to a Jefferson or a Madison. Thus, although the Founding Fathers stood solidly united on the issue of religious toleration, they were divided, if not confused, as to whether the federal government was to be viewed as strictly neutral in matters of religion or obliged to encourage systems of morality and ethics drawn from the Judeo-Christian tradition. Indubitably and until very recent years, the views of Madison were widely accepted in the pluralist society that makes up this nation, and one may legitimately be concerned that the attempt to whittle away at the Establishment clause will open a new Pandora's box. It will set religious groups and sects on opposing sides over a bundle of controversial issues previously considered outside the government's domain. It will seriously intrude on the precious right of privacy. It could impair, if not undermine, that freedom of conscience for which Madison fought so valiantly.

When Madison entered the Continental Congress as a delegate for Virginia in the winter of 1780, some of those who had not seen him before took his shyness and diffidence for self-conceit, and one delegate's wife described him as "the most unsocial creature in existence." For a time this "loner" confined himself to committee duties, which he performed with diligence and exceptional comprehension. Madison had missed by a few months making the acquaintance of John Jay, who had resigned the presidency at the end of September 1779 to undertake his mission to Spain. Nor did Madison as yet enjoy the opportunity of meeting Hamilton, who did not enter Congress until November 1782. However, Madison's diligent service on the Committee for Foreign Affairs kept him abreast of Jay's difficulties in Spain and of his peacemaking role in Paris. Madison applauded Jay's initiative in treating Congress's waiver of its claim to the free navigation of the Mississippi as a conditional one. Contrariwise, he was unhappy about the failure of Jay and his colleagues to consult the French court in negotiating a preliminary peace with England. Joining with Hamilton, by that time in Congress, the pair almost put through a resolution amounting to a vote of no confidence in the peace commissioners. Just before the vote, news reached Philadelphia that France and Spain had also signed a preliminary peace.

Congress adjourned without going on record one way or the other, thereby saving Hamilton and Madison from the absurd embarrassment of censuring peace commissioners for having achieved what would prove the greatest triumph in American diplomacy. Hamilton saw the light and quickly sent off a dispatch congratulating Jay. As for Madison, Jay was not the person to quickly forget the key role the young Virginian had played in supporting what the New Yorker considered the "unwarrantable philippic" of censure of the American peace commissioners which the French minister to the United States, the Chevalier de la Luzerne, and his partisans had futilely tried to ram through Congress.

It is in his early Congressional career that Madison's continental outlook was shaped. A careful study of the Articles of Confederation convinced Madison that Congress had implied powers which it had failed to exercise. While Article 2 had reserved to the states every power not "expressly delegated" to the "United States in Congress Assembled," Article 13 was, in Madison's judgment, a supremacy clause that vested in Congress "a general and implied" power "to enforce and carry into effect all the articles of the said confederation against any of the States which shall refuse or neglect to abide by such their determinations, or shall otherwise violate any of the said articles." This, Madison's initial assertion of the doctrine of implied powers, found support both in the Federal Constitution and *The Federalist*, and would later be pressed to its outer limits by Alexander Hamilton as Secretary of the Treasury.

Madison's remedy for the failure of the states to honor Congress's requisitions was a radical and centralizing proposition. Appointed to a three-man committee, along with James Varnum of Rhode Island and James Duane of New York, to secure remedies for noncompliance by the several states, Madison concocted for the committee a bottle of strong medicine.

It took the form of a proposed amendment to the Articles to be submitted to the states "to compel the states to fulfill their federal engagements." In case of their default, Congress would be authorized "to seize the vessels and merchandize of citizens of the offending States and to prohibit their trade and intercourse with other states and foreign countries." Congress referred the amendment to a Grand Committee representing each state, but the medicine was too drastic and they let the patient die. Significantly, the sanctions proposed against individuals, which Madison had then thought to impose and were later to be incorporated in the Federal Constitution, marked a crucial difference between the Articles and the federal charter. Madison was right in 1781, but six years ahead of his time.

Madison's concern about the nation's slippage into rampant inflation and even bankruptcy would find in Hamilton a colleague who shared his views of Congressional impotence to correct the nation's fiscal slide. That disconcerting situation both delegates attributed to the states' repeated failures to provide the revenue that Congress so desperately needed. A careful record-keeper, Madison has left us an account of the first session in which he and Hamilton joined forces on the side of enlarging the powers of the national government. In the course of a debate in February 1783, Madison proposed the setting up of permanent and adequate funds to operate generally throughout the United States.

Speaking in support of Madison's proposition, Hamilton let the cat out of the bag by insisting that the revenue be collected by officers appointed and paid by Congress. Such men, he argued, were better calculated "to support the power of Congress." Private conversations reported to Madison showed that states' rights delegates saw through Hamilton's proposition. Some members chuckled that Hamilton had "let out the secret." Madison was furious and criticized Hamilton's remarks as "imprudent and injurious to the cause which it was meant to serve."

Hence, in their very first appearance together they stood on the same side, but the Virginian was already placed on guard against what he recognized as his New York ally's impulsive and imprudent streak, an incautious proclivity that served to bolster the conviction of their states' rights opponents that Hamilton plotted to minimize state power. So did Madison, but the latter usually acted with more circumspection. What kept Madison and Hamilton together during the Confederation years was an ardent conviction that Congress must be given the power to tax and to regulate commerce—fundamental steps to make the national government effective—coupled with a mutual respect for each other's intellectual gifts. They would have gone further, but the time was not propitious.

Madison had reached the ripe age of thirty-two with a career devoid of a single recorded flirtation or courtship. More than a decade earlier, John Jay had begun his lifelong romance with the charming and socially gifted Sarah Livingston Jay, while Hamilton, a lady's man by the standards of any time, had taken one of Philip Schuyler's daughters to wife a couple of years before. Now it seemed to be Madison's turn. Lodging at Mrs. Mary House's boardinghouse, located in Philadelphia at the corner of Fifth and Market streets, close by Congress, he became acquainted with the family of William Floyd, a New York delegate and Signer of the Declaration of Independence. Inexperienced in affairs of the heart, Madison was smitten by Floyd's youngest daughter, Catherine, a teenage charmer and coquette. Never known as a great music-lover, Madison was nonetheless captivated by Catherine's renditions on the harpsichord. During his final weeks in Philadelphia he pressed his suit, and Kitty said yes. The pair even posed for the famous Philadelphia painter Charles Willson Peale, whose miniature portraits show Madison looking even younger than his pretty fiancée, whereas in fact he was twice her age.

James Madison, Jr., miniature painted by
Charles Willson Peale (*courtesy of the James
Madison Papers*).

Political events came between the pair. The Pennsylvania state militia staged a mutiny for back pay,
which Governor John Dickinson was unable to put
down. The mutineers poked their fusils through the
State House windows, where Congress sat, and therein
held the delegates prisoner. But only momentarily, for
Alexander Hamilton persuaded the Congress to end
their humiliating position and withdraw to Princeton,
where Nassau Hall was large enough to accommodate
the delegates. Madison, who did not approve of the
move, went along with the Floyd family as far as New
Brunswick. This was in fact his first trip away from
Philadelphia in three years. Then he doubled back to
Princeton to join Congress's sittings.

Meanwhile, his lightheaded fiancée was having some
second thoughts. She found a nineteen-year-old medi-
cal student named William Clarkson better attuned to
her age and temperament. For days Madison waited
for word from Kitty. Then it came. As Madison con-

Catherine Floyd, miniature painted by Charles Willson Peale, 1782 (*courtesy of the James Madison Papers*).

fided to Jefferson, the letter contained "a profession of indifference," and it was sealed with a piece of rye dough—a crowning insult! Madison's graceless figure, unstylish clothes, and high-minded, humorless conversation did not provide the right bill of fare for a romantic repast with this "capricious" youngster. The chemistry was all wrong.

Madison had suffered a shattering personal experience, a severe blow to his self-esteem. There would be no other woman in his life for more than a decade until he met and married Dolley Payne Todd, a buxom and engaging widow, who proved the ideal partner for his public career.

Five years had elapsed since Madison's blighted romance, and his overwhelming concern was now the Constitution and the need to persuade the country that it should be ratified. Madison had kept his promise to Hamilton. He would collaborate on *The Federalist*. Back in New York City by the end of September,

James Madison to Thomas Jefferson, Philadelphia, August 11, 1785. Madison informs his friend that he was jilted by Kitty Floyd. He later obtained the original and excised the personal passage (*Madison Papers, Library of Congress*).

Madison had adequate time to discuss with Hamilton his initial letter, *Federalist* Number 10, which did not appear in the New York papers until late November. Writing to Jefferson in Paris almost a year later, Madison not only disavowed any claims that the writers of *The Federalist* were "mutually answerable for all the ideas of the other," but conceded that "there was seldom time for even a perusal of the pieces by any but the writer before they were wanted at the press, and sometimes hardly by the writer himself."

One cannot believe that Madison would have gone to press with his initial contribution without showing it to Hamilton and possibly Jay as well. One can assume a visit of Madison to Hamilton's Wall Street office, where he not only announced his readiness to take over upon Jay's temporary withdrawal from the series, but gave Hamilton a chance to look over the draft. He probably admitted that he had leaned somewhat heavily on notes he had kept of remarks on the subject that he had expressed at the convention. If he had pointed out pertinent passages to his collaborator, here is what Hamilton must surely have read:

> But the most common and durable source of factions has been the various and unequal distribution of property. Those who held and those who are without property have ever formed distinct interests in society. Those who are creditors, and those who are debtors, fall under a like discrimination. A landed interest, a manufacturing interest, a mercantile interest, a moneyed interest, with many lesser interests, grow up of necessity in civilized nations, and divide them into different classes, actuated by different sentiments and views. The regulation of these various and interfering interests forms the principal task of modern legislation, and involves the spirit of party and faction in the necessary and ordinary operations of the government.

At this point Madison may have felt that he had put a scare into men of property, which was not his intention. To calm their fears, he added:

> The influence of factious leaders may kindle a flame within their particular States, but will be unable to spread a general conflagration through

the other States; a religious sect may degenerate
into a political faction in a part of the Confederacy;
but the variety of sects dispersed over the entire
face of it must secure the national Councils against
any danger from that source: a rage for paper money,
for an abolition of debts, for an equal division of
property, or for any other improper or wicked projects, will be less apt to pervade the whole body of
the Union than a particular member of it; in the
same proportion as such a malady is more likely to
taint a particular county or district than an entire
state.

Madison hardly needed to digress on his respect for
property as a fundamental right, and how he deplored
subterfuges to weaken property interests. Hamilton
shared these sentiments with his colleague, and knew
that the Virginian was equally distressed about the
great disparity between rich and poor. Hamilton, while
perhaps less concerned about the poor, was optimistic
that a more general prosperity could be obtained once
the new Constitution was adopted. He shared Madison's concern that parties were a baleful influence and
should be eschewed in the new nation. He also professed to share Madison's contention that in a republic
as expansive as that of the United States, the people
would pick their national representatives on a merit
basis and at some distance from local pressures, and
that the representatives, ideally, would share a cosmo-
politan outlook, unlike the parochial-minded Antifederalists.

Where Hamilton and Madison *privately* differed was
in their confidence that the people would exercise wise
choices. The latter was optimistic that the voters could
be persuaded to believe the leaders were convinced
that peace and prosperity could be maintained in the
extended republic that the new federal Constitution
embraced. That was the nub of the issue between the
pair, and Madison still had before him the task of
demonstrating how so large a republic could govern
vast stretches of territory awarded by the Treaty of

Peace with Great Britain and still remain steadfast to republican institutions.

Federalist Number 10 first saw the light of day in *The Daily Advertiser* of November 22, 1787. Little did Hamilton realize on the day of publication that Number 10 would be the most frequently quoted letter of all eighty-five *Federalist* essays, representing as it did the core of Madison's political thought on the role of interests and factions under the Constitution.

Charles A. Beard, whose *Economic Interpretation of the Constitution*, published in 1913 at the height of Populist-Progressive enthusiasm for economic determinism, regarded Number 10 as evidence of how the Constitution was drafted and ratified in response to the economic self-interest of its proponents. In rebuttal, others have not only denied the relevance of the evidence Beard adduced, but have argued that Madison's concern for property rights stemmed from an eighteenth-century outlook toward the protection of private property as a basic guarantee of individual liberty and an orderly society. To buttress their case, they have cited Jefferson's reference in the Great Declaration to "the pursuit of happiness" and John Adams's *Defence of the Constitutions of the United States of America*, wherein the author couples property with liberty as "surely a right of mankind." What Madison clearly envisaged was a device by which minority rights could be protected from invasion by an unchecked majority. Only by securing the public good *and* private rights, Madison reminds us, can we preserve "the spirit and form of popular government."

A NATION UNHINGED

John Jay

Looking back on the years between the Revolution and the convening of the Constitutional Convention, Dr. Benjamin Rush, physician, philosopher, and a signer of the Declaration of Independence, observed that "there is nothing more common than to confound the term American Revolution with that of the late American War. The American War is over, but this is far from being the case with the American Revolution. On the contrary, but the first act of the great drama is closed."

Having played conspicuous roles in the first act of that three-act drama, covering the years from 1776 to 1789, Hamilton, Jay, and Madison, our three "witnesses," now joined forces with other like-minded nationalist leaders in wrestling with the issues and conflicts played out in the second act. These included constitutional change, legal and social reform, and economic recovery to bring to maturity the splendid fruits of peace.

The thirteen states seemed to these leaders to be a nation of paradox. America's territory had been more than doubled by the peace, making it the largest republic in world history, one that did not, like Rome, turn into an empire. Its population had grown at a faster rate than ever before, or even thereafter. From less than two and a half million people at the end of the war, a wave of European immigration and a postwar population explosion combined to give the new country close to four million inhabitants by 1790. Included in this figure were seven hundred thousand black slaves and an additional sixty thousand free blacks. The North was initiating notable steps toward bringing about black emancipation, but in the South, save for individual cases of manumission, slavery remained untouchable.

The dominant strain of the white population claimed English origins, but in fact they constituted only sixty percent of the population. Germans, Scots, Scotch-Irish, Irish, Dutch, and French immigrants and their descendants made up most of the remainder. True, the English language prevailed, but Dutch was still spoken in the Hudson Valley; German (or a corruption thereof known as Pennsylvania Dutch) dominated the speech of the region lying between the Lehigh and the Susquehanna. In the backcountry, one heard varying English dialects spoken by the Lowland Scots, and Gaelic was the vernacular of the Highland Scots and the Irish. To form a nation—and Jay would soon coin the word—its people had to be "Americanized." As yet, few Americans had manifested resistance to the influx of foreign stock. As John Adams eloquently phrased it, "It is our business to render our country an asylum to receive all who may fly to it."

Although it was by no means united by historic ethnic roots, the population was overwhelmingly Protestant in religion if sharply divided in the manner of its observance. The postwar years witnessed a decline of the older religions—the Anglicans or Episcopalians and the Puritans or Congregationalists—and a rise in evangelical faiths—Baptists and Methodists. This transformation occurred almost in defiance of the currents of rationalism and deism that won recruits even among conspicuous leaders. The growth of these various dissenting groups proved a fillip toward the attainment of freedom of conscience.

Equality, so eloquently proclaimed in the Great Declaration, proved a most elusive goal in a society resting upon slavery and indentured servitude and among a people for whom farming was the chief occupation. Agriculture claimed the attention of great estate holders, of small freeholders, of subsistence farmers, and of a rising tenancy. Free white labor competed in many areas with slavery, that "dark gloominess hanging over the land," as the Quaker leader and antislavery advocate John Woolman described it, while women enjoyed no political rights and suffered an inferior position at law, and Indians were considered a breed apart. A minority formed an affluent society, including the *nouveaux riches* who had exploited the late war's opportunities to their own profit. Another minority was mired in poverty. Between was a large middling group, by no means untouched by the postwar business depression, but comfortably optimistic in a society that was evidencing more upward mobility and less stratification than any nation of the Old World.

If social, cultural, regional, sectional, and racial divisions kept the American people from effectively uniting, difficulties in communication conspired to discourage close physical contact among people in isolated areas. It took six days for a stagecoach to make the journey between New York and Boston, and more than three between Philadelphia and New York, a mere ninety miles. Innumerable rivers had to be forded by ferries. Save for the span across the Charles River, no significant river had been bridged prior to the convening of the delegates to the Constitutional Convention in Philadelphia in 1787. Spring and fall rains turned the highways into mud-rutted perils; winter snows contributed to the length and exhaustion of the trip, and unprepossessing inns accommodated the late-arriving traveler, who would be awakened at three in the morning for the next stage of his journey. When in March of 1784 Aaron Burr ventured the trip over the wide stretch of water between Paulus Hook and New York City, his wife was beside herself with worry over the dangers of the journey. "Every breath of wind whistled terror," she wrote. "Every noise at the door was mingled with hope of thy return."

Hence, engineers and businessmen joined forces in plans for improving inland navigation through the construction of locks, canals, and bridges, and inventors put steam engines in small craft in efforts to sail upriver. While packet boats plied between points along the Atlantic coast, the winning of the West would be as much a matter of technology as it would be a response to the yearnings of the restless pioneer and the eventual securing of the frontier against the Indians, once British troops pulled out of American territory.

As our three witnesses saw it, the disunity of the country could be put down primarily to the weak constitutional structure. The Articles of Confederation were finally ratified in 1781 by the holdout state of Maryland after Virginia, along with other states, had ceded her western land claims to Congress. The prestige of that body had fallen so low that some states no longer bothered to send delegates. Its presidency was taken so lightly that John Hancock, elected to that position in 1785 (he had, of course, served in that capacity years earlier and signed his name in bold letters to the Declaration), never bothered to come to New York for its sessions. The men who later sat in Congress were, with a few exceptions, hardly noteworthy. An encounter in 1788 with the President and several members of Congress prompted John Adams's daughter to write: "Had you been present you would have trembled for your country, to have seen, heard and observed the men who are its rulers."

The Congress was shackled, first, by its lack of powers under the Articles. It could not levy or collect taxes. It could not levy a tariff, while the states could. It had no control over commerce. Under the Articles, nine states were required for the passage of major legislation, and unanimity was required for the passage of an amendment to the Articles.

Hence, Congress lacked the power to wield the weapons of reciprocity to force Great Britain to stop discriminating against American ships and American goods. It had no funds to pay its army, which toward the end of the war seemed on the brink of mutiny, and certainly no funds to maintain a sizable one or rebuild a completely decimated navy. Lacking the ability to maintain respectable military and naval forces, it could not oust the British from the Northern and Western posts on American territory, could not force Spain to concede the navigation of the lower Mississippi to Americans, or prevent the taking of American seamen as hostages in piratical raids by Mediterranean corsairs.

Congress did not need to look abroad to see the consequences of its ineffectual powers. Over the boundaries of the states, serious conflicts soon arose. More than once, shooting wars broke out between the states. Pennsylvania and Virginia fought each other over the Pittsburgh region until they agreed upon an extension of the Mason-Dixon line (originally the southern boundary of Pennsylvania) as their boundary. Connecticut settlers, claiming the Wyoming Valley, located in Pennsylvania, were met by Pennsylvania guns and driven out. New York and Massachusetts disputed the latter's charter claims to western New York. Conspiratorial plots abounded. Land speculators and settlers threatened to bring about the cession of Kentucky from Virginia and Tennessee from North Carolina. In Tennessee, settlers actually organized the free state of Franklin, electing John Sevier as their governor, but the secessionist movement did not stick. James Wilkinson, as unsavory a character as bestrode the Western scene, a man given to lying, bullying, or fawning as circumstances dictated, devoted himself to the task of separating Kentucky from Virginia in order to turn it over to Spain, for whom he served as a secret agent. New York and Vermont quarreled over the latter's independence, and Vermont's leaders, seeking admission for Vermont as a separate state, blackmailed Congress by continuing to hold talks with the British about making their territory a province of Canada. All these secessionist claims had to be deferred until the establishment of the new federal government, when Kentucky, Vermont, and Tennessee were granted admission to the Union.

In no area was Congress's utter lack of capacity as

evident as in that of finance. At the end of the war, Congress was confronted by a debt of $40 million, not including the debts of the several states. Attempts to raise money under the old system of requisition were futile, for the system itself had largely broken down. Less than fifteen percent of the $10 million requested had been paid in by the states at the end of 1783; Congress received a mere $100,000 of a request for $3 million. Robert Morris, Superintendent of Finance since 1781, likened talking to the states to preaching to the dead. The shameful circumstances of the nation's finances were revealed when, in 1783, Congress authorized Morris to draw on the credit of loans from foreign governments which American ministers abroad had been instructed to negotiate but had not yet obtained. Fortunately, Dutch bankers rescued Congress from its embarrassment and tided the nation over for a time.

At the heart of these financial problems was the fact that Congress, under the Articles, had no power to tax. As far back as 1781, Congress sought to amend the Articles to permit a five-percent federal duty on imports to pay the interest and then the principal on the national debt, but Rhode Island refused to approve the plan. Two years later Congress again made the proposal, in modified form. This time New York, which derived the bulk of its revenue from imports, blocked it. An incensed Henry Knox, then Secretary of War, exclaimed: "Every liberal good man is wishing New York in Hell!" The states, in contrast, had paid much of their own Revolutionary War debts amounting to $13 million, although in terms of our most recent knowledge of finance, it can be argued that the state debts, by being amortized too rapidly, contributed to the deflation of the postwar period.

And that was the nub of the crisis that spawned a depression and a rebellion. Scenes such as these convinced Hamilton, Jay, and Madison that constitutional change lay at the root of the nation's unity and salvation. That sense of crisis was captured by Washington in a letter to Madison in November 1786: "No morn ever dawned more favourably than ours did, and no day was ever more clouded than the present." On this note of crisis the curtain rises on the second act.

6

Conspiracy and Depression

Madison, despite his heavy commitment to bring complete religious liberty to Virginia, would, as a delegate to the Continental Congress, seek a nationalist solution for that body's weakness. John Jay, in his first-hand contacts with foreign diplomats abroad, quickly perceived that European statesmen did not think the government under the Articles of Confederation would last. Hamilton, both as Washington's brilliant aide and later as a busy attorney in New York, would insist that the only way to bring about a change in the government was to unite the public creditors with the army and bring pressure on the country for reform. Although the methods of the trio differed, their ends were the same—a strong union under a changed constitutional system.

As early as September 1780, in a letter to James Duane, young Hamilton expounded his ideas of national sovereignty, along with the need for a national bank. In 1781, only a few months before he returned to the army to fight at Yorktown, Hamilton published a series of six *Continentalist* essays. Therein he found "something noble and magnificent in the perspective of a great Federal Republic, closely linked to the pursuit of a common interest, tranquil and prosperous at home, respectable abroad," and contrasted that with the current scene, "a number of petty states, with the appearance only of union, jealous and perverse, without any independent direction."

"The more I see, the more I find reason for those who love this country to weep over its weakness,"

Hamilton wrote Robert Morris, Superintendent of Finance, in September 1782. In order to understand what Hamilton was about, one must comprehend the situation of the nation's creditors and the army at war's end. Continental paper issued by Congress had vanished in value and was considered a "common debt" of the Revolution. Loans, however, were a different matter. Congress had obtained loans from foreign nations and foreign banking consortia. It had also secured loans from American citizens, to whom "loan certificates" bearing interest had been issued. They were held mostly in the commercial states by merchants and monied investors. With Congress on the brink of bankruptcy if not over it, that body looked now to the states for the support of the war, including funds to pay for arrears in salary and current services of the armed forces.

The people in the states blamed the radicals they had sent to Congress for the financial mess that body had gotten into, and began to replace the more radical delegates with solid conservatives, men like Alexander Hamilton, for example. Hamilton felt that the only hope of keeping the country going lay in joining the interest of the public creditors to the claims of the officers of the army. Ever a man of action, he now initiated some bold moves. Seeing the country headed for bankruptcy, even unable to pay its soldiers, he joined with Robert Morris, and his assistant Gouverneur Morris (no family relation), in a tricky move to unite the demands of the public creditors with those of the officers of the Continental army. How far Hamilton would have gone in promoting the mutinous threats of high-ranking army officers must fall into the realm of speculation, but it is clear that Washington's support was essential. If Washington would not join in the plot, Hamilton was unwilling to endorse any other military leader.

Madison, equally concerned about securing for Congress the power to levy a tax on imports, was less enamored of any program that would give to the army an activist role. He cautioned Hamilton that there was a long tradition in America that the military must be subordinate to civilian authority, and reminded him that standing armies had always been unpopular.

Threats from army officers reached Philadelphia in the last week of December of 1782. Major General Alexander McDougall, along with Colonels John Brooks and Matthias Ogden, rode into Philadelphia to petition Congress on behalf of the army quartered at Newburgh, New York. They stopped by General St. Clair's quarters, whispered their plans to him, and received his endorsement. They then paid a visit to Robert and Gouverneur Morris, where they were informed that the state of Virginia as well as Rhode Island had just killed the impost. Hence, since an amendment to the Articles required the unanimous approval of the states, the revenue plan, their last hope, was dead.

Petition Congress, the Morrises urged the officers, and let them know that your plans are no idle threat. "The army have swords in their hands!" Gouverneur Morris told Hamilton. "I am glad to see things in their present train."

Hamilton, considering all possible contingencies, asked:

"What will you do if the army disbands?"

The prestigious Superintendent of Finance replied: "I will feed them."

It was at this time that Madison and Hamilton joined forces in Congress, the former defending the demands of the officers for the half-pay that Congress had agreed to give them more than two years before. Madison found their petition reasonable and even modest, although he was somewhat disturbed about its conclusion: "Any further experiments on the army's patience may have fatal effects."

Still, despite the threatening tone of the petitioners, Madison pointed out that there was a serious defect in the Articles of Confederation in that it required unanimous consent of all the states to levy and collect a tax.

Gouverneur and Robert Morris, who advised the army officers in their campaign against Congress, portrait by Charles Willson Peale (*courtesy of the Pennsylvania Academy of the Fine Arts*).

That provision must be changed, and quickly, he warned. Hamilton followed up Madison's comments by proposing to make the army claims the basis for forcing a national fund upon the states.

After days of exhausting debates over the need to set up a permanent fund through which Congress could deal with such emergencies as the back pay due the army, James Madison, according to his own notes, joined Hamilton and several other concerned delegates in a lengthy private conversation held at the home of Thomas FitzSimons, an Irish-born Philadelphia merchant and delegate to Congress who had already been involved in setting up the first bank in America— the Bank of North America. The group listened intently to what Hamilton had to say.

Hamilton pulled no punches. He warned his listeners that it was "certain" that the army had "secretly determined" not to lay down their arms until the issue of their back pay was satisfactorily resolved, and were expected to issue a public declaration to that effect. What especially troubled Hamilton was the likelihood that the army would turn to General Horatio Gates to advance their cause. Hamilton continued: "I know General Washington intimately and perfectly," adding that the General's "extreme reserve" and his increasing "asperity of temper" were contributing to the decline of his popularity. Nonetheless, by "virtue, patriotism, and firmness" Washington could be depended upon "never to yield to any dishonorable or disloyal plan" which some in the army might have in contemplation. "I want the General to lead the army in their plans to obtain redress of their grievances," he added, because "we could count upon their being moderate and directed to proper objects." Some other leader might "foment and misguide their councils." In fact, he told the group, he had already written Washington to assume the leadership and to keep "a complaining and suffering army within the bounds of moderation."

"If the alternative is Gates," the others reminded Hamilton, "your antipathy to him is no secret. There's always been bad blood between you two."

Hamilton acknowledged that his and Gates's mutual antipathy went back a long time. He reminded them that after Saratoga, General Washington had dispatched his young aide to Gates to secure troops the General desperately needed. Puffed up with his newly won prestige in gaining a victory—credit for which, Hamilton felt, belonged to "that miserable traitor" Benedict Arnold—Gates turned Hamilton down. "No, I can't spare them," he replied curtly. Then Hamilton, a mere captain, ordered this major general "in the most explicit terms" to regard this as a "positive" order from the commander-in-chief, to dispatch without delay all the Continental troops he had under his command. Gates was furious, but he complied. In this unprecedented confrontation of a low-ranking officer with a major general, Washington had backed Hamilton. "I approve of all the steps you have taken," he wrote.

Gates, in Hamilton's opinion, never forgave him, and although now promoted to lieutenant colonel, the younger man suffered repeated and, he felt, "unprovoked" attacks on his character.

To Hamilton, Gates's disastrous rout at the Battle of Camden in mid-August of 1780 served to confirm his opinion of the latter's generalship and courage. His disdain for Gates was expressed in a letter to his friend James Duane, written not long after the battle. "What think you," Hamilton wrote, "of the conduct of this great man?" Admittedly Gates's enemy, Hamilton added, "Did ever any one hear of such a disposition or such a flight? His best troops placed on the side strongest by nature, his worst on that weakest by nature, and his attack made with these. 'Tis impossible to give a more complete picture of military absurdity." As a consequence of Gates's violations of the "maxims of war and common sense," Hamilton charged that the battle had been turned into a disaster, adding, "But was there ever an instance of a general running away, as Gates has done, from his whole army? And was there ever so precipitate a flight? One hundred and eighty miles in three days and a half. It does admirable credit to the activity of a man at his time of life. But it disgraces the general and the soldier. He is no Hector! He is no Ulysses!" Hamilton remarked disdainfully. Such a man, Hamilton was convinced, was unfit to lead the army in its present mutinous frame of mind.

Not long after this conversation at the FitzSimons home in Philadelphia, word reached the delegates in Congress that Robert Morris had just tendered his resignation as Superintendent of Finance. "To increase our debts, while the prospect of paying them diminishes, does not consist with my ideas of integrity. I must therefore quit a situation which becomes utterly insupportable," Morris declared. Despite the fact that he was distrusted by the radicals and had succeeded in collecting many enemies, Morris was recognized as a man of talent and audacity. His threatened departure struck another blow at the nation's morale. Congress persuaded him to stay on a while longer. Now Congress was confronted with a triple threat: the army delegation, the states' rejection of the impost, and the tendered resignation of the one man who had the confidence of the monied interests and was a miracle-worker at manipulating funds.

Washington took almost three weeks to reply to Hamilton's urgent letter. The General, who could be both inscrutable and taciturn, seemed to evade Hamilton's request for his active intercession and to assume the leadership of the army's cause. Insisting that he would "pursue the same steady line of conduct which has governed me hitherto," Washington assured Hamilton that he felt confident that the army, whose "just claims" he supported, gave no evidence of "exceeding the bounds of reason and moderation." He found, he said, "no proof" that "the old leaven"—meaning, of course, Gates and the anti-Washington cabal—"is again beginning to work, under the mask of the most perfect dissimulation and apparent cordiality."

Washington's noncommittal stance, so puzzling to Hamilton, the activist, was quickly shaken. Writing to Hamilton from the army headquarters at Newburgh on March 12, the General reported on the dangerous results of a visit to Philadelphia paid by "a certain Gentleman, who shall be nameless at present." That "Gentleman" was Colonel Walter Stewart, who on his returning to headquarters from Philadelphia reported to his friends that Congress planned to dissolve the army in the near future and argued that the army officers should take action to ensure that Congress would fulfill the promises it had made to them. Washington had already sent to Congress various addresses circulating at camp and obviously originating from General Gates's headquarters tent, which had suddenly become a beehive of activity. From this source emanated the letter from Major John Armstrong, Jr., an inflammatory statement denouncing the nation's ingratitude to the men who had won its independence. Armstrong pressed Gates to support a forceful memorial in the form of an ultimatum dispatched to Congress. If rejected, the army would be advised to "retire to some unsettled country, smile in your turn, and 'mock when their Congress's fear cometh on.' "

The Armstrong Address, printed as a broadside, reached Washington's headquarters and, as the General indicated in his communication with Hamilton, was promptly brought to his attention. Summoning his aides, Washington denounced it in strong language and headed off a "disorderly" and "irregular" meeting called by Armstrong for that Saturday. Now deeply aroused, Washington wrote Hamilton that he was determined to hold the army "within the bounds of reason and moderation."

Washington's handling of the mutiny proved an act of high statesmanship and decisiveness. The business was carefully stage-managed from start to finish. First the General shrewdly picked Gates to chair the meeting, which would effectively prevent the latter from talking or making motions from the floor. Then, as the troops climbed in a wintry landscape to the top of a hill and their destination, a newly constructed social hall, Washington kept them waiting. He strode into the room and requested Gates for the floor, and the chair had no course but to oblige. Then Washington tore into the would-be mutineers. He denounced the Armstrong Address, its motives, its appeal "to passions," and even charged it with "insidious purposes." "Could the army," the General asked, "really leave their wives and children and desert the country in the extremest hour of her distress? Could you contemplate anything so shocking as turning its swords against Congress and of plotting the ruin of both? Could you really cause a separation between military and civilian authority? My God!" Washington exclaimed, "what can this writer have in view? He is neither a friend of the army nor of the country, rather an 'insidious foe'!"

Adopting a more reassuring tone, Washington promised that Congress might be slow but would ultimately justify the army's faith. Then, picking up a letter from a delegate to Congress, he put on a pair of spectacles that the scientist Dr. David Rittenhouse had made for him.

"I have grown gray in the service of my country, and now find myself growing blind."

The assembly sat stunned. The tension was broken, the hostility ended. Some officers openly wept. And the Gates plan, if we can attribute it to him, collapsed. After Washington withdrew, the officers unanimously declared "abhorrent" the "infamous propositions" and disavowed "the secret attempts of some unknown persons to subvert all discipline and good order."

Did Washington realize who was behind this attempt to subordinate civilian rule to the military and set up a military dictatorship? Washington knew who was behind it, but never publicly put the blame on anyone, because in a government where the civilian authority had maintained its supremacy over the military, the character of the civilian leadership implicated might have served as a dangerous lesson for the future.

Madison had predicted that moves toward fiscal austerity would determine whether "prosperity and tranquility, or confusion and disunion" would result from the Revolution. Morris had forced the issue by discontinuing all interest payments on loan certificates and virtually stopping paying the army. That brought on, perhaps intentionally, the potentially dangerous clash between the army and Congress that we have examined. Now the army quickly disbanded, most officers left, and the rank and file were down to a pitiful force of seven hundred men.

And what did these men face on their return home? First, a false prosperity brought on by a burst of buying to satisfy pent-up demand. British merchants took advantage of the war's end to unload their heavy inventory of manufactured goods on the American markets. Such excessive imports stifled native industries that had been springing up during the war, and drained away precious gold and silver. Neither a national tariff nor an embargo could be seriously proposed, for Congress under the Articles lacked the power to regulate commerce, while retaliatory action taken by individual states against British imports had proven ineffectual. Thus, when Massachusetts tried to prevent dumping, New Hampshire readily absorbed the imported goods.

Other trade grievances compounded the business difficulties. Once the American states had won independence, they were no longer a part of the British Empire and therefore no longer eligible for the preferential trade treatment accorded British (including American colonial) ships and goods. Southerners no longer enjoyed the bounties that had been paid for naval stores and the special treatment that had been accorded rice exports. New England and the middle states, which had traditionally exported fish and lumber to the British West Indies in exchange for sugar, rum, and molasses, were now barred from that area.

Trade restrictions between the states themselves, and retaliatory actions by states discriminated against, compounded the problem. Some states enacted protective tariffs, taxing both foreign goods and products made in other states. As business pursued its downward spiral, commodity prices continued to sink, wages withered, and unemployment soared. Businessmen were concerned about currency instability, and debtors sought paper money as a way out of their straitened circumstances. Rhode Island was on the blacklist of American businessmen. In that state, a debtor lobby had pushed a bill through the legislature that made it obligatory for creditors to accept paper money. Soon tested in the courts, the law was declared unconstitutional, but most of the judges who handed down this unpopular decision were ousted for their presumption by the voters at the next election.

Barred now from trading with the British West Indian islands, New Englanders suffered acutely. In Boston, Gloucester, and Newburyport, fishermen, ropewalkers, and shipyard workers pounded the streets; the wharves were idle. In New York City, hundreds of families were on poor relief. As bankruptcies, foreclosures, and jailing of debtors became the order of the day, the only unity that the country now enjoyed was a unity in misery.

A mountain of data can be gleaned from account books, court dockets, shipping records, commodity price lists, and other statistical reports to depict the postwar depression that struck the country most severely by the year 1786. For that year one could have obtained a comparable and equally comprehensive view by dropping in at a busy attorney's office at 58 Wall Street. There Hamilton handled his practice in a room lined with lawbooks, containing shelves bulging with parchments tied with red ribbons, and a huge desk and several tables piled high with papers, briefs, and correspondence. Had one assumed that Hamilton chucked all his papers in a dustbin when he was through with a case, he might have been surprised to learn how, unlike most other lawyers of those years, he held on to most of his legal correspondence, pleadings, and briefs, and that Betsey Hamilton in later years managed to persuade Hamilton's executor to preserve them, along with the rest of his papers.

Hamilton could be seen seated at his desk. Time was at his heels. *Rutgers* v. *Waddington* had brought him a host of Loyalist clients, along with creditors whose collections of prewar debts were held up by a recently enacted Citation Act passed by the state legislature. Litigation growing out of the depression inundated his law clerks and scriveners, and found Hamilton making the circuit of the courts—scurrying to the Mayor's Court, where he argued civil suits, then to the state's Supreme Court, and at other times handling cases in Chancery, where New Yorkers, following English precedent, had traditionally dispensed equitable relief.

One can imagine a typical review of current cases conducted by Hamilton with his office manager, Balthazar de Haert, and one of his law clerks, Joseph

Strang. As they summarized the cases for him, Hamilton would be jotting down the "point" at issue, a process at which he had shown himself a past master.

Despite a huge case load, Hamilton managed to be buoyant and often irrepressible, as he would thumb through the batch of papers on his desk and comment on others being summarized by his associates. The very first one he might have picked could have come both as a shock and a sad reminder to him. It was from Henry Laurens, the South Carolinian. Hamilton could hardly forget the tale of the former President of Congress, who, dispatched on a diplomatic mission abroad during the war, had been captured by the British and confined to the Tower of London, charged with carrying treasonous correspondence. Like a good common-law attorney, Hamilton regarded Laurens's confinement in the Tower for some two years as a travesty of that justice of which the British boasted: no habeas corpus; no trial; an old man thrust in prison and left to rot away until good friends posted bail and made possible a last-minute appearance of Laurens at the preliminary peace talks in Paris.

What particularly disturbed Hamilton about Laurens's letter was that it contained a request to recover a black man whom the British had carried off from Laurens's South Carolina plantation and who was now reputed to be in New York. Hamilton was baffled by the contradiction between Laurens's former professions—that slaveowners like himself should heed the assertion of equality in the Declaration of Independence and proceed to free their slaves despite the custom of the country—with his present stance. Turning the letter aside, he reminded his two co-workers of his close friendship with Henry Laurens's gallant son John Laurens. Before John's death in one of the last military incidents of the Revolution, he had joined with Hamilton in a proposal to Congress to enlist slaves in the Patriot army with an offer of freedom, a proposal that Congress sidetracked. Compounding Hamilton's distaste for the assignment was his promi-

nent membership in John Jay's New York Society for
the Manumission of Slaves, set up to safeguard free
blacks and to make sure they were not unjustly deprived of their freedom. To Hamilton, as he remarked
to his aides, the request was morally repugnant and he
would not touch the matter.

As the young clerk and the office manager huddled
with Hamilton over the correspondence and legal documents being reviewed, they noted that letters were
swarming in from one trouble spot after another. Strang
showed his employer a request from an Albany client
to recover a debt from a New York City man. Hamilton picked up another from Jeremiah Wadsworth, an
affluent Connecticut entrepreneur and stout Federalist
who was worried about his stock in the Bank of North
America. One client, Isaac Moses, whom Hamilton
characterized as "an honest ironmonger," was peti-
tioning for bankruptcy. De Haert summarized for Hamilton another batch of papers from Stephen Delancey,
who was pressing a dozen law suits on debts due him.
Strang handed him another letter from a Philadelphian
suing on a bond.

Considering the lengths to which he had gone to see
that justice was done to Loyalists and British creditors, Hamilton found it supremely ironic when he noted
the request from one Nathaniel Hazard that he urge
the legislature to hold up a pack of suits pressed by
British creditors against a group of Americans, who,
the writer contended, would be "ruined." The State
Senate had incautiously let Hazard's bill go through,
but the Assembly took no action. Now Hazard turned
to Hamilton and asked him, of all people, to lobby the
bill through the lower house.

Hamilton needed no reminder from his good friend
John Jay that the passage of such an act would be in
violation of the treaty with Great Britain and would
serve to undercut every effort the Secretary for Foreign Affairs had expended to get the states to repeal
such discriminatory legislation. Hamilton's stand in
Rutgers would have been ample assurance to Jay that

the former would remain steadfast in upholding national treaties, and that the United States would lose all credence abroad if a treaty could be violated by any state. At the same time Hamilton, as a realist, recognized how impossible it was for a group of debtors to discharge their own debts when others in turn had failed to make remittances due them. The fault, he acknowledged ruefully, was not theirs, but the times'.

The pile of letters, petitions, and documents that Hamilton and his two aides had been reviewing comprised in microcosm a picture of a critical situation that stretched nationwide. To Hamiton, the crisis cried out for a strengthened national government with energy to act.

Among the letters in the pile Hamilton had been examining was one from John Barker Church, Angelica's husband, enclosing a power of attorney along with a request to collect monies due him. Pushing a heap of papers aside, Hamilton took a quill pen and wrote a note to Angelica, who he assumed had left America for good: "Judge the bitterness it gives to those who love you with the *love of nature* and to me who feels an attachment for you not less lively. . . ."

Hamilton was not likely to forget the nation's first depression and the misery that it brought to so many families. In the twelfth *Federalist* he argues that if we had the kind of strong government that the Constitution provided for, these economic difficulties could be reversed. Congress could levy a tariff that would force the British to come to terms, and then there would be no need for heavy land taxes. But it required great diplomacy to get concessions from foreign nations, and as we shall see, that task, among a host of others, Congress assigned to its new Secretary for Foreign Affairs, John Jay, who was elected to that office even before his return from his triumphs in Paris.

Aside from the inability of Congress to levy tariffs, Madison, back in Virginia, laid the depression to an erosion of the value of money. He saw tobacco planters in Virginia going broke as a result of the crash in tobacco prices and a similar collapse in corn. He was determined that paper-money remedies like those resorted to in Rhode Island would not contaminate Virginia. In a notable speech before the state legislature in November 1786, he denounced the issuance of paper money without the taxes to back it. He called it unconstitutional—a device for partial confiscation of property by partial payment for it. Enough paper was afloat in tobacco notes and public securities. More would only vitiate morals, foster luxury, and cut off funds for Congress. It would destroy confidence between individuals and enrich sharpers. Should Virginia join the paper-money states of that day—Pennsylvania, New York, North and South Carolina—she would be conspiring "to disgrace republican government in the eyes of mankind." Madison's speech, with its evangelical overtones, decided the issue, and the legislature overwhelmingly defeated more paper. Here was a case where Madison the statesman acted against his own economic interest because he and his family were all in debt and pinched for money. Like the states' regulation of commerce, the states' issuance of paper money, Madison found, was starting to shake a very rocky Confederation.

These thoughts Madison would bring both to the convention in Philadelphia and to his contributions to *The Federalist*. In *Federalist* Number 44 he defended the prohibition in the Constitution against the issuance of bills of credit by the states. This prohibition, Madison rather optimistically observed, "must give pleasure to every citizen in proportion to his love of justice and his knowledge of the true springs of public prosperity." He continues:

> The loss which America has sustained since the peace, from the pestilent effects of paper money on the necessary confidence between man and man; on the necessary confidence in the public councils; on the industry and morals of the people, and on

the character of Republican Government, constitutes an enormous debt against the States chargeable with this unadvised measure, which must long remain unsatisfied; or rather an accumulation of guilt, which can be expiated not otherwise than by a voluntary sacrifice on the altar of justice, of the power which has been the instrument of it. . . .

Debtors themselves at times, Hamilton and Madison joined in upholding the sanctity of contracts, the inviolability of property, and the just claims of creditors. To them, that was the main lesson of our first great depression.

Nowhere do we find in capsule form as graphic an account of the effects of a weak national government upon the economy as in John Jay's masterly *Address to the People of the State of New York*, written not long after his final contribution to *The Federalist*, his letter Number 64, relating to foreign affairs. Jay, in the *Address*, hammered away at "this new and wonderful system of government" that had left unprovided "almost every national object of every kind." As a result, other nations, "taking the advantage of its imbecility, are daily multiplying commercial restraints upon us." Like a good prosecuting attorney, Jay then cited the results on the American economy of such nonaction:

> Our fur trade is gone to Canada, and British garrisons keep the keys of it. Our ship-yards have almost ceased to disturb the repose of the neighbourhood by the noise of the axe and the hammer; and while foreign flags fly triumphantly above our highest houses, the American stars seldom do more than shed a few feeble rays about the humbler masts of river sloops and coasting schooners. The greater part of our hardy seamen are ploughing the ocean in foreign pay, and not a few of our ingenious shipwrights are now building vessels on alien shores.
>
> Although our increasing agriculture and industry

extend and multiply our productions, yet they constantly diminish in value; and although we permit all nations to fill our country with their merchandises, yet their best markets are shut against us. Is there an English, or a French, or a Spanish island or port in the West Indies to which an American vessel can carry a cargo of flour for sale? Not one. The Algerines exclude us from the Mediterranean and adjacent countries; and we are neither able to purchase nor to command the free use of those seas. Can our little towns or larger cities consume the immense productions of our fertile country? Or will they without trade be able to pay a good price for the proportion which they do consume?

The last season gave a very unequivocal answer to those questions. What numbers of fine cattle have returned from this city to the country for want of buyers? What great quantities of salted and other provisions still lie useless in the stores? To how much below the former price is our corn, and wheat, and flour, and lumber rapidly falling? Our debts remain undiminished, and the interest on them accumulating; our credit abroad is nearly extinguished, and at home unrestored; they who had money have sent it beyond the reach of our laws, and scarcely any man can borrow of his neighbour. Nay, does not experience also tell us that it is as difficult to pay as to borrow; that even our houses and lands cannot command money; that lawsuits and usurious contracts abound; that our farms fall on executions for less than half their value; and that distress in various forms and in various ways is approaching fast to the doors of our best citizens?

Now, when the tide of the depression washed the doorsteps of "our best citizens," it seemed obvious that it was a time to act. If foreign powers would not make the first move to exploit American weakness, a rising by the afflicted people might well force the issue.

7

The Years of "National Humiliation"

"Almost the last stage of national humiliation." Thus does Hamilton, in his *Federalist* Number 15, depict the years between 1784 and 1789, years when Congress and the thirteen states suffered one inglorious setback after another at the hands of foreign powers. England recognized the United States as too weak to force her to comply with the request of her erstwhile colonies to grant them a commercial treaty that would lift the trade restrictions against America, restrictions embodied in British Orders in Council that had contributed so heavily to the continuing depression in the states. Britain refused to remove her troops from frontier posts on American soil. She stirred up Indian attacks to keep settlers from moving north of the Ohio and even into western New York. France insisted on giving its consuls extraterritoriality in America and controlling the emigration to this country of Frenchmen who wanted to come over. In the Mediterranean the Barbary pirates were intercepting American merchant ships and imprisoning American seamen, who were held as hostages. Finally, Spain's readiness to grant America a commercial treaty was tied to her positive refusal to permit Americans to freely navigate the Mississippi, thereby thwarting the ambitions of America's western settlers and the long-range interests of the South.

Dismal indeed seemed the prospects of resolving these postwar problems. In 1784, Congress dumped

John Jay, Secretary for Foreign Affairs, portrait by
Joseph Wright, painted in 1786 (*courtesy of The New
York Historical Society, New York City*).

these unresolved issues with the Great Powers into the
lap of John Jay, electing him to the post of Secretary
for Foreign Affairs. Jay accepted the post only on
condition that his terms be met: that Congress, temporarily in Trenton, decide on a set meeting place; that
he have the right to appear and address Congress
anytime he wished, a power not granted any other
department head; and that all correspondence both
from foreign states and American state governors be
first transmitted to him. He was even given the power
to open the mail, a secret intelligence authorization
that he never appears to have exercised.

Jay set up modest offices at Fraunces Tavern, at
the foot of Broad and Pearl streets, where it is still
standing. For a staff he had just a single undersecretary, two clerks, a couple of part-time transla-
tors, and a messenger-doorkeeper. To these offices
flowed a steady stream of discouraging dispatches from
abroad.

*   *   *

The year is 1785. Reports that Jay passed on to Congress, along with the recollections of survivors, preserve for us a humiliating story of American hostages taken along the southern Mediterranean coast. They transport the reader to a dark, dank, noisome dungeon in Algiers. Stepping cautiously over the brick floor, one encounters the bodies of American seamen, tattered and emaciated, and half asleep. Added to the vermin that their clothing houses, swarms of mosquitoes find ready and helpless targets. Morning comes. Some of the captives are seen shackled, dragging heavy weights, and walking a treadmill, their bare backs showing evidence of severe beatings. Others are dragged, similarly shackled, to a small piazza opposite the mosque of the fishermen, where they squat among other prospective slaves of many nationalities. Their shackles removed, they are made to run to and fro so that the prospective buyers can listen to their heartbeats by placing their ears against their naked chests. Then, prying their mouths open, the merchants peer within to verify their age by the condition of their teeth. One by one they are sold off, prices varying with their physical condition.

The survivors from among the work force return to their dungeon quarters that evening. An American ship captain is heard shouting to his fellow captives: "Congress has forgotten all about us! Since we were captured by the Algerines, they have left us here to be sold as slaves or worked to death." One of the captured crew mutters: "I hear they are holding us as hostages. There is a price on our heads—thirty thousand guineas!" The remarks plunge the captives into a mood of deep despondency.

A year passes. The delegates of Congress assembled at New York's old City Hall request information about the Mediterranean crisis from their new Secretary for Foreign Affairs, John Jay. The Journal of Congress reveals Jay's discomfiture as well as his resolve. First of all, Jay informs the delegates how he and his fellow peace commissioners at Paris anticipated the current Mediterranean troubles once American ships and crews lost the protection of the British navy as a result of winning independence. In vain had the Americans sought to incorporate in the Definitive Treaty a provision pledging the British to intervene on behalf of the United States against piratical depredations. The fact is, as Jay patiently explains to Congress, the British see every advantage to themselves in declining to assist their former colonies and new trade rivals.

Ship seizures had their beginnings almost a year before Jay assumed his new post. Moroccan pirates initiated them with the seizure of the ship *Betsey* and her crew. Negotiations for the release of the American hostages were progressing, and Jay had counted on bringing Congress news of peace, informing them that, through the good offices of Spain and American negotiators abroad, the crew held by Morocco was released. While that release had been effected, Algiers had now come into the picture with the seizure of two American brigs, their cargo and crew. Worse yet, as Jay had just been informed by John Paul Jones, Algiers had declared war on the United States.

Congress and Jay jointly faced a dilemma. Should America pay or fight? Congress first toyed with the notion of propitiating the Mediterranean corsairs by buying treaties with each of the Barbary states, including Tripoli and Tunis as well as Morocco and Algiers. However, save for Morocco, from whom such a treaty was obtained by purchase, the sum Congress authorized to ransom the Algerine captives fell far below the expectations of the avaricious intermediaries employed by the Barbary powers.

Should we meet such incredibly high demands? Congress asked Jay. His answer was an emphatic negative. Congress, he pointed out, had no such sums in its treasury, and it would be imprudent to authorize commissioners abroad entrusted with the negotiations to borrow such a sum, even if they could. For his own part, Jay declared, to the surprise of the delegates, he preferred waging war to paying tribute.

These were brave words, but Jay then had sober second thoughts. America's wartime navy had been sunk, demolished, or sold. Before war could be waged in foreign waters thousands of miles from America's coast, a new navy had to be built. For Congress to divert money at this time to such an effort, Jay felt, was unrealistic. A nation that could not protect its own frontier or pay its debts was in no position to build and maintain an adequate naval force.

Congress was insistent. What should be done? Jay was asked. His answer: put the problem up to the states. "Until such time as they furnish Congress with their respective portions of the sum needed to redeem the hostages," Jay warned, "the depredations of those barbarians will, in all probability, continue to increase." As a humane person Jay deplored the situation, but as a committed nationalist he was aware that these continued humiliations would further underscore the weakness of the central government under the Articles of Confederation and spur action for creating the kind of government with powers to act in such a situation, to forge a union that would earn the respect of foreign powers great and small.

"Shall we wage war or pay tribute?" Jay returned the question to Congress. "That, gentlemen, is a question you yourselves must decide." The Confederation Congress and the thirteen states refused to face the issue, and American seamen continued to rot in North African jails. Two decades were to pass before the first of the successful expeditions was launched by a rebuilt American navy toward securing unmolested transit of American merchantmen through the Mediterranean. Indeed, the humiliation of having to meet continued ransom demands was not finally ended until 1815, with Stephen Decatur's victory against Algiers.

As Congress recessed for the day after one of these futile debates, Jay could be seen striding rapidly down the steps leading out of City Hall and hastening along Broad Street. Entering his headquarters in Fraunces Tavern, he mounted the stairs to his private office. On his desk he found two piles of memoranda systematically arranged, and a batch of letters that had arrived on the latest packet from abroad. A quick glance revealed that his French translator, John Pintard, had left him a pile of *arrêts* and other French decrees that Thomas Jefferson, the minister to France, had included in his latest dispatches from Paris. Alongside them lay another batch. These were also systematically arranged, with translations prepared for him by his part-time Spanish-Portuguese translator, Isaac Pinto, and involved the sticky issues that were still holding up negotiations with the Portuguese court. Portugal was procrastinating about signing a commercial treaty, one that Jay had reason to assume met the demands of both parties.

Before he had a chance to pore through these two piles, Jay opened a couple of letters just received from London, one from his good friend John Adams, minister to the Court of St. James's, and the other from Adams's son-in-law, William Stephens Smith. Adams, with his customary bluntness, declared he was "regarded by the British court as a cipher." Smith's letter compounded Jay's pessimistic assessment of the possibility of concluding quickly with a half-dozen European powers the commercial treaties he was counting on to improve America's foreign trade. European monarchies, so Smith informed him, were praying for the United States to collapse, and "like the ancient Grecian republics, fall prey to some ambitious prince." Prussia, Jay had heard, was a prime example. Even though the United States had successfully negotiated a treaty with that country, its prideful monarch, Frederick II, was quoted as having said, "I am much persuaded that this so-called independence of the Americans will not amount to much."

Jay knew it would take decisive action on the part of both the states and Congress to prove the arrogant

Prussian wrong. The notorious weaknesses of "the United States in Congress Assembled" were only exacerbated by the deliberate delaying tactics on the part of the European powers, anticipating a breakup of the Confederation. Negotiations with America's ally, France, provide a good example. Hardly had Jefferson arrived in Paris to assume his duties as Franklin's successor when, as he wrote Jay, he was "astonished to find all the public papers filled with accounts of the anarchy and distractions supposed to exist in America." Meanwhile, Jay was still holding up a treaty that Franklin had made with France, which gave their consuls the right to operate extraterritorial courts on United States soil and permitted them to scrutinize French emigrants to America and ship them home to France, a concession, he told Congress, that that body should not think of making. That treaty had now been dropped in Jefferson's lap, and finally a treaty in a form acceptable to America was ratified by the two parties.

A commercial treaty with Great Britain, ending that nation's deliberate policy of trade discrimination against the new United States and its ships and people, was proving one of the two toughest nuts for Jay to crack. The tone of John Adams's letters from London was discouraging, and Jay's talks with Sir John Temple, the British consul-general in New York, seemed to dim further any optimistic conclusion about the course of negotiations deemed by Jay as so vital to a return of American prosperity.

To Jay the British seemed intransigent. They had declined to dispatch a person with the rank of minister to the United States and had continued to keep their troops on American soil in violation of the Treaty of Peace. They justified the latter by insisting that the United States had broken the treaty before they did. They buttressed their argument with citations of laws that states were continuing to enact confiscating Tory property, contrary to the Definitive Treaty, and by stressing the obstacles that the state courts continued to erect to keep legitimate British creditors from col-

lecting bona fide prewar debts owed them. The debtors who sought protection in their state legislatures
and courts were principally the tobacco planters of
Maryland and Virginia. Many of them, but by no
means all, had no intention of ever paying back the
principal owed, aside from the mounting interest, which
they also ignored. In turn, the British refused even to
consider paying for the slaves their army took away
from the Southern planters when they evacuated. On
that last score the British surmised that Jay, with his
pronounced antislavery convictions, would not be likely
to put up much of a fight.

John Jay was both thorough and fair. He wanted the
facts, and to ascertain them he wrote to all the state
governors, requesting copies of their laws relating to
the enforcement of the Treaty of Paris. After a careful
review of the evidence, he concluded that the British
were in the right, and that the states had started vio-
lating the treaty before the British did. Jay then confronted Congress with his findings. Congress took the
news badly. Even fair-minded men find it hard to
acknowledge unpalatable truths. Not so James Madison, however. True, some of the reasoning on the
subject of the debts would be rather grating to Virginia, but Madison acknowledged that Jay had given
Congress a fair and able presentation of the issue.

At Jay's request, Congress swallowed the medicine.
It resolved that treaties constitutionally made became
"part of the law of the land, and [were] not only
independent of the will and power of such Legislatures, but also binding and obligatory on them." Finally, Congress called upon the states to repeal laws
repugnant to the treaty. Adopted only a few months
before the signing of the Constitution, this resolution
may be considered the basis of its supremacy clause
(Article VI, Section 2).

Not satisfied with telling Congress that America had
sinned first, Jay also told Sir John Temple, who in
turn relayed the information to his Foreign Secretary.
This indiscretion on Jay's part earned him the reputa-

tion in England as one of that nation's well-wishers. Jay might have been more cautious in drawing conclusions had he been privy to the correspondence between the British government and Canada's officials. He would have been astonished to learn, from records now available, that on April 8, 1784, Lord Sydney, the Secretary of State for Home Affairs in the Pitt Cabinet, had addressed a dispatch to Sir Frederick Haldimand, Governor-General of British North America, instructing him that in view of the vagueness of the treaty's stipulation for evacuation "with all convenient speed," such a move might be delayed "at least until we are enabled to secure the fur traders in the Interior Country and withdraw their property." The very next day, George III proclaimed the ratification of the treaty and promised "sincerely and faithfully" to observe the provisions. If there was duplicity, it was not the monopoly of one party!

Finally, the point should be made that about a decade later, John Jay, on a special mission to England, succeeded in winning modest commercial concessions from the British and persuading them to remove their troops from American soil, the latter action not unrelated to an American military defeat of the Indians, an event that rendered the British occupation untenable.

To Jay, the recurring question was, How long would the nation tolerate its humiliations at the hands of the great powers? His answer, in a letter penned at this time to Lord Lansdowne, formerly the Earl of Shelburne, the friend of America who had accepted the Preliminary Peace terms and, for his concessions, had been forced out of public life: "I cannot persuade myself that Providence had created such a nation, in such a country, to remain like dust in the balance of others."

Of all the serious issues confronting the Confederation, the one most likely to rip the Union asunder was the contest with Spain over the Mississippi. It arrayed North against South, commercial interests against agrarian, Western settlement against Eastern expansion, and John Jay against James Madison, men soon to

identify themselves on the same side sharing the pseudonym of "Publius."

From its earliest instructions to its wartime unac-
credited minister to Spain, Congress had demanded
the free navigation of the Mississippi to the Gulf. Jay
had pressed America's case when in Spain, even after
Congress had backed down. When in Paris, Jay had
again advanced America's claim, in a futile attempt to
win over both Vergennes and the Conde de Aranda.
The Mississippi proved the main stumbling block in all
Spanish-American negotiations between 1780 and the
end of the Confederation years.

Spain and France, relying on a corpus of contemporary international law, held that a nation such as the
United States, which did not control both banks of a
river, could not justifiably claim the freedom of shipping and an outlet to the sea—in this case the Gulf of
Mexico. Americans could cite one authority in their
favor, the Swiss jurist Emmerich de Vattel. They also
asserted that the Revolutionary government had succeeded to the easement of the east bank of the Mississippi, which England had secured at the end of the
Seven Years' War, giving the British the right of passage to the Mississippi. Since the Spaniards had recovered the Floridas at the end of the American Revolution
and were solidly planted in New Orleans, at the mouth
of the great river, these arguments were to no avail.

To forestall any aggressive movements on or toward
the river by the Americans, Spain, at war's end, formally closed the river to American shipping, fortified
points that would curb westward settlement by Americans, and seized American boats at Natchez, confiscating their cargo. This series of actions was calculated to
turn the Southwest, if not the whole South, against a
diffident Congress, should that body not come up with
some kind of acceptable compromise short of war.

War itself was hardly a viable option for America,
unless France was prepared to join forces with its
wartime ally to procure this vital claim. Jay checked
this point with Jefferson, only to be informed by the

latter that France could not be counted upon for either military or diplomatic backing of America's territorial claims or navigation rights.

Was this the kind of issue that was worth a war, even if America was prepared to fight? No less a personage than George Washington uttered a resounding "No!" At that time he had founded the Potomac Company, concerned with developing, through a system of locks and other engineering projects, a direct waterway connection between Chesapeake Bay and the Ohio River. This would bring Western trade east, and even as far south as Maryland and Virginia, whereas trade movements down the Mississippi would divert trade from the Atlantic states. What Washington feared was the rapid settlement of the West, one that would be accompanied by a mad scramble for land, by lawlessness, and even by a separation of the trans-Appalachian region from the rest of the country. What he preferred was "a progressive settling." He went on record opposing the demand for the navigation of the Mississippi "at this time" (the underscoring was his own). Richard Henry Lee, President of Congress, was completely persuaded by Washington, as was Henry Lee, when he took his seat as a delegate to that body. Contrariwise, James Madison was shocked, as he wrote Jefferson, that "many minds were tainted with so illiberal and short-sighted a policy."

Encouraged by Washington and a few other Southern leaders, and unaware of the depth of contrary sentiment in the South, Jay approached the negotiations with Spain in a conciliatory spirit. In fact, the Spanish-American talks were long, tortuous, and contentious, reaching a climactic turn in the late summer of 1786, on the eve of the convention at Annapolis, which urged wider commercial powers for Congress and other changes for which a federal convention was needed.

Jay's opposite in the Spanish negotiations was Don Diego de Gardoqui, an old acquaintance from Madrid, dispatched to the United States as special plenipotentiary, bearing the title *encargado de negocios*, or chargé d'affaires. His arrival in New York seemed a favorable omen to Jay, for Gardoqui's father had headed a Spanish firm that had been the go-between in the funneling of secret military stores to the American Revolutionaries.

Gardoqui had been given formal instructions and had some ideas of his own as to the best manner to proceed. From his knowledge of Jay gained during the war, Gardoqui made some unusual suggestions to be incorporated into his instructions. "The American" (referring to Jay), he observed to Spain's Principal Minister, the Conde de Floridablanca, "who is generally considered to possess talent and capacity enough, covering in great part a weakness natural to him, appears (by a consistent behavior) to be a very self-centered man, which passion his wife augments, because, in addition to considering herself meritoriously and being rather vain, she likes to be catered to, and even more to receive presents. This woman, whom he loves blindly, dominates him and nothing is done without her consent, so that her opinion prevails, though her husband at first may disagree. From which I infer that a little management in dealing with her and a few timely gifts will secure the friendship of both, because I have reason to believe that they proceed resolved to make a fortune." The Jays were not to be considered isolated targets, Gardoqui added: "He is not the only one in his country who has the same weakness, for there are many poor persons among the governing body, and I believe a skillful hand which knows how to take advantage of favorable opportunities, and how to give dinners and above all to entertain with good wine, may profit without appearing to pursue them."

Gardoqui may have been right about Jay's bump of self-esteem and abiding affection for his wife, an affection that was beyond the capacity of this Spanish diplomat to comprehend, but he was far wide of the mark in labeling the pair as fortune-hunters. Throughout his long public career, Jay was the soul of propriety. Even the royal gift to Jay from King Carlos III of a Spanish horse would not be accepted until he received the consent of Congress, and the American Secretary for Foreign Affairs politely declined Gardoqui's presents intended for Jay's wife. As regards Congress, we can have less confidence in its probity, considering that a number of its delegates managed to be on the payroll of the French foreign office during the late war, a fact of which Gardoqui must have been apprised.

Gardoqui's hands were tied by specific instructions. He could not accept the northern boundary line of West Florida laid down in the British-American Treaty of 1783. He dared not relinquish Spain's right to the exclusive navigation of the Mississippi River where it ran between Spanish banks. He was urged to trim the westward territorial claims of the United States, but these territorial issues remained negotiable. Finally, he was permitted to agree to commercial treaty, one providing both sides with "most-favored nation" privileges, including liberal treatment of American ships at Spain's peninsular ports and European islands.

Jay's instructions in turn offered him little leeway. He was to insist on the territorial bounds defined by the British Treaty of 1783 as well as the free navigation of the Mississippi through its length to the sea, and it was this last—the free use of the Mississippi—that proved the real sticking point.

Fortunately both Jay and Gardoqui kept records of their talks, but unfortunately their memoranda do not agree on all points. Jay saw the possibility of a deal with Spain which would lift the country, particularly New England, out of the depths of depression, a commercial treaty that would open up the peninsular ports of Spain to American commerce, of which the most substantial item was fish. This commerce promised the quick revival of the New England fisheries, a sick industry, and a stimulus for provision states like New York and Pennsylvania. To procure that trade agreement, Jay was ready to "forbear" the use of the Mississippi for twenty-five or thirty years, by which time, he thought, following Washington's reasoning, the United States would be invincible in that area. It should be noted that he did not propose to cede America's *claim* to the Mississippi, an assertion of right that he had stubbornly and even eloquently defended for almost seven years.

Backed by Washington and the Lees, Jay assumed that the South might be willing to accept a compromise. Knowing that the vote would be close, however, he proposed to Congress that henceforth he be guided in his negotiations with Spain by a committee to be named by Congress. To sound out the Southern reaction, in December 1785 Jay had a talk with James Monroe, a delegate from Virginia. Instead of letting Jay know how bitterly opposed he and other Southerners were to such a proposition, Monroe coolly reminded the New Yorker that Virginia had instructed

James Monroe of Virginia, who carried on a personal vendetta against John Jay over the proposed Mississippi deal with Spain (*Independence National Historical Park Collection*).

its delegates to the contrary on the Mississippi proposition. The more Monroe pondered what was an innocent exploration of views, the more he became convinced that there was a dark conspiracy of Northerners to enrich themselves at the expense of the South, and the more he fantasized the aims of the North as seeking to dismember the nation and to go it alone. His paranoiac charges threw Governor Patrick Henry and James Madison into a state of alarm, and prompted Monroe to journey privately to the Middle States to do some lobbying on his own against Jay's proposal.

Jay's recommendations to Congress on the score of consummating a treaty of commerce with Spain and forgoing for a time the navigation of the Mississippi precipitated the stormiest debates in the brief annals of the Confederation Congress. A committee appointed to study the question and make recommendations threw the entire issue into the lap of Congress sitting as a committee of the whole. Congress asked Jay to appear in person, which he did on August 3, 1786. Jay described the treaty as good for America, and contended that to forgo temporarily the navigation of the Mississippi was "not *at present* important." "We lost nothing," argued lawyer Jay, since "they who take a lease admit the right of the lessor," and after twenty-five or thirty years the West would be so heavily populated that Spain would recognize the impracticality of denying the right. Suppose, instead, we reject the treaty? Jay asked, and then proceeded to paint a gloomy picture of the alternative. "Unblessed with an efficient government, destitute of funds, and without public Credit either at home or abroad, we should be obliged to wait in patience for better days, or plunge into an unpopular and dangerous war with very little prospect of terminating it by a peace, either advantageous or glorious."

Jay's speech mobilized the Southern delegates to combine forces in a series of savage attacks against the treaty. Charles Pinckney denied that the commercial treaty offered real reciprocity, reminded the delegates that the sale and disposition of the lands in the Western territory had always been considered by Congress as providing a sufficient fund to discharge the domestic debts, and predicted that ties between East and West would be permanently severed. The Southerners also revealed a darker side of their motivations to reject the treaty. Having for years speculated heavily in Western lands, they now argued that restraints on land expansion in the Southwest would make the "vacant lands" of the East appreciate in value, and their workers would stay at home, thereby keeping wages down. The East would gain what the South lost.

William Grayson, a Virginia delegate, bluntly confessed that the proposed treaty "would destroy the hopes of the principal men in establishing the future fortunes of their families." Such an open avowal of interest was made by this delegate at a time when he was suffering from a nervous disorder and was, as Monroe found him, "often delirious" and "afflicted with strange fancies and apprehensions." Whether or not Grayson knew how much of the game he was giving away, his remarks could not go unanswered.

Rufus King, a Massachusetts man who had just married into the wealthy Alsop merchant family of New York, where he would shortly make his permanent residence, bore much of the brunt of the Northern battle for the treaty proposal. He parried the thrust by accusing Grayson and his supporters of "sacrificing the interest and happiness of a million people to promote the views of a few speculating landjobbers."

In truth, neither side was disinterested, and some Southern land speculators were hoping to make a killing by Western expansion. The real issue, however, was not one that Monroe acknowledged or Grayson understood. Louis Otto, the French chargé who was in cahoots with James Monroe during these months, disentangled "the secret motives" of the great sectional fight, and stated them concisely in a letter to the Comte de Vergennes. The resistance to the treaty was an expression of resentment by the South over what they felt was the preponderance of the Northern states. Southerners widely expected that the new territories would gradually be admitted to statehood, a movement that would greatly augment "the mass of the *southern states*," Otto shrewdly pointed out.

As for Monroe and Madison themselves, they had only just taken a flier in New York's Mohawk Valley lands and could hardly have been quick beneficiaries of expansion toward the Mississippi. To shift the power and weight of government from North to South was in essence what the Mississippi controversy was all about, and such calculations over power would continue to play a large role in the political battles that lay ahead.

King and other Northerners failed to move the South. When the treaty came to a vote, seven states favored it (all from the North); five opposed. Thus the treaty fell two states short of ratification under the provisions of the Articles of Confederation.

Although Monroe was the ringleader, Madison carried on what was becoming a personal vendetta against Jay. He moved that the negotiations be taken out of his hands and placed in Jefferson's, but Congress voted him down. He then slipped through a bill cutting Jay's salary by five hundred dollars, a rather mean-spirited gesture against one who was so soon to collaborate with him on a series of great state papers.

Meanwhile, one cannot imagine that Gardoqui was an idle bystander. A practitioner of prodigal entertainments, the Spaniard gave a series of lavish balls at his residence, the handsome Kennedy mansion on New York's lower Broadway. We can see him standing in the foyer leading to his magnificent ballroom, while a liveried footman announces the guests as they enter. With Congress sitting in New York, the guest list at one time or another could not have excluded Nathaniel Gorham, that body's President, or the Jays, it goes without saying, or General Henry Knox, the Secretary of War, and his wife—the entry of this florid Bacchanalian figure and the equally ponderous Mrs. Knox would always cause a stir. Gardoqui was too much the diplomat to ignore the state's governor, George Clinton, or the city's mayor, James Duane. The small foreign diplomatic circle was customarily included: the French chargé, M. Otto; the minister from the United Provinces, Pieter Johann Van Berckel; and the British consul-general, Sir John Temple, and Lady Temple. The Hamiltons were frequent guests, along with Baron von Steuben, who was temporarily residing with them, and it is highly unlikely that Gardoqui would not have high on his visiting list so influential a delegate as James Madison, a man to be wooed if the Spanish mission was to succeed.

On an occasion such as this, the guests would come dressed in the height of fashion, save for the plainly habited Mr. Madison. Men would favor velvet or satin in a variety of colors, ruffled shirts of silk, and stockings and vests. Precious buckles would adorn their shoes, and their hair would be powdered and curled. Most of them would be fitted with wigs, John Jay being the exception. They would leave their cocked hats on a table in the foyer, but carry their snuffboxes. The ladies would be counted on to rival each other in the complicated Paris-styled coiffures of the period, with fashionable silk gowns, hooped skirts, and enormous hats.

As the formal ball would begin with the band striking up a minuet, one would be tempted to forget that this was the nadir of depression days, that in one month a notable preConstitutional meeting would assemble at Annapolis, and that already rumblings of unrest were being heard among the farmers of western Massachusetts.

Were Madison and Jay to meet on such an occasion, we can be sure that the unsocial Madison would try to maneuver John Jay into an anteroom adjoining the ball. Madison would get to the point, and Jay would quietly defend the compromise he was proposing. Then Madison would again remind him that the passage of such a treaty would lead to dismemberment, and that Jay would have to come up with two more votes than the seven he had in hand to make the treaty's passage legal. Jay would then remind his tormentor that he was aware of the constitutional restraints and that as an advocate of a stronger union, buttressed by a stronger constitutional structure, he shared some of Madison's concerns. We might hear him telling Madison what he was soon to tell Congress: "A treaty disagreeable to one half of the nation had better not be made, for it would be violated. If I find that to be the case, I will not only withdraw the proposal but *come out against it*." Surely Madison must have realized that the Union was Jay's first concern, not the profits of a few Eastern businessmen.

Their private chat ended, we can see them joining the guests now grouped in a circle watching some gypsies dance to an eighteenth-century Spanish tune, as the assemblage clap and stamp in step with the intoxicating dance rhythm.

Gardoqui, despite his duties as host, must have observed the pair and given Jay a quick look on the latter's return to the ball. A shake of the head from Jay, and it should have been clear that the deal was dead.

What Jay could have told Madison, he *did* tell Congress. When the votes in Congress were tallied, John Jay found that his treaty could only command seven votes out of thirteen, not the two-thirds required by the Articles of Confederation. Jay did not press ahead. "The Spanish project sleeps," Madison reported to Jefferson in March of 1787, after one of his numerous private visits to Gardoqui. Jay not only announced that the treaty had better not be made, "for it would be violated," but in September 1788 he admitted that his proposal of forbearing to use the Mississippi now seemed more questionable than had appeared to be the case when he considered the issue originally. Therefore he urged Congress to reassert the nation's right to the river's navigation and its intention never to cede it. By these remarks, John Jay, a foremost continentalist and spokesman for enlarging the powers of the central government, should have put to rest the wild rumors, so lacking in foundation, that he had been spearheading a drive to break up the Union.

That Jay had acted from high motives was conceded by James Madison. In the course of debates over the ratification of the Constitution in Virginia, Madison replied to a question from Patrick Henry on the Mississippi in these words: "With respect to the secretary of foreign affairs, I am intimately connected with him. I shall say nothing of his abilities and attachment to this country. His character is established in both respects. He has given a train of reasoning which governs him in his project. If he was mistaken, his integrity and probity more than compensate for the error."

Jay did have an indirect hand in resolving this contentious issue, however. The treaty he negotiated with Great Britain in 1794 so alarmed the Spaniards, who considered America as now having allied herself with England, that they yielded to Thomas Pinckney, specially dispatched as an envoy extraordinary to Spain, virtually everything they had refused to give Jay eight years earlier.

Jay never forgot his experience at treaty-making and his observations of treaty-breaking by both the states and the British. Although he was not a delegate to the Constitutional Convention, the supremacy clause in that document drew upon the resolution he wrote for Congress in 1787. In the sixty-fourth *Federalist*, which appropriately was assigned to him because of his grasp of foreign affairs, he reminds the readers that treaties are part of the supreme law of the land. Interestingly enough, the Convention delegates had not forgotten the shock when the proposed Jay-Gardoqui treaty carried by seven states to six, and had insisted on incorporating in the Constitution a clause requiring a two-thirds vote of the Senate to ratify a treaty (in effect, the equivalent of the nine votes out of thirteen required by the Articles, save that the Senators now voted as individuals and not as state units). At Philadelphia, the ghost of the close vote over the Spanish treaty stalked the East Room of the historic State House.

Jay never forgot James Monroe, either, nor did Monroe ever forgive him. When Monroe, as America's minister to France, learned in 1794 that John Jay had concluded a treaty with Great Britain, he wrote Jay requesting a copy of the text. The demand seemed extraordinary to Jay, since the treaty had not as yet even been submitted to the President or the Senate, nor had it been ratified. Jay also knew that the Virginian Francophile, notorious for his indiscretions in France, would rush over to a French foreign ministry, apprehensive and suspicious of the Jay mission to England, and give them the substance of the agreement. Instead, Jay had the secretary of his mission, the artist John Trumbull, commit the entire treaty to memory and journey to Paris. There, Trumbull offered to recite the treaty word by word to Monroe with injunctions of the strictest confidentiality. Astonished and infuriated, Monroe sent Trumbull packing.

8

---•---

Move and Countermove: Annapolis and the Shaysites

A Rump Session at Annapolis

For the United States and its people, 1786 was truly the year of decision. Time was running out on steps to strengthen the Union. In March of 1785, commissioners from Virginia had joined commissioners from Maryland in a meeting, first at Alexandria and then, with George Washington acting as host, at Mount Vernon. Washington abstained from participating directly, but in fact the subject of the conference—settling the jurisdiction between the two states over the Potomac River for purposes of improved navigation—was of great personal interest to him and to the Potomac Company, of which he was president.

Washington's company was about to embark upon an ambitious engineering and navigation program with the objective of bringing the Potomac to the Shenandoah and Ohio valleys by a series of locks, making possible a successful penetration of the interior by a waterway system. Thereby East and West would be joined, to the advantage of the Potomac and Chesapeake regions. The Potomac Company was preparing to construct a set of locks to bypass a formidable obstacle to Washington's long-range program—the Great Falls of the Potomac, that surging, roaring cataract thirty-five feet in height, forming a series of rapids about fifteen miles from the present city of Washington, where the river descends some ninety feet. At a time when steamboating on the Potomac was being seriously considered, but its execution held up by the fiercely contested rival claims of "inventors" James Rumsey and John Fitch, the navigation of the interior waterways was now gaining national attention.

By March 28, 1785, the commissioners had come to a meeting of the minds, and they drew up an interstate compact that went beyond tidewater navigation and considered a multitude of problems relating to navigation and commerce: entrance and clearance of vessels, duties on imports and exports to be the same for both states, equality in the valuation accorded the current money of the two states, as well as foreign gold and silver coin. Realizing that their plans for expanding the navigation of the Potomac involved a route through Pennsylvania, the commissioners on their own addressed the President of the Executive Council of Pennsylvania, urging the legislature of that state to provide rights-of-way for vessels from Maryland and Virginia, while asserting that the same rights of navigation be accorded the citizens of the whole United States, thereby stressing the notion that transportation on navigable or inland waters was a national concern.

In sum, the commissioners had raised questions of great national import, timed to express a general consensus of the needs of a nation still in deep economic depression. Both states ratified the compact. In the Virginia legislature, James Madison, who inadvertently was never notified of the time and place of the Mount Vernon Conference, although he had been designated one of Virginia's commissioners, acted as floor manager, successfully carrying the fight in his own state's legislature to adopt the Mount Vernon Conference resolution.

Scholars differ, however, as to whether Madison kept the initiative and inspired the next move, one of national consequence, the calling of the Annapolis Convention. Certainly Madison was coy about his original identification with the idea. In a letter to Jefferson he attributed the proposal not to himself, but to John

Tyler. A Revolutionary patriot and later governor, Tyler's fame rests in no small measure on his having sired a president of the United States, the first to achieve the office by succession rather than election. Whether Tyler took the initiative, as Madison wanted people to believe, or Madison put him up to it—a political strategy not atypical of Madison—there is no question that some political figure who was by no means committed to the nationalist cause would arouse less suspicion than would Madison. As John Jay had regretfully discovered, in those times everybody seemed suspicious of everyone else's motives.

We do know that Madison had discussed such a convention with George Washington late in 1785. We also know that when Tyler put the proposition to the Virginia legislature, Madison privately expressed skepticism as to its outcome. "Better than nothing" was the way he described the ideas for the Annapolis Convention. Tyler's proposal was passed by the Virginia legislature, which moved ahead to appoint commissioners to join delegates from other states. They were invited to convene at Annapolis, Maryland, in September 1786 "for the purpose of forming such regulations of trade as may be judged necessary to promote the general interest." Annapolis was chosen, as it was not the beehive of commercial activity that towns like Boston, New York, Philadelphia, or Charleston were, and because of its central geographical location between North and South.

Madison's skepticism seemed justified. The first shock came from Maryland, the host state, where the authorities, considering such a meeting as transgressing the powers of Congress, refused to appoint commissioners of their own to attend its sessions. Recognizing this augury of potential failure, Madison, on a trip that took him to New York and Philadelphia, gave the outward appearance of one ready only to tinker and mend the creaky structure of national government under the Articles. To intimate friends, however, he indicated that he had bolder objectives, toward which he had been moving for many years.

Hamilton, one of the delegates from New York, was equally known for his nationalist views. Not long after the Virginia summons to the other states, he had drafted a petition to the legislature of his own state urging that body to comply with the requisitions of Congress for an impost, which New York had just turned down.

"Government without revenue cannot subsist," Hamilton exhorted. "That Government implies trust," he continued, "and every government must be trusted so far as is necessary to enable it to attain the ends for which it is instituted; without which insult and oppression from abroad, confusion and convulsion at home." This Cassandra-like declaration proved right on target. Already rumblings were coming out of Massachusetts which held promise of an insurrection.

That "convulsion" broke out almost a month before the commissioners assembled at Annapolis, and continued until the end of the year. Indeed, it was in the midst of this insurrection by debt-ridden farmers far off in western Massachusetts that commissioners from only five of the thirteen states managed to reach Annapolis in time to take the decisive step. What was especially curious was that the delegates from New England, most likely to benefit by uniform commercial regulations laid down by the federal government, failed to arrive in time, and that the host state, along with Georgia, South Carolina, and Connecticut, did not participate, nor did North Carolina. Hence, only the Middle States and Virginia were represented; John Dickinson, now a resident of Delaware, was elected chairman, but the slim attendance convinced the twelve delegates that it would be useless to proceed to a study of interstate commercial problems.

The failure to obtain a forum for full and careful deliberations must indeed have been a blow to James Madison, for no statesman of his day ever prepared for a meeting more carefully than did he. He had devoted the spring of 1786 to setting down for the

Annapolis meeting a set of "Notes on Ancient and Modern Confederacies," a draft representing years of reading and reflection. Confederacies, he concluded, were fragile creations continually tending toward dissolution or impotency, and unless we took proper steps, ours would suffer the same fate. There was no time for these arguments at the abbreviated sessions, nor was it the place to consider Madison's cure for the survival of federal republicanism—giving a veto to the federal government on local and state legislation. His proposal was not considered at Annapolis, and to his great disappointment, it was turned down at the Federal Convention.

Madison had all along been pessimistic about the prospects of the Annapolis Convention's achieving any meaningful increase in the powers of the federal government except for adopting some commercial reforms. Hamilton, with his audacity and decisiveness, would press forward with characteristic activism.

During this brief but historically significant stay at Annapolis, one can focus on the behind-the-scenes activities of the two main nationalists who attended the convention. Madison reached Annapolis around September 6, and immediately took lodgings at George Mann's Inn, a leading hostelry in the capital and the scene of the famous farewell banquet given to General Washington the day before he resigned his commission on December 22, 1783. Madison was impatient to learn from the proprietor which delegates had already arrived, and especially whether Alexander Hamilton had yet made an appearance. Mann was not too comforting. Only a few delegates had signed the register, and Hamilton's name was not among them.

Three days later Hamilton showed up. In warmly greeting Madison, he professed that the exercise and fresh air of the horseback journey he had taken from New York via Philadelphia had restored his health and spirits, both of which had been somewhat dampened of late. Hamilton's journey from New York took a whole week, and he was heard to complain about the lack of bridges in New Jersey and the intolerable delays at the ferries, and to praise the sensible efforts in Massachusetts to complete a bridge across the Charles River. More such internal improvements were needed, he felt, to forge a closer union, whose present ties were weakened by poor communication among the thirteen states.

Hamilton learned that delegates from only five states had shown up thus far, and that this rump group had even proposed calling off the meeting, or trying for another site. To either option Hamilton was emphatically opposed. To him, the troubling news from Massachusetts demanded prompt action, even if the rest of the delegates did not make an appearance.

Madison took the same line and informed Hamilton of a conversation he had had the previous evening with Abraham Clark, a delegate from New Jersey. Clark had brought good news. He had informed Madison that his delegation was authorized not only to consider commercial arrangements but "other important matters"—matters that might be necessary to the "common interest and permanent harmony of the several states."

In addition, Hamilton had a chance to read a communication from Tench Coxe, one of the Pennsylvania delegates, an ex-Loyalist but now a fervent nationalist. Coxe, who would become a close adviser to Hamilton when the latter headed the Treasury Department, relayed the advice that his state had recommended a broad reconsideration of the commercial laws of the individual states because of the discrepancy of the duties they were levying on foreign goods, as well as the discriminatory duties one state was imposing on imports from another. Pennsylvania urged that all vessels belonging to citizens of the United States pay the *same* tonnage duties, and took the occasion to argue for a "blending of interests" of the various states, which "must cement the Union of the States." This fair-minded advice, long advocated by both Madison and Hamilton, animated their spirits.

As further evidence of a nationalist tide, Hamilton was told that Virginia's attorney general, John Randolph, was drafting a resolution to embody the larger objectives that the New Jersey delegates encouraged. When Hamilton had a chance to look through the Randolph draft, he was enthusiastic. Madison, however, less impressed by Randolph's literary talents than Hamilton's, proposed that the latter prepare a draft resolution to be passed around to the other delegates for their reactions. Knowing Hamilton's capacity for both audacity and indiscretion, he cautioned the New Yorker to keep the tone moderate. They had not only the task of persuading the uncommitted, but of securing Randolph's approval, and the attorney general was well known for shilly-shallying whenever the topic of giving greater powers to the central government arose. One should not be deceived by his present posture, Hamilton was warned.

Hamilton took only a few hours to prepare a draft for the attorney general's scrutiny. Randolph looked it over and felt that the tone was perhaps too bold. If Hamilton wondered why so much attention should be paid to Randolph's feelings, he quickly learned that Randolph was being widely talked about as Virginia's next governor, upon Patrick Henry's retirement from that office in a few months. Holding such a position, he might well turn Virginia against a nationalist posture.

A few hours later Hamilton was ready with his revisions, and the Convention, which by that time comprised a mere twelve delegates representing just five states (a minority of the thirteen), unanimously adopted Hamilton's draft. As recorded by New York's Egbert Benson, the convention secretary, the resolution urged:

That there are important defects in the system of the Federal Government is acknowledged by the acts of all those States, which have concurred in the present meeting; that the defects, upon a closer examination, may be found greater and more numerous than even these acts imply is at least so far probable, from the embarrassments which characterise the present State of our national affairs—foreign and domestic, as may reasonably be supposed to merit a deliberate and candid discussion. . . . In the choice of the mode your Commissioners are of opinion, that a Convention of Deputies from the different States . . . for supplying such defects as may be discovered to exist, will be entitled to a preference from consideration, which will occur, without being particularised. . . .

Your Commissioners, with the utmost respectful deference, beg leave to suggest their unanimous conviction, that it may essentially tend to advance the interests of the Union, if the States meet at Philadelphia on the second Monday in May next, to take into consideration the situation of the United States, to devise such further provisions as shall appear to them necessary to render the constitution of the Federal Government adequate to the exigencies of the Union and to report such an Act for that purpose to the United States in Congress Assembled, as when agreed to, by them, and afterwards confirmed by the Legislatures of every State will effectually provide for the same.

Though your Commissioners could not with propriety address these observations and sentiments to any but the States they have the honor to Represent, they have nevertheless concluded from motives of respect, to transmit Copies of this report to the United States in Congress assembled, and to the executives of the other States.

By order of the Commissioners

Dated at Annapolis
September 14th, 1786.

The copy of the resolution among the Hamilton Papers includes the signatures of all twelve delegates from the five states attending the convention, while the copy submitted to Congress is merely signed by the Convention chairman, John Dickinson of Delaware, but curiously, "Js. Madison Jr." is listed below the signature as one concurring in the report. Madison, in an unusually cheerful frame of mind, was last seen at Annapolis settling his bill at Mann's Inn for £17/7/2 for a ten-night stay. He then headed toward Philadelphia, along with Hamilton, where the pair parted.

In both their minds lay a single question: Would they meet there again next May? That still was highly speculative, for Congress showed no great warmth toward the proposal. It referred the invitation to a committee on October 11, but not until February 21, 1787, was a cautious endorsement of the proposal adopted. On that day Congress described as "expedient" a convention *"for the sole and express purpose of revising the Articles of Confederation* and reporting in Congress and the several legislatures such alterations and provisions therein."

An impatient five states—Virginia, New Jersey, Pennsylvania, and South Carolina—had already named delegates to the Philadelphia Convention without waiting for Congress's call. Significantly, eight of the twelve states to be represented at the Philadelphia Convention instructed their delegates to operate under the Annapolis formula, while the remaining four confined them merely to revising the Articles as authorized by Congress. The thirteenth state, Rhode Island, mired down in paper-money experiments, refused to name a delegation. With these conflicting instructions facing them, the big question was how far the delegates would go. Would they scrap the Articles and start all over? The nationalists had their plan and were ready to scuttle the Articles. Would the rest of the delegates go along, and then would the people accept the results? These crucial questions would all be answered in time, and Messrs. Madison, Hamilton, and Jay helped resolve them.

Shays' Rebellion

What had shocked James Madison most on his return to Virginia from Princeton more than a decade earlier was the contrast between the scenes of poverty he observed existing side by side with the luxurious life-style of the planter class. That failure of the affluent to bestir themselves about the desperate conditions of common folk was a failure by no means confined to Virginia. In New York, John Jay denounced "the universal rage and pursuit of private gain," which, as he saw it, with other causes, accounted for the inability to improve "our condition." That sense of burdens unequally borne by common folk, farmers, artisans, and the laboring man lay behind the insurrection in Massachusetts—a crisis commonly known as Shays' Rebellion—which commenced while the sessions at Annapolis were being held, and continued down to the very eve of the Constitutional Convention. Perhaps more than any single condition or event, it produced a sense of crisis that had a profound effect on the forthcoming deliberations in Philadelphia.

Unlike Virginia, in Massachusetts the disparity in economic resources lay along geographical lines. The subsistence farmer in the interior, in debt to his eyeballs, stood arrayed against the affluent commercial creditors dwelling mostly in the coastal towns. In essence, the postwar depression, an inequitable system of taxation, and a biased and oppressively expensive court system combined to create a climate of opinion that favored resorting to force to procure economic justice after all other means had failed.

To comprehend the immensity of the debtor problem in Massachusetts and the fate that befell delinquents, we might first look at the statistics and then observe how delinquent debtors fared. In the two-year period beginning with August 1784, the Court of Common Pleas in Hampshire County prosecuted 2,977 cases of debt, a 262 percent increase over the years 1770–72. Some 31.4 percent of the county's male citizenry over sixteen were stuck with debts they could not repay, almost three times as many as in the earlier period. Even somewhat darker statistics can be unearthed in the Worcester County court records. In sum, from Berkshire County in the western part of the state to Essex along the coast, the courts were deluged with suits against debtors, nor was that condition confined to Massachusetts; the contagion of debt had spread its symptoms throughout New England from Connecticut to New Hampshire and Vermont.

The creditors who brought suit were almost all shopowners who, in turn, had borrowed heavily from wholesale importers along the coast, and were being pressed for payment. The shopowners found that they had been too optimistic in the amount of credit they had advanced to the small farmers, on the assumption that the postwar demand for goods would last forever instead of a relatively brief span. The depression caught creditors unawares and found debtors facing jail or servitude.

A debtor was something more than an item of statistics. The plight of impoverished farmers at the hands of the county justices can be uncovered from court judgments, newspaper accounts, and reminiscences. Lacking hard money for the payment of state taxes and personal debts, they saw their farms and homesteads, their cattle and personal belongings, sold at auction for a fraction of their value. If foreclosure sales infuriated a suffering populace, their indignation was fanned by the prospect of confinement in debtors' jail or even of being sold into servitude to pay unsatisfied judgments.

Under the prevailing law, a person lacking sufficient property to settle his debts faced an indefinite jail sentence. In the tavern jail at Great Barrington, Massachusetts, they would be confined in small, cramped cells whose floors and walls were mildewed and spotted with mold. Isaiah Thomas, the famous newspaper editor, reported that some debtors confined to the Worcester jail suffered impairment of health, some even dying "by means of being confined in a place which disgraces humanity." A Massachusetts House committee found in one jail some twenty-six prisoners languishing without proper food or ventilation. Samuel Ely, soon to be a Shaysite leader, reported that in an earlier Bristol County incarceration he managed to stay "alive, and that is all, as I am full of boils and putrefied sores all over my body and they make me stink alive, besides having some of my feet froze which makes it difficult to walk."

The western debtors first tried all the democratic processes that had been tested in the years of the Revolution. They petitioned the legislature against what they considered high and inequitable taxes; they demanded paper money and stay laws; they held local and county conventions; but their demands were ignored. In fact, in the year 1786 the legislature sharply raised taxes to pay off the state debt. The protesters then stopped the courts from holding sessions, as they had done in pre-Revolutionary days. Their next move was military action, counting on a leadership heavily recruited from former officers and veterans. Their leaders, including Daniel Shays, Samuel Ely, and Luke Day, were average men—little men, neither wedded to a revolutionary ideology nor willing to earn the kind of immortality that the Christian martyrs gained in the Roman arenas. When the heat was on, their resolve melted. But for the better part of a year they enjoyed the support of a substantial segment of the whole commonwealth, and kept the state government in disarray.

True, the leaders did possess a streak of demagoguery, as their critics charged, but behind the leaders were a host of others, so considerable that conservative Eastern businessmen raised funds to support a military force to put them down. An alarmed Congress increased its own mini-army, ostensibly to crush nonexistent frontier threats from the Indians, but carefully picked its forces from New England, where they could be deployed if necessary. Called Regulators, the dissidents largely hailed from western Massachusetts. More popularly, they were known as Shaysites, followers of a thirty-nine-year-old farmer and Revolutionary War veteran, Daniel Shays. Crowded inside Conkey's Tavern in Pelham, for example, they would quickly fall under the spell of their leader.

Shays held his auditors captive. He would confess that while he still owned his farm, he did not think he could hold on to it. He would fire the crowd with attacks on the courts and lawyers, charging them with being in cahoots with fat Eastern creditors. He would attack the rapacity of the attorneys, pointing out that at the ridiculously high fees they charged, only rich men could hire them. Then, the nub of his talks. The courts, he would remind his listeners, were under their thumb. Without mercy, he charged, they were grinding out foreclosures, taking away the farms of little men, sending them to jail, or selling them off as servants. No relief could be expected from the government officials in Boston. He charged that they kept raising the taxes on farmlands, and that many of those he was addressing did not own enough property to vote the legislature out of office. In any event, since the legislators adjourned at the beginning of the summer, it was clear they had no intention of listening to him and his followers.

When someone in the crowd would ask, "What shall we do?" Shays was ready with his answer. "Close down the courts! Then they can't take our property away or throw us into jail." Even before he spoke, his advice had been anticipated. A Shays ally, Job Shattuck, broke up the session of the court of common pleas at Cambridge. Crowds had shut down the courthouse at Concord. Similar actions were taken at Northampton, Worcester, Taunton, and Great Barrington. The law had ground to a close, shut down by a disgruntled citizenry.

Now Shays and his followers, bloated with success, threw caution to the winds, grabbed up their rifles, and moved toward Springfield, where they could not

Daniel Shays and Job Shattuck, leaders of Shays' Rebellion, contemporary woodcut, c.1787 (*courtesy of the National Portrait Gallery, Smithsonian Institution*).

only stop the court but get themselves some more guns from the arsenal there. When Shays was reminded that the arsenal belonged to the federal government, he retorted: "To hell with Congress! That crowd is too weak to act."

With the armed overthrow of the state government as their apparent goal, the Shaysites had set off a quick counterreaction on the part of the government leaders and the propertied class. Seeing that the federal government was cautious and irresolute, men of property raised and recruited their own military force, a special army of 4,400 troops commanded by Benjamin Lincoln, a former Revolutionary War general. Anticipating a serious confrontation as the crisis approached its greatest intensity, General Rufus Putnam arranged to meet privately with Shays to warn him against the course he was pursuing. He reported his talk to Governor Bowdoin, and from the conversation Shays hardly emerges as a heroic figure, but one cautious enough to disavow treasonable intent. Putnam informed Shays that an earlier amnesty would not be renewed. He could count on no general pardon.

"Then we must fight it out," Shays replied.

"That is as you please, but it's impossible you should succeed, and the event will be that you must either ruin your country or hang, unless you are fortunate enough to bleed."

"By God! I'll never ruin my country!" Shays retorted.

Putnam reminded him that in a previous conversation Shays had admitted that "it was wrong in the people ever to take up arms as they had." Shays weakly argued that he took command "to prevent the shedding of blood."

"Well, then, why didn't you stop there?" Putnam challenged.

"I did not pursue the matter; it was noised about that the warrants were out after me, and I was determined not to be taken."

"That won't do," Putnam pressed. "How come you to write letters to several towns in the county of Hampshire to choose officers and furnish themselves with arms and sixty rounds of ammunition?"

Shays flatly denied doing so. "It was a cursed falsehood!" He continued to deny that he had ever assumed command of any but county forces. When pressed to answer what course he would pursue if he were denied a pardon, Shays replied, "Why, then, I will collect all the force I can and fight it out; and, I swear, so would you or anybody else, rather than be hanged."

Putnam then asked Shays whether he would be willing "to set off this night to Boston and throw" himself "upon the mercy and under the protection of Government."

Shays's reply was, "No, that is too great a risk, unless I was first assured of a pardon."

Putnam answered that there was no risk. "If your submission is refused, I will venture to be hanged in your room."

"I don't want *you* to be hanged, in the first place," Shays answered, "and, in the next place, they would not accept of you."

Putnam reported the conversation to Governor James Bowdoin, adding the observation that he thought Shays could be "bought off." If that was contemplated, it was now too late.

The Putnam interview occurred with the crisis approaching its greatest intensity. Already, on December 26, Shays had marched into Springfield and forced the courts to cease business. When General Benjamin Lincoln, who was now acting as head of the expedition against the insurgents, learned that Shays was situated six miles south of Springfield and that Luke Day and his followers were holding West Springfield, he set off in relief of General William Shepherd, who was defending the Springfield arsenal, property of the United States government. Had Luke Day executed his part of the plan agreed upon by the two rebel leaders and joined forces with Shays, the results might have been quite different. But Day sent a message to Shays informing him that he could not join him for the planned attack on January 25, 1787, but needed an extra day. This message was intercepted by Shepherd's men. Unknowing, Shays went ahead with his attack on the scheduled date, assuming that Day would join him. Marching his men up to the arsenal, he brought them within a hundred yards of Shepherd's forces.

Shepherd warned, "Come any nearer at your peril!" and followed with cautionary salvos of artillery. When Shays's men edged closer, Shepherd fired two more warning salvos. Shays's men ignored them. A third, through the center of the column, caused the attackers to hesitate. A fourth and fifth caused a complete rout. Had Shepherd been disposed to charge upon their rear and flanks, he could have cut them to pieces, but he forbore further action in his desire to avoid unnecessary bloodshed.

The rest was anticlimax. Lincoln's forces cut off Day's retreat, and those who could do so took to the woods. Shays now retreated to Pelham, and during surrender negotiations that Shays rejected, his main body marched to Petersham. In a memorable night march through a deep winter snowstorm in subzero temperature, Lincoln advanced his forces some thirty miles in thirteen hours. Their front reached Petersham at nine in the morning, and the complacent insurgents were thrown into complete confusion by the seemingly impossible feat. The body of the insurgents was captured; their leaders fled to adjacent states.

The insurrection was over, but it had a profound effect both on the voters and their state government.

The voters registered their disapproval of their state government in no uncertain terms. In the election held in the spring of '87, John Hancock, running on the popular party program of amnesty for the rebels, defeated the inflexible opponent of the Shaysites, Governor James Bowdoin, by a vote of three to one. Only a quarter of the members of the new House of Representatives had sat in the former one. Thus, defeated on the field of battle, the insurgents had the satisfaction of seeing many of their recommendations carried out by the new legislature. Laws were enacted exempting clothing, household goods, or tools of trade from debt process, allowing personal property or real estate to be used in payment of debts, and providing that imprisoned debtors might obtain their freedom by taking the pauper's oath, avowing that they were destitute of means. A new fee bill was passed, reducing court charges. No direct tax whatsoever was enacted for 1787, and in the years following, the tax burden was much lighter than it had been at the time of the crisis. John Hancock voluntarily cut his own salary by three hundred pounds, an action prompting the uncharitably inclined James Madison to observe that Hancock's merits were "not a little tainted by a dishonorable obsequiousness to popular follies."

On perhaps a lesser scale, backcountry resistance to debt and tax collection was a contagion that spread from New England to pockets of law defiance evident from New Jersey to South Carolina. In June of 1786 "a tumultuous assemblage of the people" closed down Maryland's Charles County courthouse, and boycotts against the sale of debtor property were spreading rapidly in other parts of Maryland. In South Carolina, farmers attacked the Camden courthouse and sent the judges scurrying home. In Virginia, some farmers boycotted auction sales of property, and flooded the legislature with petitions for paper money and legal tender laws. In May of 1787 a mob burned down the King William County courthouse, destroying all the records, and court proceedings were blocked in other county courts as well. A shocked Madison wrote Jefferson on the very eve of the Constitutional Convention that Virginia's officials watched "the prisons and courthouses and clerks' offices willfully burnt." Again: "The nearer the crisis approaches the more I tremble for the issues."

Shays' Rebellion sounded alarm bells throughout the country. Secretary of War Henry Knox, in a letter to Washington, attributed to the Shaysites the doctrine that since "the property of the United States has been protected from the confiscation of Britain by the joint exertions of all, it therefore ought to be the common property of all; and he that attempts opposition to this creed is an enemy to equality and justice, and ought to be swept from the face of the earth." In short, Knox added, "they are determined to annihilate all debts public and private, and have agrarian laws, which are easily effected by the means of unfunded paper money, which shall be a tender in all cases whatsoever."

John Jay, who was disheartened by his experiences with Congress over the Spanish treaty, could not help being perturbed by further evidence of disunity. When the so-called Connecticut Wits pilloried the New England radicals in satirical verse entitled the *Anarchiad*, a pitiless exposé of mob rule, currency inflation, and other nostrums, John Jay significantly clipped from the New York *Daily Advertiser* a few verses:

> Shall lordly Hudson part contending powers,
> And broad Potomac lave two hostile shores?
> Must Alleghany's sacred summit bear
> The Impious bulwarks of perpetual war?

and he underscored the two concluding lines:

> On you she calls! attend the warning cry:
> *"Ye Live United, or Divided Die."*

While Jay insisted that "Justice must have a sword as well as a balance," he observed that a little virtue and common sense "would bring order out of chaos."

At the Philadelphia Convention, the ghost of Shaysism was not easily laid to rest. The nightmare of an irresolute Congress, lacking powers under the Articles of Confederation to intervene in Shays' Rebellion, haunted the halls of the Convention. The answer was found in the Guaranty Clause (Article IV, Section 4), a protection inspired by the combined threats of civil unrest, fears of splitting the Union, and loose talk of monarchy. Under this provision "the United States shall guarantee to every State in this Union a Republican Form of Government." The Article then proceeds to require the United States to protect each state against "Invasion" and "on Application of the Legislature, or of the Executive (when the Legislature cannot be convened) against domestic Violence." Another response came in the form of the framers' denial to the states of the power to emit bills of credit. John Langdon of New Hampshire, who would have endorsed the use of federal troops to put down insurrections even without state application, is reputed to have declared that "rather than the states should have the power of emitting paper money, he should consent to make General Washington despot of America."

Broken and discredited though their leaders may have been, the followers of Shays in western Massachusetts put up a vigorous stand against their state's ratification of the federal Constitution, which they visualized as setting up a strong central government benefiting the commercial interests of the seaboard and endangering personal liberties. Still, the Antifederalists were overpowered in a relatively close vote of 187 to 168, and Massachusetts did join the Union.

One might have expected Alexander Hamilton to exploit this series of episodes of defiance of law to hammer home a lesson to doubters about the need for a responsive republican government. Hardly an apostle of revolution in the postwar period, he expressed the view in *Federalist* Number 28 that "if the representatives of the People betray their constituents, there is then no resource left but in the exertion of that original right of self defense which is paramount to all positive forms of government," and that in single states where the subdivisions had no distinct government to oppose a usurper, "the citizens must rush tumultuously to arms, without concert, without system, without resource, except in their courage and despair." Thus, and perhaps unwittingly, Hamilton had the last word on Shays' Rebellion.

A NATION
UNITED

James Madison

In the choice between constitutional modification and root-and-branch change, between revision and creation, there could be no doubt where our three witnesses would be aligned. "An union of sovereign states, preserving their civil liberties, and connected together by such tyes as to preserve permanent and effective government is a system not described. It is a circumstance that has not occurred in the history of man." In such fashion did the North Carolina delegates to the Constitutional Convention choose to inform their governor, Richard Caswell, of what was in the process of being created in Philadelphia in June of 1787.

It was appropriate that Mount Vernon and Annapolis would set the stage for the last act of a drama in which the nation was to embark on a perilous experiment toward achieving unity without sacrificing liberty.

The principal questions raised at the Convention magnified the inventiveness of the answers. One question, coming out of Mount Vernon and Annapolis, addressed itself to the economy. In a society that was in the course of discarding an older economic order in favor of an emergent capitalist system, a market economy international in scope, and even banking institutions, could best be underwritten by creating a system of nationwide uniform regulation of monetary and commercial affairs.

The Confederation years had witnessed a contrary trend. States violated treaties, blocked the claims of foreign creditors, and were unable to prevent mob action from closing the courts, which would stop judges from continuing to enter judgments on behalf of domestic creditors. States had forced businessmen to accept depreciated paper money and had shown serious disregard for private property. Our three witnesses shared the view that order and good faith had to be restored and that a new constitution was urgently needed to support the emergent new economic order.

An even more complex question involved setting up on a permanent basis a federal republic that could govern a vast territorial expanse without transforming it into a colonial empire. To do so, it was first of all necessary for the Framers of the Constitution to transcend the limitations imposed by the Articles of Confederation. Article II of the Confederation's constitution had, regrettably, provided: "Each state retains its sovereignty, freedom and independence, and every Power, Jurisdiction and right, which is not by this confederation expressly delegated to the United States, in Congress assembled." The federal Constitution omitted the fatal word "expressly," nor does it appear in the Ninth and Tenth Amendments, which retained for the people, in the case of the former, rights not enumerated in the Constitution, and in the latter, reserved to the states or the people powers not delegated to the United States or prohibited to the states respectively.

Instead of a federal system, the Confederation's Article II had set up a league of states held together by a Congress, which, while supreme in war and foreign affairs, found its powers severely limited otherwise. It created a system of dual sovereignty, which brought competition and conflict rather than cooperation and reconciliation. It deprived the central government of energy to initiate change, and removed its cloak of respectability both at home and abroad.

As the authors of *The Federalist* viewed it, the new Constitution would, when ratified, successfully perform a juggling act. While preserving the internal sovereignty of the states and guaranteeing that they remain republican, it grasped for the central government broad powers, delegated, implied, and inherent. What emerged was a unique system of federalism, a latter-day model for emerging nations who found that it also suited their conditions. The Constitution set up a federal system in fact far more centralized than any confederation known to the contemporary world, one that would endow the central government with energy and capacity while permitting the states to retain a broad range of powers in their internal management, thereby recognizing their variant social, cultural, and economic problems.

To the theme of federalism, James Madison as "Publius" addressed a number of papers, notably his tenth, thirty-ninth, and fifty-first *Federalist* letters. Even to a man possessing extraordinary talents of originality and improvisation, the task of balancing the claims of the central government against those of the states proved a feat of great subtlety. Madison's thirty-ninth *Federalist* is not transparently clear about how much and in what areas the government is "national" and not "federal," respective roles that each generation has found it necessary to reassess. The Virginia statesman's solution to governance over a vast expanse of territory, his "extended republic," was revealed in the diversity of the American population. That divergence of often conflicting interests would prevent a minority from thwarting the public will, while at the same time the system of separation of powers and checks and balances built into the Constitution (notably the President's qualified veto) would serve to protect minority rights. If Madison was so confident that men could transcend private gain for public good, why was it necessary, one might ask, to hamstring government by the mechanisms of control incorporated in the Constitution? The answer seemed to suggest the existence of a darker side to human nature, and all three of the *Federalist* authors had witnessed that side in action during the years of the Confederation. At most, one can say that the Constitution is testimony to the cautious optimism that prevailed over a widely shared and deep-seated pessimism about human nature.

One major step was taken contemporaneously with the sessions of the Philadelphia Convention, which would nail down a program of national expansion and assure new territories that theirs would not be a long period of colonial subordination. Sitting in New York in July of 1787, Congress provided for the government of the territories recently acquired by the peace with Great Britain. Back in 1784, Thomas Jefferson had proposed a territorial program that would have allowed the entire West the fullest possible measure of self-government, with provisions for adult male suffrage and the eventual admission of the territories into the Union. Even though some of its more liberal provisions (notably the barring of slavery in all the territories both North and South) were watered down in the justly celebrated Northwest Ordinance of 1787, that statesmanlike measure constituted a repudiation of colonial imperialism. It involved compromises, to be sure, and the Framers of the Constitution in Philadelphia were doubtless aware of what was taking place ninety miles away. As a concession to Eastern conservatives, the Ordinance introduced a "first stage" of tutelary administration by officials appointed by the federal government. The Ordinance applied only to the territory north and west of the Ohio, wherein slavery was forbidden. By implication, its expansion might well be permitted in the territories lying to the west of the Old South, thereby allaying the deep concerns of that region.

The Ordinance also set in place the machinery for admission of territories to statehood on the basis of absolute equality. This innovative concept assured prospective settlers that regardless of where they chose to put down stakes on the continental domain, theirs was not to be a permanent colonial subordination; they could look forward to participating in the Union of the states "on an equal footing" with the original thirteen. Indubitably, this fair and even generous settlement contributed to a climate that proved hospitable to the opening of the West, with speculators, be it said, rivaling homesteaders in their eagerness for a quick killing.

If, under the new federal system, any vestige of ambiguity remained as to the subordinate role of the states, it vanished with the inclusion of Article VI, which reads:

> The Constitution, and the Laws of the United States which shall be made in Pursuance thereof; and all Treaties made, or which shall be made, under the Authority of the United States, shall be the supreme Law of the Land; and the judges in every State shall be bound thereby, any Thing in the Constitution or Laws of any State to the Contrary notwithstanding.

In the enforcement of the supremacy of treaties and laws of the United States, much reliance was placed by the Framers on the judicial branch, whose authority is concisely outlined in Article III of the Constitution, so concisely in fact that, as a supplement to the seventy-seven "Publius" letters published in the public press, Alexander Hamilton felt obliged to add several more letters in his two-volume edition of *The Federalist,* issued in the late spring of 1788. Although he took some pains to reassure his readers that the judicial branch would also be the "weakest of the three departments of power," he had no hesitancy in declaring that the federal courts had the right to declare invalid laws contrary to the Constitution. Significantly, he assumed that judicial review would encompass all legislation, whether by state legislatures or by the federal Congress. To disabuse his readers of the notion that he was arguing that the legislative branch was inferior to the judicial—whereas in fact under the Constitution all three branches are coequal—Hamilton argued that to deny to the judiciary the power to invalidate unconstitutional laws "would be to affirm that the deputy is greater than his principal; that the servant is above his master; that the representatives of the people are superior to the people themselves; that men acting by virtue of powers may do not only what their powers do not authorise, but what they forbid." Accordingly, he refused to concede that the legislative branch was the constitutional judge of its own powers, and that the construction it put upon them was conclusive upon the other departments.

That the Constitution was drafted with such expedition and that it won ratification by the people attests, first of all, to the recognition by our three witnesses at its creation—a recognition shared by their nationalist colleagues—that the objections raised by their opponents were weighty and had to be answered by reasoned arguments and even a promise of concessions. As Hamilton conceded in his opening *Federalist* letter, the measures adopted at Philadelphia saw "wise and good men on the wrong as well as the right side of questions of the first magnitude to society."

Its adoption was also a tribute to a broad consensus that a nation, not a league of states, was what was wanted, and that such a nation must be structured on a solid and secure foundation if the fruits of revolution and the aspirations of the American people for a better life for themselves, their children, and the generations ahead were to be fulfilled.

To achieve that "more perfect union" at which the Framers had set their sights, one had to build a more just society. No one phrased it more eloquently than James Madison in his fifty-first *Federalist:* "Justice is the end of government. It is the end of civil society. It ever has been, and ever will be pursued, until it be obtained or until liberty be lost in the pursuit."

9

Behind Closed Doors

In the steaming hot summer of 1787, fifty-five delegates met in convention in the State House of Philadelphia and devised a new national government for the thirteen states and all those that were to enter the Union thereafter. The delegates sat almost daily for four months and argued out their ideas in long, heated sessions in secret and behind closed doors. On September 17 they gave to the people the final document, five pages of parchment setting forth a plan of union calculated "to secure the Blessings of Liberty to ourselves and our Posterity." This document is our Federal Constitution. It provided for a sovereign government with broad, if clearly defined, powers and responsibilities.

The spare, eloquent language, much of it attributed to the talented Gouverneur Morris, outlined a republican government that steered a course between the equal dangers of tyranny and ineffectualness by providing by implication for a separation of powers among the three coequal branches of the government: Congress, the President, and an independent judiciary, all curbed by a system of checks and balances.

It created a unique system called federalism, in which the central government was delegated authority in international and national affairs, including the power to tax and to regulate commerce, to provide for the common defense and the general welfare, and to make all laws necessary and proper for carrying into execution the powers vested in the Constitution. As its Preamble declares, it is a government of the people, not of the states, and lines of demarcation between the national government and the states were laid down. It guaranteed to the states a republican form of government and declared the Constitution and the laws and treaties of the national government to be the supreme laws of the land. Finally, it wisely provided for a method of amendment.

That delegates from so many regions of the country and with such widely diverse interests could unite in creating an entirely new governmental system was, for George Washington, who presided over the Convention, "little short of a miracle." It was also testimony to the fact that, with a few exceptions, the delegates who attended were committed to a more national frame of government than the Articles of Confederation had provided, and were in general agreement about the powers to be conferred on a central government. On much else there was a sharp disagreement and heated debate, but the spirit of compromise that prevailed attested to the common wisdom and common sense of the participants.

It is more than chance that both the Great Declaration and the Constitution were adopted at the Pennsylvania State House in Philadelphia, a shrine now called Independence Hall. Both documents enlisted the wisdom and statecraft of many of the same men. These men recognized that merely winning independence did not suffice. They knew the newly emerging nation would have to be soundly structured.

In London, John Adams declared the Convention "the greatest single effort of national deliberation that the world has ever seen." Thomas Jefferson was later to refer to the Convention as "an assembly of demigods," for, with a few notable exceptions, virtually all of America's big names were found on the roster of delegates. Indubitably, the Convention's greatest asset was the presiding officer, George Washington, the unanimous choice to chair its sessions, and one who could count on advice from a prestigious delegation from his own state. Pennsylvania's delegation claimed

Benjamin Franklin, then eighty-one years old, as its senior member; he brought to the assemblage his wit, common sense, and unrivaled experience in the service of empire, colonies, state, and nation, as well as his international renown as diplomat, scientist, and humanitarian. Virginia's most erudite member was James Madison, an ardent nationalist with whom we are now familiar. And there were first-class legal minds like James Wilson of Pennsylvania, who never lost his Scottish burr, John Rutledge of South Carolina, and William Livingston, the learned and witty governor of New Jersey.

The only state to dispatch an Antifederalist delegation was New York, where an Antifederalist legislature, under prodding from Governor George Clinton, passed over John Jay, certainly one of the best qualified for the task at hand, but grudgingly included Alexander Hamilton, who, as the author of the Annapolis resolution, could not conceivably be left out, but curbed his independent authority by including two antinationalists in the delegation, John Lansing and Robert Yates, both upstate lawyers. Since the pair consistently outvoted Hamilton and then left the Convention in disgust, the state that Hamilton represented was, in effect, deprived of a vote. How well Hamilton could operate under these handicaps was, as we shall see, the special concern of his fellow nationalists and well-wishers of his hometown.

How wisely the delegates performed their task may be judged from the ability of their instrument of government to surmount the trials and crises of two hundred years. The prescience, innovative capability, drafting skills, and awareness of the need to compromise on the part of the Convention's delegates are attested to by the Constitution's durable qualities. Over a period of two centuries, dozens of constitutions adopted in other countries, whether in imitation of the American model or based on quite different plans, have gone into the scrap heap. The United States Constitution has outlived all its successors.

Fortunately for posterity, James Madison chose a seat up front. Not missing a single day, the diligent and meticulous Virginian took systematic notes, providing us with the principal record of the debates in the convention. The ordeal, he later said, "almost killed" him; but having undertaken the task, he was "determined to accomplish it." Some nine others also took notes, but none are as full, as impartial (despite

Madison's notes of debates at the Constitutional Convention: a page from his notes of July 14, 1787, including a portion of remarks by Elbridge Gerry and concluding with a portion of a speech by Luther Martin (*Madison Papers, Library of Congress*).

some corrections that Madison, some forty years later, saw fit to make), or as accurate as Madison's. It is through James Madison chiefly that we are let in on the secret debates by which the most delicate and crucial issues were resolved and a constitution drafted and adopted between May 25 and September 17, 1787.

Although he was not present at Philadelphia, Jay's views were known to the most influential delegates, and he even indulged in a bit of lobbying while the Constitutional Convention was in session. Jay's nationalist outlook had been heightened by a deeply felt sense of crisis. As President of Congress in 1779, he had taken the position that the Articles of Confederation, which most states had ratified, were already a functioning body, since in their final form the Articles contained no provision regarding the number of states needed for their ratification. He had stressed the supremacy of the judicial rulings of Congress over those of state courts. He had cordially endorsed the notion of judicial review expounded in Hamilton's "Phocion Letters." He had drafted the 1787 resolution of Congress on the supremacy of treaties. He had consistently supported augmenting the powers of Congress in the areas of taxation and the regulation of commerce, and he had been one of the earliest advocates of the separation of powers and checks and balances.

"I have long thought," Jay wrote Jefferson in 1786, "and become daily more convinced that the construction of our Federal government is fundamentally wrong. To vest legislative, judicial, and executive powers in one and the same body of men and that, too, in a body daily changing its members, can never be wise. In my opinion, these three great departments of sovereignty should be forever separated, and so distributed as to serve as checks on each other." Again, and only shortly before the Convention, he wrote at Washington's solicitation: "Let Congress legislate. Let others execute. Let others judge."

Jay's republicanism did not preclude his advocacy of

a strong executive possessed of the powers with which the Constitution would endow such an office, including a veto over bills enacted by a dual-chambered legislature. "While other experiments remain untried," he was not prepared to settle for a king. Thus he dismissed as vapid murmurings the crop of rumors that gripped the country on the eve of the Convention. Von Steuben had been spreading gossip that Prince Henry of Prussia had been sounded out about establishing a limited monarchy in America. The approach to the Prussian was reputedly made by Nathaniel Gorham, lately President of Congress and now designated as a delegate from New Hampshire to the Constitutional Convention. There was also talk about bringing over Frederick, Duke of York, George's second son, and making him king. A Frederick for a George! To a stout republican like Jay, both ideas were abhorrent, but perhaps they were less so to his friend and associate Alexander Hamilton, who came to Philadelphia prepared to argue for a life presidency. Finally Jay, who wanted a new Constitution based directly on popular sovereignty, would have preferred to have the delegates to the Convention elected by the people and not by the state legislatures. The state attachments of others proved too strong, however, and the process that Jay advocated was reserved for the Constitution's ratification, not for the selection of its Framers.

On two occasions Jay felt moved to let his views be known to the Convention, although, like most others, he was still in the dark about the direction toward which that body was moving. On July 25 he wrote to Washington, proposing, in the form of a question, "whether it would not be wise and reasonable to provide a strong check to the admission of foreigners into the administration of our national government, and to declare expressly that the commander-in-chief of the American army shall not be given to or devolve on any but a natural-born citizen." Fortunately for the nation, Jay's first suggestion ran counter to prevailing sentiment and was rejected, but not before the notion touched off a heated debate on the convention floor. Jay's "anti-foreigners" proposal appears to have been reflected in the motion that Elbridge Gerry made on the floor of the Convention in August that representatives in the lower house in future be confined to native-born Americans. As might have been expected, Alexander Hamilton was quick to rebuke the sponsor. Not only did Hamilton oppose "embarrassing the government with minute instructions," but he insisted, while conceding some possible dangers, that "the advantages of encouraging foreigners were obvious and admitted." "Persons in Europe of moderate fortunes," he reminded his listeners, "will be fond of coming here when they will be on a level with the first citizens." His motion that eligibility to the lower house be based merely on "citizenship and inhabitancy" was enthusiastically seconded by Madison but, oddly enough, was then defeated by seven states to four. Finally, prior citizenship of seven years was adopted as a qualification for the House of Representatives.

Jay's views about the qualifications for the commander-in-chief were shared far more widely by convention delegates. The provision that the Framers incorporated in the Constitution dealing with the executive branch confers upon the President the powers of commander-in-chief and bars any person from holding that office "except a natural-born Citizen, or a Citizen of the United States, at the time of the Adoption of the Constitution." The delegates decided on this point on September 7, a good number of weeks after Jay's letter had reached their presiding officer. The saving clause, of course, opened the door to such foreign-born and highly qualified Americans as West Indies–born Alexander Hamilton; the Scot, James Wilson, soon to be an Associate Justice of the Supreme Court; and Swiss-born Albert Gallatin, later to become Secretary of the Treasury.

Jay was sorely tempted to lobby the Convention when rumors reached New York that the delegates

were, through one device or another, prepared to give
a constitutional sanction to slavery. The final draft of
the Constitution, with its three-fifths clause, its clause
for the recovery of fugitive slaves, and its delayed
barring of the slave trade showed that Jay's suspicions
would be well founded. Sitting in New York, one
could not be sure, however, for on July 23, Congress,
in its Northwest Ordinance, had barred involuntary
servitude from the territory north of the Ohio. We
now know that the details of the drafting of the Northwest Ordinance were readily available to the Philadelphia delegates. Some key figures among them had
already conferred with the Reverend Manasseh Cutler, a lobbyist for an Ohio land company, who claimed
to be extremely knowledgeable about the drafting of
the Ordinance.

The South seemed reconciled to the Northwest Ordinance since it implied an open door to slavery in its
own adjacent territories, where that institution had in
fact already taken root. By this date the issues between the large and small states had been largely
resolved and supplanted by divergences, as Madison
saw it, between North and South over the institution
of slavery. Already, antislavery forces had been making themselves felt in the North, notably in Pennsylvania and New York, and no public figure in this section
of the country was more aroused over the issue than
was John Jay, who had accepted the presidency of the
New York Society for the Manumission of Slaves.

On August 16, 1787, Jay presided over a meeting of
the society which was held in the home of a Quaker
businessman in New York City. The society's first
order of business was to consider a proposal of
Melancton Smith, soon to be known as a leading
Antifederalist, that the society instruct its president to
draft a petition to the Constitutional Convention con-
demning slavery and urging that the traffic in slaves be
prohibited.

Jay, as we have already seen, could write at top
speed when properly motivated. In this case he was

back at the society the very next day with a petition along the lines that had been proposed. This time, unlike the previous evening, Alexander Hamilton, a society member, was present. He had visited Philadelphia for a few days in mid-July, had met with Cutler, and, from talks with delegates, had recognized the peril of pressing the slavery issue. Enlightened Southerners, particularly from the Upper South, might well have shared the views of the New York Society, but even the opponents of slavery from that region hoped that the institution would wither away with time. So prestigious an Enlightenment figure as Benjamin Franklin, who doubled as Convention delegate and president of the Pennsylvania Antislavery Society, had personally declined to present a similar petition from his own group, fearful that it might strike a fatal blow to the unity so essential to framing an acceptable Constitution. If Franklin did not consider the time opportune, he would not wait too long. His last public act before his death in 1790 was to affix his signature to a memorial to Congress for the abolition of slavery.

_ Reluctantly, Jay's group withheld their petition, while Jay himself continued to identify himself with the antislavery cause. He had long favored gradual emancipation, consistently opposed both political and civil discrimination, and, later, as governor of his state, had the satisfaction of signing legislation providing for the gradual termination of the institution of slavery in New York.

As for Alexander Hamilton, his constitutional views, as we have already noted, had matured by the early 1780s. An activist, thoroughly disillusioned by the ineffectual role of Congress under the Confederation, he pounded away on the theme of more power to the central government. Sometime after March 26, 1783, when he had unsuccessfully proposed that Congress be empowered to nominate its own officers to collect the revenue (a proposal made in conjunction with Madison's initial effort), Hamilton prepared a set of resolutions, but abstained from presenting them to Congress.

The time, he felt, was not opportune. In his draft he recommended that the several states send delegates to meet in convention "with full powers to revise the Confederation, and to adopt and propose such alterations as to them shall seem necessary." The memorandum was endorsed in Hamilton's hand: "Intended to be submitted to Congress in 1783—but abandoned for want of support!"

The essence of Hamilton's constitutional thinking was embodied in this draft. Therein he urged enlarging the powers of the central government and separating the legislative, executive, and judicial branches as in "the most approved and well founded maxims of free government." He would have conferred upon Congress "a general superintendence of trade." He disapproved of the ambiguity he found over how much and what power Congress had over Indian affairs in the Articles of Confederation. He disapproved of the requirement in the Articles that nine states must endorse important matters and seven must approve all others, "a rule destructive of vigour, consistency or expediency from day to day." He favored consolidating the national debt to place the responsibility back in the hands of Congress, not in those of the states. Three years passed, and at the Annapolis Convention Hamilton would grasp the opportunity to summon the federal convention he and Madison had been urging for so long.

When that convention eventuated, Hamilton, contrary to widespread expectations, failed to seize the initiative and come forward with a comprehensive plan that would unite the rival sections, calm the jealous states competing with the federal government for sovereignty, and reassure the citizenry that republican institutions would be preserved. True, he did oppose the move to have the representatives in the lower house of the legislature elected in such manner as the state legislatures should direct, instead of by the people. According to one unfriendly delegate-reporter, he asserted that direct election by the people was essential to the "democratic rights of the community." While this remark might have been calculated to shore up Hamilton's republican credentials, it probably was motivated by a nationalist credo that stressed popular sovereignty and minimized state power in the affairs of the central government. His obeisance to "democratic rights" served only to alarm the two states' rights diehards in his own state delegation.

In sum, it remains a conundrum to this day whether Hamilton adopted his highly centralized posture and manifested his obeisance to the British constitutional system as a tactical maneuver to undercut the demands of the small states for equality, or whether he was motivated by the sincere conviction that this was the road to take.

No man went to the Convention better prepared than Madison. During the past twelve months he had delved deeply into the history of ancient republics and confederacies. In April 1787 he had prepared a memorandum on "Vices of the Political System of the United States," in which he denounced the state legislatures for failing to honor the requisitions of Congress, and he had concentrated his attention on the people and their division into factions according to economic interest, regional allegiances, and "the different kinds of property" they possessed. What made a government republican, he felt, was that decisions were made by a majority, and unless there were adequate checks, the interests of individuals or minorities might well be threatened. Herein, of course, was the substance of the tenth *Federalist*.

Unlike Hamilton, however, Madison came to the Convention with a plan, which he had previously outlined in letters to Jefferson, to Edmund Randolph, and to George Washington. In this correspondence he stressed the need for the *ratification by the people* of the new plan of government. He urged arming "the federal head" with a "negative in all cases whatsoever in the local Legislatures." Finally, he advocated drastically changing the representation in Congress under the Articles, proposing instead that it be made proportional to the population of the states, thereby depriving the small states of the equal vote they presently enjoyed. He was confident that in the long run the South would gain "superiority under such a change." He sought a middle ground between independent state sovereignty and consolidation into "one simple republic," with "a due supremacy" accorded the national authority but leaving to the states unspecified subordinate powers.

Madison also proposed that "this national supremacy be extended" to the judiciary department, with an appeal lying to the national tribunal "in all cases which concern foreigners, or inhabitants of other States," and that admiralty jurisdiction be fully assumed by the national judiciary.

The legislative branch he envisioned was to comprise two branches: one larger in numbers, elected for a shorter term; the other relatively small, but serving for a longer term "and going out in rotation." In this house (the Senate) he was prepared to lodge the veto over state laws.

Finally, he proposed a "National Executive," but he did not delineate the authority with which it was to be clothed, nor the manner in which it was to be selected. And he stressed the importance of conferring upon the national government "the right of coercion" by sea or land. Whether the proposed veto power would provide such a coercion, or whether investing Congress with control over taxation and commerce was the solution, he was not prepared to clarify.

Madison's views thus constituted the core of the Virginia Plan, and its details seemed to have been hammered out in the eleven days in which the Virginia delegation caucused at Mrs. House's lodgings prior to the convening of the Convention. George Washington had been whisked away by Robert Morris, but was doubtless apprised of the deliberations of the state delegation of which he was so prominent a member.

The Virginia caucusing had come to an end with the

eve of the Convention. Madison could be found still at work, seated at a desk piled high with papers in a quiet corner of Mrs. House's drawing room. If the harpsichord resting in an opposite corner brought back humiliating memories of Kitty Floyd and the scenes in which he had participated four years earlier, he showed no signs of them. Instead, he was absorbed in earnest conversation with Governor Edmund Randolph, reassuring him that the days the Virginians had spent there had not been wasted, that the delayed opening of the sessions of the Convention, with most delegates caught in the rain and mired down in mud, gave the Virginians the opportunity to unite on the plan that Randolph was to submit. Again, Madison chose to stay behind the arras until his plan was expounded. He was the prompter; another took the stage.

Madison prodded Randolph that, following the opening organizational formalities of the Convention, the governor must be prepared to get the Virginia Plan on the floor before any of the other delegations came up with theirs. The ever-cautious Randolph scrutinized the plan in its final form. What he read shocked him. He found the proposal to scrap the old Articles a revolutionary action and urged a conciliatory tone to keep the fur from flying. Jefferson called Randolph "the poorest chameleon I ever saw, having no colour of his own and reflecting that [of the person] nearest him." This apt characterization fitted both Randolph and the timid and tiny revision he was proposing. It was contained in the opening paragraph that he read to Madison and his fellow Virginians:

> Resolved that the Articles of Confederation ought to be so corrected and enlarged as to accomplish the objects proposed by their institution; namely, "common defense, security of liberty, and general welfare."

Randolph felt that he was hitting the right note, one that would not alarm listeners still attached to the old

Articles. However, when the delegates listened further, they would be hearing the voice of Randolph mouthing the program of Madison. In essence, they were given a constitutional proposal radically new and enormously variant from the existent system.

The following day, May 25, a quorum of seven state delegations were seated in the East Room of the State House. Here the Declaration of Independence had been signed, and here the old Congress had mostly sat until they were humiliatingly driven out by an insubordinate state militia wanting back pay. The East Room, forty by forty feet, with a twenty-foot-high plaster ceiling, proved adequate for the business at hand. The delegates seated themselves at tables covered with green baize, three or four delegates to a table. Before the session began, Washington talked informally to the delegates, urging them to create a plan of government of which they could be truly proud. As Gouverneur Morris later reminisced, Washington exhorted them, "Let us raise a standard to which the wise and honest can repair! The event is in the hands of God."

The first order of business was the election of a presiding officer. In the absence of the senior delegate, Benjamin Franklin, who was indisposed that day, Robert Morris moved that General Washington be the presiding officer, a motion seconded by John Rutledge. Unanimously elected, Washington was escorted to his chair by his two co-sponsors. In a brief speech he thanked his fellow delegates for the honor conferred upon him, and asked their indulgence for any errors he might commit in the execution of that post. Then the delegates picked as secretary William Jackson, a former army officer, and decided on the rules to be followed.

It was agreed that a majority of the states present could decide any question, each state to have an equal vote. This was an initial victory for the small states, and one that conformed to the voting rules of the Continental Congress. Then a rule of secrecy was adopted, the delegates feeling that they could talk more freely and be willing to modify their declared positions if word of what they said did not leak to their constituents back home. The rule, with strict injunctions laid down by Washington, was vigilantly respected. The wide, lofty windows ranging on both sides were nailed shut. Guards were posted outside the doors. Throughout a torrid summer the delegates sweated it out, but in the main what was happening inside never got outside. No one raised the issue of the public's "right to know," although Jefferson, from his post in Paris, protested privately to John Adams in England that the "precedent" of "tying up the tongues of the delegates was abominable." What came out of Philadelphia on September 17 has been called "an open covenant secretly arrived at." And years later Madison would insist that "no Constitution would ever

A Session of the Constitutional Convention with George Washington presiding (*from an engraving at the Independence National Historical Park Collection*).

have been adopted by the convention if the debates had been public."

The initial victory of the small states would quickly prove abortive. The Virginia delegation now seized the initiative. On May 29, Governor Randolph rose from his seat at a nod from General Washington and, with a degree of modesty concealing his own indecisiveness, declared:

"I regret that it should fall to me, rather than those of greater standing in life and longer experience, to open the great subject of this mission. But my colleagues from Virginia imposed this task on me.

"I need not comment on the crisis that confronts us, on the weakness of the Union under the Articles of Confederation, and on the dangers of our situation. But here is the remedy I am offering, which I am proposing in the form of a resolution."

Randolph, to reassure his listeners, began with the timid resolution proposing that the Articles be "corrected and enlarged." Ahead lay the real shockers, the fourteen following resolutions, which in essence proposed to demolish the Articles of Confederation and erect in their stead a strong national government on a popular foundation. The resolutions set up a bicameral legislature, the lower house chosen by popular election, the upper house picked by the lower from the candidates named by the state legislatures. Each house's representation was to be proportional to population. This Congress would have the authority to make laws "in all cases in which the separate states are incompetent" and to nullify any state laws contrary to the Federal Constitution.

The Virginia Plan provided for a President to be called the National Executive, who was to have all the executive powers granted Congress under the Articles. With the concurrence of a number of federal judges, the President would have veto power over the acts of Congress. He was to be chosen by Congress and would serve for a term of seven years. The plan also proposed to set up a system of federal courts.

This audacious plan transcended a mere revamping of the Articles, placing in its stead a different constitutional structure embracing a balanced government of three branches, supreme over the states.

The Convention now went into a committee of the whole. For a few moments the response to the Virginia Plan seemed auspicious. On the motion of Gouverneur Morris, the Convention voted six to one "that a *national* government ought to be established consisting of a *supreme* Legislative, Executive, and Judiciary." The dissenting state was Pennsylvania, whose delegation yielded to Benjamin Franklin's long predilection for a unicameral legislature, such as had been operative in Pennsylvania. Once taken and never reversed, the vote on the Morris resolution was perhaps the most significant made by the Convention, amounting as it did to a commitment to set up a supreme central government.

Other parts of the Randolph Plan provoked serious debate. The proposition that "the first branch of the legislature" should be elected by the people quickly raised two questions: First, how much democracy did the Founding Fathers really want? And second, how much power were the states ready to yield to the people? Perhaps to the surprise of most delegates, two old Patriots with long-established radical credentials quickly sought the floor to contest this proposition.

The first to do so was Roger Sherman, a delegate from Connecticut, signer of the Declaration of Independence, onetime shoemaker, and one of the few ex-artisans present at the Convention. The second was Elbridge Gerry, the fiery maverick from Marblehead, who stunned some of his colleagues with his uninhibited antidemocratic outpourings, among them:

> The evils we experience flow from the excess of democracy. The people do not want virtue, but are the dupes of pretended patriots. Just look at Massachusetts. There it would seem to be a maxim of democracy to starve the public servants. There has

been a perfect clamor to reduce salaries, and even the governor has had to cut his salary. I have been too republican, heretofore; I am still republican, but I have been taught by experience of the dangers of the leveling spirit.

The nationalists who looked to the people, not to the states, for support of their program, could not let these remarks go unchallenged. George Mason, more democrat than nationalist, rejoined: "I am for an election of the larger branch of the legislature by the people. That is to be the grand depository of the democratic principle of government. We ought to attend to the rights of every class of the people. Perhaps we have been too democratic in the past, but let us not now run into the opposite extreme. However indifferent the affluent may be on this subject, let me remind you gentlemen: Every selfish motive, every family attachment, ought to recommend such a system as would provide no less carefully for the rights and happiness of the lowest than the highest orders of citizens."

Mason had brought the class issue out in the open. Two others, more enthusiastically nationalistic, now manifested their concern about attaching the people to the national government. James Wilson wanted to raise "the federal pyramid to a considerable altitude," and for that reason "to give it as broad a base as possible." He warned that "no government could long subsist without the confidence of the people." To put elections in the hands of the state legislatures would only increase their weight rather than reduce it.

Madison had impatiently waited his turn on an issue so vital to the nationalist cause. He contended that to have one branch of the national legislature elected by the people was "essential to every plan of free government." "The excessive flirtations" of indirect elections now being practiced in some of the states, was, in his opinion, being "pushed too far." He was prepared to have such indirect elections for the second branch of the legislature as well as for the president and the judiciary. But the great fabric to be raised would be more solid and durable "if it should rest on the solid foundation of the people themselves." Then he first enunciated the theme he would later expound in the tenth *Federalist:*

> All civilized societies are divided into different sects, factions, and interests, as they happen to consist of rich and poor, debtors and creditors, the landed, the manufacturing, the commercial interests, the inhabitants of this district or that district, the followers of this political leader or that political leader, the disciples of this religious sect or that religious sect. In all cases where a majority are united by a common interest or passion, the rights of the minority are in danger.

Madison then developed his notion of the need to protect minority rights, expressing what may well have been the first reference to race persecution at the Convention, a theme usually avoided:

> We have seen the mere distinction of color made in the most enlightened period of time, a ground of the most oppressive dominion ever exercised by man over man. What has been the source of those unjust laws complained of among ourselves? Has it not been the real or supposed interest of the major number? Debtors have defrauded their creditors. The landed interest has borne hard on the mercantile interest. The holders of one species of property have thrown a disproportion of taxes on the holders of another specie. The lesson we are to draw from the whole is that where a majority are united by a common sentiment, and have an opportunity, the rights of the minor party become insecure. What is the remedy in a republic, then? The only remedy is to enlarge the sphere, and thereby divide the community into so great a number of interests and parties, that in the first place a majority will not be likely at the same moment to have a common interest separate from that of the whole or of the minor-

ity; and in the second place, that in case they should have such an interest, they may not be apt to unite in the pursuit of it. Let us try this remedy, and frame a republican system on such a scale and in such a form as will control all the evils which have been experienced.

How far the delegates were prepared to trust the judgment of the people was reflected in the stirring debate over the method of electing senators. Once the committee of the whole had approved by a vote of six states to two the election to the "first branch" (the House of Representatives) by the people, how was the "second branch" (the Senate) to be picked? Randolph, arguing in support of his original proposition that the Senate be elected by the House, maintained that the "second branch" should be small enough "to exempt it from the passionate proceedings to which numerous assemblies are liable."

This proposal was entirely unacceptable to James Wilson, who took his nationalistic notions of popular sovereignty seriously, and favored having both branches elected by the people. John Dickinson, a man of elitist inclinations, strongly disagreed. The senators, he insisted, would more accurately reflect the "sense of the states" if they were picked by their respective legislatures. Such a method, in his judgment, was better calculated than election by the people to attract "the most distinguished for their rank in life and their weight of property." The model that he had in mind for the Senate was the House of Lords, and he wanted the second branch to conform as closely as possible to that aristocratic chamber.

Over this issue the committee of the whole was deadlocked. Neither Wilson nor Madison, each supporting different proposals, was impressed by Dickinson's arguments. Neither saw the least danger that the states would be devoured by the national government if their senators were elected either by the people, as Wilson urged, or by the House of Representatives, as

Madison preferred. Wilson flatly denied the applicability of the British model. "Our manners, our laws, the abolition of entails and of primogeniture, the whole genius of the people, are opposed to it," he contended. On this point Madison concurred, and thereupon he began a wrangle with Gerry over whether the people or the legislatures had been responsible for the paper-money experiments that Madison loathed.

With no agreement obtainable, the issue was put off for another week. Madison reaffirmed his support for the Virginia proposition. Arguing for a relatively small Senate, he asserted that the more the senators "partook of the infirmities of their constituents, the more liable they would come to be divided among themselves either from their own indiscretions or the artifices of the opposite faction." Contrariwise, when the weight of a set of men "depends on the degree of political authority lodged in them, the smaller the number, the greater the weight."

Dickinson entered a persuasive plea for his own proposition on the ground that "the preservation of the states in a certain degree of agency is indispensable." It would preserve a useful check on the popularly elected House. After further debate and over Madison's persistent objections, Dickinson's motion for the appointment of the senators by the state legislatures was adopted nine to two, only Pennsylvania and Virginia registering negative votes.

The Senate as chosen Dickinson's way would in later times be perceived by the public as having become the tool of big business combines. Wilson's vision proved the sharpest. The Seventeenth Amendment, providing for the direct election of senators by the people, ratified in 1913, vindicated his judgment on this issue.

How long should the senators serve? Terms varying from nine years down to four were proposed, but in the end the Convention was persuaded by Randolph's plea for rotation, along with Madison's argument for a considerable duration of term "in framing a system which will last for ages." It was finally agreed that senators would serve six-year terms, one-third to be up for election biennially.

The Convention, having resisted a renewed effort to have the state legislatures elect the House of Representatives, now had to deal with the ticklish issue of whether representation should be equal, as in the old Congress, or proportionate to population, and, if the latter, how the population was to be counted. George Mason pointed out that under the existing Confederation, Congress represented the *states* and *not* the people of the states, and that the acts of Congress operated on the states and not the people. The new plan he advocated of election to the House by the people would reverse this. While favoring having the people vote from large districts, he was silent on the issue of proportional representation. But since Virginia, Pennsylvania, and Massachusetts—the largest states in population—had the most at stake in pressing their demand for proportional representation, and the smaller states the least, the issue brought on a direct confrontation between the larger and smaller states.

For a time it seemed that the nationalist momentum would be stalled. New Jersey, in the person of William Paterson, insisted that the convention was acting *ultra vires,* as the delegates were expected to proceed under a commission to amend the Articles of Confederation. "We have no power to go beyond the federal scheme," he declared, "and if we had, the people are not ripe for any other. We must follow the people; the people will not follow us." Arguing that a confederacy "supposes sovereignty in the members composing it, and sovereignty supposes equality," he warned that his state would never part with her sovereignty.

Thus far the method of election to the legislative branch had been determined. The most troublesome issue remained to be resolved. How would representation in each house be apportioned? That issue, arraying the small states against the large, consumed a large portion of the Convention deliberations for a full month and was not to be settled until the middle of July. The debate it precipitated revolved around a major question: Would the government be a consolidated nation, with the national government holding its authority directly from the people, or would it be a federal union in which some degree of sovereignty would be recognized as proper to the states and some check be placed upon popular rule?

Initially, attention focused on the "first house" (the House of Representatives). Connecticut's Roger Sherman proposed that representation be proportionate to the numbers of free inhabitants; Rutledge, that it be according to the respective quotas of contributions. The issue seemed clearcut: people against wealth. In supporting his fellow South Carolinian, Pierce Butler reminded the delegates that "money was power and that the states ought to have weight in the government in proportion to their wealth." Rufus King rejoined that, if voting were made proportionate to revenue, nonimporting states like New Jersey and Connecticut would suffer serious discrimination.

At this point Benjamin Franklin, that unreconstructed democrat, in a paper read for him by James Wilson, urged that voting be proportional to population, citing the case of England and Scotland, whose union failed to bring about adverse actions in Parliament against minority Scottish interests. He even advanced a formula to equalize the contributions of the states, but his rather diffuse proposals seemed to perplex the delegates.

By a vote of seven to three the committee of the whole voted for proportional representation in the first house, without settling the most troublesome point, *who* would be represented? James Wilson's answer: representation and direct taxation should be based proportionate "to the whole number of white and other free citizens and inhabitants of every age, sex, and condition, including those bound to servitude for a term of years, and three-fifths of all other persons, except Indians not paying taxes."

When it was proposed, few realized that, after furious debate, Wilson's formula would be adopted, for he had unwittingly touched a sensitive chord among Northerners opposed to slavery and unprepared to grant the slave states the advantage in numbers that this proposal embodied. Gerry promptly voiced a vigorous dissent. "Are we to enter into a separate compact with slaves?" he asked, responding to his own query with a vigorous "No!" In his customary blunt style he amplified his question by raising a second one: "Why should the blacks, who were property in the South, be in the rule of representation more than the cattle or horses of the North?"

Ultimately Wilson's motion prevailed, thereby encouraging the nationalists to press their victory. Wilson and Hamilton now proposed that the right of suffrage for the second house (the Senate) be the same as for the first house. The vote was close—six states in favor, five against, a forecast of an ominous division ahead.

Meanwhile, the nationalists had pushed through agreements on the supremacy of the laws of Congress and national treaties, on giving necessary and proper powers to Congress, and even on allowing the national government a veto of state laws contravening the Constitution, the clause on treaties being added by Franklin.

The long-brewing confrontation between the large and small states began on June 14. Regardless of whether a final settlement would apportion seats in the national legislature according to taxes paid or according to the number of the state's free inhabitants plus three-fifths of the slaves, the small states saw themselves completely outvoted in a national legislature by a few large states.

On June 15 it was clear what form an alternative proposal would take. Its spokesman was William Paterson, New Jersey's former attorney general, a rather diminutive figure whose modest demeanor cloaked respectable learning and oratorical talents. Paterson now split the convention apart by proposing the Small-

State or New Jersey Plan in the form of nine resolutions. These called for a one-house legislature elected by states regardless of population, with a plural executive elected by Congress and a Supreme Court chosen by the executive. Paterson made one obeisance to the national system. He was prepared to declare the acts of Congress and all treaties "the supreme law of their respective states," binding "upon the State courts," regardless of state law to the contrary. Otherwise, save for granting Congress the right to tax and regulate commerce, the New Jersey Plan would have continued almost intact the old Articles of Confederation.

Franklin had always been congenial to a unicameral legislature such as his own state possessed, to the dismay of conservatives. The Old Doctor caused some gossip by reputedly letting slip to a friend his concern about a bicameral system. The latter he compared to a snake with two heads. "One head chose to go on the right side of the twig; the other on the left. So that time was spent in the contest; and before the decision was completed the poor snake died of thirst."

But even Franklin's metaphor could not save Paterson's unicameral proposal, which moved against the tide of delegate opinion. From the moment Randolph initiated his proposals, it had become evident that the delegates would not content themselves with an amended set of Articles. Paterson's proposal was too little and came too late. After three days of sharp debate, the New Jersey Plan was defeated seven to three, a decisive vote that amounted to a complete rejection of the Confederation frame of government and of any notion of returning the nation to where it had been before the Annapolis Convention. That point was driven home by New York's Lansing. "New York," he declared, "would never have concurred in sending deputies to the Convention if she had supposed the deliberations were to turn on a consolidation of the states and a national government."

Lansing's negativism was too much for Paterson, who now sought to strike a more constructive tone.

He was not opposed to a national government, nor were the people, he conceded. What he did oppose was the inequality of the present plan, which, as in Great Britain, "has ever been a poison contaminating every branch of government." Without restraint on the legislative authority, he asked, is there not danger of "a legislative despotism"? Randolph responded with a spirited defense of the Virginia Plan.

Now it was Alexander Hamilton's turn. He had said very little over the first three weeks, but Paterson's proposals struck alarm bells in his ears. He foresaw a fatal compromise that would in effect seriously reduce the powers of the national government. Perhaps to bring the delegates back to their senses, perhaps because he was not noted for his discretion, on June 18, the day before the New Jersey Plan was rejected, Hamilton revealed his own plan in what was probably the most controversial speech he ever would make, and one that was as damaging as any to the people's perception of him as a republican leader.

Neither the Virginia nor the New Jersey Plan appealed to him, he confessed, but he found the latter more unpalatable. His own proposals amounted to reducing the states to mere subdivisions. An executive in each state would be appointed by the national government, while the Chief Executive would be elected for life by electors. Hamilton was brutally frank. Arguing that two sovereignties could not coexist within the same lines, he sought to mollify his shocked listeners by arguing that if the states were extinguished, great economies could be effected.

Piling one sledgehammer blow on top of another, Hamilton proposed a Senate chosen for life and invested the executive with an absolute veto. Beyond that, he denounced both the Virginia and the New Jersey plans as too democratic. Since Hamilton was a rational man, the extremist solutions that he offered, solutions that shocked even the ultranationalists, were proffered evidently to offset the Paterson proposals rather than with any expectation on his part that his own notions would prevail. As time would show, Hamilton, despite his indiscreet remarks of June 18, would in essence back the basic Virginia Plan as the best obtainable.

Could a republican government be established over so great an extent of territory? Hamilton asked. While he was not prepared to offer an alternative, he did hold up the British political system as "the best in the world." Hence there should be a life Senate, since no temporary Senate, he asserted, not even one of seven years, "will have firmness enough to answer the purpose. When a great object of government is pursued which seizes the popular passions, they spread like wildfire and become irresistible." A hereditary monarch, like the King of England, was, he declared, "above the dangers of being corrupted," and to guarantee such executive incorruptibility he called for a National Executive chosen for life.

Is this a republican government? Hamilton asked his now thoroughly aroused audience. His answer: "Yes, if all the magistrates are appointed and vacancies are filled by the people or a process of election originating with the people." Thus, to Hamilton, the Randolph Plan did not go far enough. Hamilton confessed that he was offering what was merely a sketch, not a set of formal propositions, but with the idea of further underpinning the Randoph Plan as it evolved in the convention.

Hamilton consumed most of the day, and when he gathered up his papers, his auditors sat stunned and silent. Then the committee of the whole rose and the house adjourned.

Hamilton's audacious assault on the weaknesses of the constitutional proposals thus far submitted left their imprint. On the very next day the New Jersey Plan was defeated, but not before James Madison had torn it to shreds. He attacked it as too "federal," as fantasizing the idea of the large states combining against the small, and prophesied that if the New Jersey principle were admitted, it would "infuse mortality into a Constitution which we wished to last forever."

Debate on the Randolph Plan was resumed, but the small states were not content, insisting on an equal vote in the Senate. Some ten days elapsed before a compromise could be hammered out. Hamilton took the occasion of the last speech he was to make for a considerable time to characterize the issue as "a contest for power, not for liberty, but for *their* liberty," meaning the states'. "States," he pointed out, "are a collection of individual men. Which ought we respect most, the rights of the people composing them, or the artificial beings resulting from the composition? Nothing would be more preposterous or absurd than to sacrifice the former to the latter." Reminding his hearers that "this was a critical moment for forming a respectable government," he urged that the delegates "should run every risk in trusting to future amendments." If we do not act now, he warned, while we still have some sentiments of union, now when we are weak and sensible of our weakness, it may be too late when we are "feeble and the difficulties greater."

In one version of Hamilton's closing, he charged that "the people are gradually ripening in their opinion of government. They begin to be tired of an excess of *democracy*—and what even is the Virginia plan, but *pork still, with a little change of the sauce.*"

A stunned audience sat in silence. Hamilton had gone the furthest in advocating a centralist plan that would forever label him as undemocratic and promonarchical. Outvoted by the two other New York delegates who soon quit the Convention, thereby depriving him of a vote, and depressed by the depth of what he felt to be states'-rights sentiment, Hamilton left the Convention on June 29 and headed for New York on the pretext of private business.

Hamilton did not depart without administering one more shock. The day before he quit, the debate on the Convention floor over the suffrage in the lower house reached a state of such acrimony that Benjamin Franklin, never celebrated for his religious orthodoxy, called on the delegates to invite a clergyman to offer prayers at the beginning of each session. Hamilton, among others, contended that this action would spread word out of doors that dissensions within the Convention had suggested a measure that had not been initiated at its start. One later version, as has already been noted, had Hamilton express confidence that the convention could transact the business entrusted to its care without "the necessity of calling in foreign aid." He could not have timed his departure more opportunely.

The Great Compromise

Even before Hamilton temporarily quit the Convention, animated debate had begun over a compromise plan proposed by the Connecticut delegation and effectively argued by Roger Sherman, Oliver Ellsworth, and William Samuel Johnson. Dr. Johnson eloquently reminded his fellow delegates that the United States was for many purposes "one political society" composed of individuals, while for other purposes the states also constituted political societies with interests of their own. These notions, Johnson observed, were not contradictory. "They were halves of a unique whole," and as such "ought to be combined" to the end that "in *one branch* the *people* ought to be represented, in the *other* the states."

The Connecticut Compromise, providing for equality of the states in the Senate, elicited strong rejoinders from the nationalist camp, whose notable leaders now were James Madison and James Wilson, and the debate waxed fierce. On the critical motion for equal representation in the Senate the nationalists succeeded in obtaining a tie vote. The resolution of the issue was now assigned to a special committee made up of one member from each state, an arrangement favorable to the small-states group. On July 5, that committee reported in favor of the Connecticut Plan, and a week later the convention agreed that representation and direct taxes in the lower house should be based "in proportion to the whole number of white and other free citizens and inhabitants of every age, sex, and condition including those bound to service for a term of years and three-fifths of all other persons not comprehended in the foregoing description, except Indians not paying taxes." This proposal had been advanced by James Wilson some weeks before to gain Southern support for basing representation on population rather than property, that population to be determined by a census ordained by the Constitution. While in essence this adopted motion became Article I, Section 2 of the final Constitution, the drafters avoiding spelling out distinctions of color, substituting the phrase "the whole number of free persons" for "white and other free citizens," but continuing to abstain from mentioning slavery by referring to the enslaved blacks as "all other Persons." In this form the rule of representation survived until the Civil War and the ratification in 1868 of the Fourteenth Amendment.

Eleven days later the Convention removed the last element in the controversy by accepting the principle of equal representation in the Senate. It should be noted that for proportioning representation no distinction of sex was made either in the free or slave population. Hence, for purposes of representation, women were to be counted, but since qualifications for voting were left to the state legislatures to determine, women gained no rights of suffrage—except in New Jersey by an accident of legislative drafting, and then for all too brief a time.

For James Madison, his defeat on the composition of the Senate, a proposal advantageous to his own state of Virginia but only to be scuttled by the Connecticut Compromise, convinced him of the need for executive independence and separation of powers, thus making it much easier for him to collaborate on *The Federalist* with the two other contributors who had long voiced these views.

The Slavery Concession:
The Sections in Confrontation

Back in Philadelphia, earlier in August, the Convention agreed to give Congress the power to regulate commerce with foreign nations and among the several states, and added, on Madison's motion, "with the Indian tribes." Although all had agreed that conferring power over commerce on the national government was a prime motive for calling the Convention, Southern delegates were shocked by the notion that this clause would work out purely to the North's advantage. Charles Cotesworth Pinckney wanted to restrict commercial legislation to a two-thirds vote of each house rather than a simple majority, and George Mason, in support of the two-thirds vote, declared:

> The southern states are the *minority* in both houses. Is it to be expected that they will deliver themselves bound hand and foot to the eastern states, and enable them to exclaim in the words of Cromwell, on a certain occasion—"The Lord hath delivered them into our hands"?

James Madison, countering in one of his most effective speeches, pointed out that "as we are laying the foundation for a great empire, we ought to take a permanent view of the subject." The great object, he pointed out, was "the necessity of securing the West India trade to this country." Madison prevailed, and Congress won the power to regulate commerce.

Nonetheless, every regional concession brought its price and begot a compromise. Thus the great slavery issue, which hitherto had been swept under the rug, came to the fore when the delegates took up the matter of import and export duties. A fortnight after the commerce clause victory, the South proposed that Congress be forbidden from levying a tax on the importation of slaves, both into and between the states, and from prohibiting such importation altogether.

To the consternation of most Northerners, Roger Sherman favored the proposition. He disapproved of the slave trade, he explained, but felt it expedient to offer as few impediments to the proposed scheme as possible, especially when one realized, he remarked in an optimistic vein, that "the abolition of slavery seemed to be proceeding throughout the United States." If the Connecticut Yankee's support for leaving the slave trade unrestrained provided an agreeable surprise to Southerners, their equanimity was short-lived. Virginia's elder statesman, George Mason, took the floor and shocked the delegates from the Lower South with his tirade against what one day the South would defend as its "peculiar institution." While attributing the blame for the original slave traffic to British merchants and to the refusal of the British government to allow the colonies to prohibit the traffic, Mason painted an ugly picture on a broad canvas, one that did not spare his fellow Southerners. Mason's blast stands out as one of the most stirring speeches of the Convention:

> The present question concerns not the importing states alone, but the whole Union. The evil of having slaves was experienced during the late war. Had slaves been treated as they might have been by the enemy, they would have proved dangerous instruments in their hands. But instead they were as foolish in dealing with the slaves as they were with the Tories. Maryland, Virginia, and North Carolina have prohibited the importation of slaves. But all this would be in vain if South Carolina and Georgia remained at liberty to import them. The West is calling out for slaves, and will fill their country if the states in the Lower South remain at liberty to import. Slavery discourages arts and manufactures. The poor despise labor when performed by slaves. Slavery prevents whites from immigrating, and produces the most pernicious effect on manners. Every master of slaves is born a petty tyrant. They bring the judgment of heaven on a country. As nations cannot be rewarded or punished in the next world they must be in this. By an inevitable chain of

causes and effects providence punished national sins by national calamities. I hold it essential to every point of view that the General Government should have power to prevent the increase of slavery.

Rutledge, replying for the Lower South, was unimpressed by the moral and economic arguments Mason had marshaled. He warned that "the people of those states would never be such fools as to yield on so vital a point nor agree to the plan of union unless the right to import slaves were untouched." Charles Cotesworth Pinckney reaffirmed Rutledge's threat.

With the Northern delegates divided between those from Connecticut, who preferred not to meddle in the slave trade, and others, like John Dickinson and New Hampshire's John Langdon, who placed the issue on the high moral ground of honor and conscience as well as safety, the Convention was prepared, as Randolph suggested, to find "some middle ground." The signal contribution to such "middle ground" was the proposal now forthcoming from New Jersey's governor, William Livingston, Jay's father-in-law. No prohibition shall be permitted before the year 1800, he recommended. Mollified by this spirit of concession, Charles Cotesworth Pinckney substituted "the year 1808" for Livingston's 1800.

Despite Madison's objection that "twenty years will produce all the mischief that can be apprehended from the liberty to import slaves," and that a term of that length was "dishonorable to the American character," the "Father of the Constitution" was overruled once again. With minor modifications of phraseology, the Convention voted eight to four to bar prohibition of the slave trade before 1808. Even the North divided on this crucial vote, nor was there a solid South, as Virginia voted "nay."

The word "slavery," Abraham Lincoln would someday note, was "hid away in the Constitution, just as an afflicted man hides away a wen or cancer, which he dares not cut out at once, lest he bleed to death."

Instead we find, "The migration or importation of such persons as any of the states now existing shall think proper to admit, shall not be prohibited by the Congress prior to the year one thousand eight hundred and eight; but a tax or duty may be imposed on such importation, not exceeding ten dollars for each person" (Article I, Section 9). Thus slavery was in effect validated by this and the two other compromises—the three-fifths rule for representation and direct taxes (Article I, Section 2), and the provision for the return to their owners of fugitive slaves ("persons held to Service or Labour" is the description used) crossing state lines (Article IV, Section 2). By these three compromises with Southern sensibilities, the Framers negated the Great Declaration's assertion that all men are created equal.

These concessions to the slave states allayed but failed to end the tensions between North and South, tensions that had earlier emerged during the Confederation years over the issue of the West and the Mississippi, and now would embrace slavery, the last a smoldering source of contention, which one day would erupt in a tragic conflagration.

In the meantime, since numerous issues had already been settled, the Convention adjourned on July 26 until August 6 to give the Committee of Detail an opportunity to "report a Constitution conformable to the resolutions passed by the Convention." The committee was composed of John Rutledge of South Carolina, Edmund Randolph of Virginia, James Wilson of Pennsylvania, Oliver Ellsworth of Connecticut, and Nathaniel Gorham of Massachusetts. Randolph wrote a preliminary draft and Wilson the revised draft that formed the final report. The committee did more than adopt the resolutions previously carried. It amplified them and provided innovations of its own. Thus, it took the very brief resolution on the "National Judiciary," and itemized in some detail the jurisdiction of the "Supreme Court" more or less in the form that it appears in the final Constitution. Again, it transformed the vague powers conferred on the national legislature into a series of specific powers, including the crucial "necessary and proper" clause that permitted the broad or "Hamiltonian" construction of the Constitution that was to govern the Supreme Court for many years to come. It adopted or paraphrased a number of clauses in the old Articles of Confederation, perhaps to convey the illusion that the Constitution was a mere revision of the Articles—a fiction that was transparent to everyone.

The Committee of Detail's report, submitted to the Convention on August 6, was debated until September 10, when the Convention adjourned to await the work of the Committee of Style, which had been named to prepare a new version of the Constitution. Since the Convention continued to make changes, such as in the mode of electing the President, and removing from the Senate the power to make treaties and appoint Supreme Court justices, the Constitution that emerged from the Committee of Style had to take these matters into consideration, but the Committee of Detail's report remained the core of the final version.

Numerous divisive issues continued to be resolved even after the Committee of Detail had completed its work. One of the most important was the manner of electing the President. Should he be elected by Congress, as the original Virginia Plan proposed, or should he be elected directly by the people rather than by the states; Those committed nationalists, James Wilson and Gouverneur Morris, eloquently pleaded the case for having the President elected by the people, while the aristocratic George Mason, although himself a foremost civil libertarian, considered Wilson's proposal to be as unnatural as asking a blind man to pick out colors. The final decision, after countless proposals, was to have the President elected by electors who would be chosen in each state "in such manner" as its legislature might "direct." The electors would vote by ballot for two persons, of whom one could not be an inhabitant of the same state. The person having the greatest number of votes would become President; the second highest Vice-President. It was Roger Sherman who proposed that if no one person gained a majority of the electors, the House of Representatives should choose the candidate from among the top five, each state's delegation casting one vote. The plan, perhaps conceived to propitiate the states, proved instead a victory for both nationalism and democracy, for very shortly after 1789 nearly all the state legislatures provided for the election of their states' presidential electors by popular vote.

How long should the President's term be, and should he be eligible for reelection? Hamilton, who, on his return to the Convention, took an active and constructive role, had originally indicated his preference for a life term, others for a seven-year term without eligibility to run again; toward the end, Hamilton opted for a mere three years. The Convention finally settled on a four-year term without placing a limitation on the President's right of reelection.

A vexing issue at the Convention was where to locate the power to declare state laws unconstitutional. Even ardent nationalists shied away from granting the power to Congress. In the end it was a bitter states'-rights man who hit upon a satisfactory solution. Drawing upon the phraseology of the now discarded New Jersey Plan, slovenly Luther Martin, whom one delegate castigated as "an insufferable bore and blustering obstructionist," inserted a clause making the Constitution and the laws and treaties of the United States "the supreme law of the land," binding upon the judiciary of each state. The supremacy clause, as it is called, which had its origins in a resolution drafted by John Jay for the old Congress, became the cornerstone of national sovereignty in 1789, when Congress passed a judiciary act providing for appeals from state courts to the federal judiciary. The Convention prudently abstained from spelling out just what body would have the right to declare acts of Congress unconstitutional, but from the sense of the debates it was implied that the federal judiciary would exercise the power.

A large number of dissenting Christian sects, along with the Jews, had a stake in the outcome at Philadelphia, but no way of knowing for sure whether religious tests for officeholding, such as still existed under some of the state constitutions, would be incorporated into the Federal Constitution still in the drafting stage. In Pennsylvania, for example, the state constitution required members of the assembly to subscribe to a declaration that ended in these words: "I do acknowledge the Scriptures of the Old and New Testament to be given by divine inspiration." Most states had removed, or were about to remove, such effective bars to officeholding, but the disqualification in the Maryland Constitution of 1776 barring Jews from public office was not removed until 1825. Rhode Island, once the home of religious liberty, did not secure equal rights for the Jews until the adoption of the state constitution in 1842, and North Carolina not until 1868. In the main, though, the religious minorities were beneficiaries of the movement in the original thirteen states to remove religious bars to public office holding.

It was the federal government rather than the states that provided the most vigorous impetus to the movement. The old Congress, on July 13, 1787, ordained in the very first article of the Northwest Ordinance that "no person, demeaning himself in a peaceable and orderly manner, shall ever be molested on account of his mode of worship, or religious sentiments in the said territory."

Would the Federal Convention meeting simultaneously in Philadelphia adopt so liberal a stance? The answer was soon forthcoming. On August 20, Charles Cotesworth Pinckney had submitted to the Convention, for reference to the Committee of Detail, a number of propositions. Among them was this: "No religious test or qualification shall ever be annexed to any oath of office under authority of the United States." This proposition was referred to the Committee of Detail without debate or further consideration. When the committee reported back on August 30, Charles Pinckney then moved to amend the article with the addition of these words: "but no religious test shall ever be required as a qualification to any office or public trust under the authority of the United States." Roger Sherman thought the clause unnecessary, "the prevailing liberality being a sufficient security against it." But Gouverneur Morris and Charles Cotesworth Pinckney approved the motion, which was agreed to unanimously. The entire article was adopted, with only North Carolina and Maryland divided.

Not knowing what had transpired, Jonas Phillips, a longtime patriot of New York of the Jewish faith, who had removed to Philadelphia before the start of hostilities and had served in the Philadelphia militia, memorialized the Convention on September 7 to omit from a test oath the phrase regarding the divine inspiration of the New Testament, so that "the Israelites will think themselves happy to live under a government where all religious societies are on an equal footing." Phillips, along with persons from other minority religious groups, appears to have been unduly concerned. In its final form, Article VI of the Federal Constitution requires all federal and state officials to take an oath or affirmation to support the Constitution, with the provision "but no religious Test shall ever be required as a qualification to any office or public trust under the United States."

Although Article VI was adopted with little debate, it was a particular target for that Antifederalist diehard, Luther Martin. At the Maryland ratifying convention, Martin singled out the supporters of the article, contrasting them, in his customary vein of heavy sarcasm, with "some members *so unfashionable* as to think that a *belief of the existence of a Deity,* and of a *state of future rewards and punishments* would be some security for the good conduct of our rulers, and that, in a Christian country, it would be *at least decent* to hold out some distinction between the professors of Christianity and downright infidelity or paganism."

Martin's harangue did not deter proponents of religious freedom, nor did it keep James Madison from including as the first article of the Bill of Rights a prohibition of Congress from making any "law respecting an establishment of religion, or prohibiting the free exercise thereof."

What stands out in the debates of the Convention are the points of similarity among the various plans proposed, rather than their differences. Both the Virginia and the New Jersey plans had granted Congress the power to levy and collect taxes; and every plan presented at the Convention gave Congress the right to regulate foreign and interstate commerce. The Convention was unanimous in vesting in Congress the power to pay the debts and "provide for the common defense and general welfare of the United States." There was, too, widespread agreement about incorporating into the Constitution a prohibition of the issuance by the states of paper money.

With the basic charter of government hammered out, the Constitution was entrusted to the skillful hands of the Committee of Style, to which some of the most talented writers among the delegates were named. William Samuel Johnson was the committee's chairman, with Gouverneur Morris, Madison, Hamilton, and Rufus King serving under him. It was Morris, however, who was largely responsible for the final phraseology of the Constitution, producing in a mere two days a document distinguished for its precision of language and clarity of style. Morris's most noteworthy contribution was in changing the wording of the Preamble. Since the new government would go into operation upon ratification of nine states, and no one could be certain which states would ratify, Morris very sensibly reworded the Preamble as drafted earlier by the Committee of Detail. Instead of "We the people of the States of New Hampshire, etc., . . . do ordain, declare, and establish the following Constitution for the government of ourselves and our posterity," Morris's Preamble designated the people as the source of authority, thereby elevating the sights of government and couching its purposes in eloquent language. As he reworded it, the Preamble read:

> WE THE PEOPLE *of the United States, In order to form a more perfect Union, establish Justice, insure domestic Tranquility, provide for the common defence, promote the general Welfare, and secure the Blessings of Liberty to ourselves and our Posterity, do ordain and establish the* CONSTITUTION *for the United States of America.*

One other point: While the attribution is not certain, it is most probable that Alexander Hamilton persuaded his colleagues on the Committee of Style to add a clause forbidding any state from passing any "law impairing the obligation of contracts." Property interests would not be neglected.

Just two days after the Committee of Style submitted its final draft to the Convention, it was approved, and on September 17 the Convention adjourned. On that closing day the engrossed Constitution was read and adopted, but not before a number of moving speeches were heard.

Hamilton conceded that no man's ideas were "more remote" from the final plan than his were known to be, but offered the delegates the choice "between anarchy and Convulsion on one side, and the chance of good to be expected on the other." Randolph surprised his fellow delegates by disclosing that he would not sign because he wanted to feel uncommitted as to what his final judgment would be about the Constitution—an odd admission from a man whose initial plan provided the basis of the charter finally adopted. The prolix Elbridge Gerry warned that the Constitution would promote dangerous divisiveness in his state. He

The Constitution of the United States, signatory page. The designation of the States in the handwriting of Alexander Hamilton (*National Archives, Washington, D.C.*).

could not sign the document because he would not pledge himself to abide by it.

Old Doctor Franklin expressed certain reservations, but admitted that if he lived long enough he might change his mind. "The older I grow," he remarked, "the more apt I am to doubt my own judgment and to pay more respect to the judgment of others." He did not consider himself infallible, and told of the French lady, who in a dispute with her sister, remarked, "I don't know how it happens, sister, but I meet with nobody but myself who is always in the right—*il n'y a que moi qui a toujours raison.*" Franklin's enthusiasm for the Constitution burgeoned on reflection. About a month later he wrote to an old friend of America, Ferdinand Grand, the Paris banker, suggesting that if the Constitution succeeded in being ratified, "I do not see why you might not in Europe carry the project into execution by forming a federal union and one grand republic of all the different states and kingdoms; by means of a like Convention, for we had many interests to reconcile." In Europe that grand constitution still seems a remote dream. Despite monarchical "Concerts of Europe," and the more recent Common Market and the European Parliament, the latter exercising far less authority than did the American Confederation under the Articles, Europe is today as sharply divided between East and West as it was in the days of Napoleon between puppet republics and reactionary monarchies.

Of the original fifty-five delegates who attended some or part of the sessions, thirty-nine signed. Washington's diary tells us that after that last session the delegates "adjourned to the City Tavern, dined together and took a cordial leave of each other."

They were no longer behind closed doors.

10

"With Trembling Anxiety"

In a triumphant, if often turbulent, session over a span of less than four months, a remarkably innovative charter of government had been adopted. The relative speed with which agreement was reached attests to the broad appeal that the idea of national union commanded among all the states, large and small, as well as to the basic consensus among most delegates, even among those who contested some of the many detailed commitments embodied in the final document. They had committed themselves to a structure that deliberately bypassed direct democracy and substituted rule by popular majorities through elected representatives. They had incorporated checks by Congress upon the President, and by the President upon Congress, and had established with remarkable brevity a judicial branch that would act as guardian of the Constitution. They had set up a unique federal system, providing for the supremacy of the national government in crucial areas, and impliedly reserving rights to the states in others.

Now the doors were open. By mail or newspaper, the Constitution was available for everyone to examine. How would it be received?

The answer was not long in coming. Madison, who had returned at once to New York to make sure that Congress would give its blessing to a document that consigned to the waste-heap the old Articles upon which that body functioned, kept a close check on public opinion. For some weeks the Antis were shocked into silence. "The advocates for it come forward more promptly than the adversaries," Madison reported to Randolph on October 7. Everywhere along the seacoast, he found that the people seemed "fond of it." Soon he was to be better advised. He learned that in his own state Richard Henry Lee and Patrick Henry were against the Constitution, that the paper-money faction in Rhode Island adopted a fiercely negative stance, and that every sign pointed to a fight brewing in the interior of Pennsylvania.

In short, by the end of October the tide seemed to be turning against the Constitution. In Virginia, Randolph found the bar, the judges, and those in debt to British creditors sounding outraged or betrayed. Thus far it was a trickle. Then it swelled to a torrent— pamphlets, newspaper letters, mass meetings—all the authority and voices that the Antifederalists could muster. There was James Winthrop from Massachusetts, whose "Agrippa" letters attacked on two fronts: the Constitution gave too much power to the central government, left too little to the states, and would create a *permanent* aristocracy. From Virginia, Richard Henry Lee, in his widely read *Letters from the Federal Farmer*, charged that the "change now proposed is a transfer of power from the many to the few." Melancton Smith, in an *Address to the People of the State of New York*, warned that the Constitution would create an "aristocratic tyranny" that must soon terminate in "despotism."

The Antis challenged the practicality of the notion that a federal republic could govern over so vast an extent of territory, found fault with the kind of dual sovereignty the Constitution envisioned, and condemned its omission of a bill of rights. Its absence became a special target for George Mason's broadside, *Objections to the Proposed Federal Constitution*, hardbiting propaganda emanating from the pen of the renowned author of Virginia's Declaration of Rights. If federal law were paramount, the state bills of rights would be rendered nugatory, Mason argued. Hamilton, in his closing *Federalist*, took occasion to refute these charges. He pointed out that the Constitution forbade bills of attainder and *ex post facto* laws, provided for trial by jury, and banned titles of nobility. Hamilton went further. He insisted that the bill of rights now envisioned by its proponents was not only unnecessary but positively dangerous. "Why declare that things shall not be done for which there is no power to do?" Hamilton asked, but in this case his answer failed to resolve serious misgivings by many fair-minded persons.

More extreme critics than Mason charged that the Constitution had been framed by a *"dark conclave"* of "monarchymen," bold conspirators who sought not only an elective king and a standing army, but "an aristocratical Congress of the *well-born.*" Among such critics was Luther Martin, the Maryland delegate who had left the convention before it had completed its work and who had not had the occasion to refuse to sign. He now set forth his objections in a series of letters called *The Genuine Information,* which were run in the Baltimore papers. The states, Martin insisted, were better judges of the construction of tax laws than the federal judiciary, and as for an inferior federal judiciary, that would be superogatory, giving rise to an army of federal officials at enormous expense. If only Martin had lived to see the fattened federal bureaucracy of our own day!

The severe drubbing that Martin administered to Article III of the Constitution was impressively disposed of in the later *Federalist* letters that Hamilton wrote, and to which we have already had reference. In the course of his diatribes, Martin disclosed some of the secret proceedings at Philadelphia, especially the lineup of voting by the states. His violation of the secrecy agreement prompted a rhymester to send a verse to the newspapers, and it was reprinted rather widely:

> Did not the devil appear to Martin
> Luther in Germany for certain?
> And can't the Devil, if he please,

> Come o'er to Maryland with ease?
> This being admitted, then 'tis certain
> He has got into L——r Ma——n.

Ridiculed in rhyme, Martin was also lambasted by Oliver Ellsworth, a future chief justice, who attacked the Marylander for his garrulity, his vanity, his capacity for putting delegates to sleep, and for the contradictory stands he had taken on the floor of Congress from those he now espoused in his present literary effusions.

More specific points of substance and mechanics were to be scored by the Antifederalist side in the state ratifying conventions that lay ahead. In essence, the Antis disclosed themselves as state-centered men, parochial in their vision, generally living isolated from the arteries of trade, and debtors of varying degrees and backgrounds. Those holding positions of state and local leadership were tenacious in their determination to hold on to their power.

Madison, who was obsessed with property and paper-money considerations, would have laid their opposition to a desire to maintain the supremacy of the state legislatures in order to print money and violate contracts, but in fairness to many sincere and thoughtful critics, the opposition to the Constitution transcended narrow economic motivations. The Antifederalists were concerned with individual liberty, which, they believed, rested on republican virtue, and that in turn depended on maintaining the primacy of the states. Contrariwise, the Federalists considered themselves to be the elite, boasting the best talent and the best speakers. Posing as the pure and virtuous who knew what was best for the country, they had a special genius for rubbing their opponents the wrong way. They proffered their propositions in every confidence that the people would defer to them, not only as regards the kind of government that was needed, but concerning the kind of men who should run it. The Antis, just as self-righteous, presumed that they alone spoke for the common man.

The great weakness of the Antis, despite certain well-founded objections they raised to the Constitution, lay in their lack of an alternative plan. It was the principal task of the three authors of *The Federalist* to demonstrate that the rejection of the Constitution would create a vacuum of power, a return to the irresolute and impotent Confederation. At the same time, they felt obligated to show that a republican federalism would both provide effective government and preserve liberty without endangering the often separate and different interests that governed in the various thirteen states. In the ninth *Federalist*, Hamilton was at pains to point out that "the excellencies of republican government" might "be retained and its imperfections lessened or avoided." Through such devices as checks and balances, courts composed of judges holding office during good behavior, representation of the people in the legislatures by deputies of their own election—all these provisions, Hamilton argued, would "tend to the amelioration of popular systems of civil government.

It was the task of "Publius" to assure his readers that the government they were debating was *federal* rather than *national*. Hamilton essayed the task in the thirty-second *Federalist*, wherein he expatiated on the concurrent and coequal authority of the United States and the individual states. The fact that the people of *each* state rather than a *whole majority* of the people must establish the Constitution, and that it could not be slipped through by a mere *majority* of the states, was urged to reassure the localists. "It must result from the *unanimous* assent of the several States that are parties to it," Madison reaffirmed in *Federalist* Number 39. As regards the House of Representatives, the government is *national*, not *federal*, but as regards the Senate, with its principle of state equality, the "government is *federal*, not *national*."

The presidency, on the other hand, was portrayed as being in its selection of "a mixed character, presenting at least as many *federal* as *national* features." Furthermore, since the proposed government "extended

(*National Archives and Records Service, Washington, D.C.*).

to certain enumerated objects only, and left to the several states a residuary and inviolable sovereignty over all other objects," the government could not be deemed "a *national* one." As Madison conceived it, the amending process was neither wholly *national* nor wholly *federal*.

As Hamilton envisioned it, the Constitution set up a filtering-down process under a system of representative government, but certainly at the start it was not to be all-embracing. In the thirty-fifth *Federalist* he castigated occupational representation as "visionary," arguing that mechanics and manufacturers would "always" be inclined to give their votes to merchants because of the interconnections between manufacturing and mercantile interests. The landed interests, on the other hand, he accepted as "perfectly united from the wealthiest landlord down to the poorest tenant." The landholder, the merchant, and the members of the learned professions, he contended, could be counted on to understand and judge the concerns of the other parts of society. "Let every considerate citizen judge for himself where the requisite qualification is most likely to be found," he concluded rather smugly. Here, Hamilton signally failed to anticipate the great issues over the tariff, for example, between commerce, manufacturing, and agriculture, which divided the country for more than a century, or the hordes of lobbyists today that serve occupational groups so effectively.

Some time later, Madison in his fifty-first *Federalist* sought to assure his readers that a republic could oper- ate over so huge an area as that of the United States by reason of the functioning of the separation of pow- ers within the national government and between the latter and the states themselves. "Hence a double security arises to the rights of the people." Thus, the judicious modification and mixture of the *federal principle* would guarantee to the people of an ex- tended republic with "the great variety of interests, parties, and sects which it embraces, a coalition of a majority of the whole society, could seldom take place on any other principles than those of justice and the general good," while providing essential safeguards to minority rights.

Of equal concern to Madison was the necessity to moderate the passions of the people while making sure at the same time that devices were introduced to limit the abuses of government. After all, was not govern- ment "but the greatest of all reflections on human nature?" he asked in the fifty-first *Federalist*. "If an- gels were to govern men, neither external nor internal controuls on government would be necessary. In fram- ing a government which is to be administered by men over men, the great difficulty lies in this: you must first oblige it to controul the governed; and in the next place oblige it to controul itself. A dependence on the people is no doubt the primary controul on the gov- ernment; but experience has taught mankind the ne- cessity of auxiliary precautions."

Hamilton had the last word. He declared a bill of rights unnecessary and even "dangerous," asking in the eighty-fourth *Federalist*, "Why, for instance, should it be said, 'the liberty of the press are not to be restrained', when no power is given 'by which restric- tions may be imposed'?" Hamilton went so far as to argue that the Constitution was in itself a Bill of Rights. Then, in his closing letter, he criticized the under- current of anti-elitism that ran through the Antifederalist literature. Perhaps revealing a bit too much of his own lack of communion with the common man, Hamilton declared: "The perpetual charges which have been rung upon the wealthy, the well-born, and the great, have been such as to inspire the disgust of all sensible men." After charging the Antifederalists with "unwarrantable concealments and misrepresentations," and warning that a defeat of the Constitution would hazard anarchy and civil war, "and perhaps the military despotism of a victorious demagogue," he concluded with a grand peroration: "A nation without a national government is, in my view, an awful spectacle. The establishment of a Constitution, in time of profound peace, by the voluntary consent of a whole people, is a prodigy to the completion of which I look forward with trembling anxiety."

The delegates at the Constitutional Convention were sober realists. They knew that the greatest battles lay ahead. The Convention had overstepped its instructions. It had scrapped the Articles instead of amending them. Having defied Congress, the Convention decided to pursue what amounted to a revolutionary course by declaring the ratification by nine states sufficient "for the establishment of this Constitution between the States so ratifying the same." In other words, the Constitution was being submitted *directly to the people* through ratifying conventions. Not even Congress, which had summoned the Convention, would be asked to approve its work. Still, Congress, after acrimonious debate, and without endorsement or disavowal, did submit the Constitution to the state legislatures, to be submitted in turn to conventions in accordance with Article VII of the Constitution, providing that once nine states had ratified the Constitution, it would go into effect between the affirming states. Above all states, all factions, and all interest groups stood the people, as the Preamble felicitously reminded the country, and it was to the people through ratifying conventions that the federal Convention appealed for endorsement of its handiwork. In utilizing an institution innovated by the Massachusetts ratifiers in 1780, the Convention shrewdly bypassed the state legislatures, attached as they were to states' rights, and which required in most cases the agreement of two houses. If speedy ratification was a reasonable objective, then the single-chambered, specially elected state ratifying conventions rather than the state legislatures seemed to hold the greatest prospect of agreement.

As soon as the Constitution was in the hands of the state ratifying conventions, Madison, Hamilton, and Jay kept in close touch with nationalist leaders in the various delegations. The results had been more or less predicted. The small states, once reassured by the crucial Connecticut Compromise, which gave them an advantage beyond their numbers or wealth, fell into line, and quickly. Thus the Constitution, which Washington felicitously called the "child of fortune," was ratified in haste and with little or no discussion by Delaware, New Jersey, Connecticut, and Georgia.

The battles, it grew evident, would be waged in the large states. The first occurred in Pennsylvania, and it took on all the characteristics of a comic opera. The Antis sought frantically to delay action; their pretext was a need for more information. They refused to attend a session of the legislature, thereby preventing a quorum and keeping that body from taking action. In retaliation, a band of Constitutionalists broke into their lodgings, dragged the Antis through the streets to the State House, and forcibly kept them in the Assembly until a vote was taken to call a ratifying convention.

The feverish haste with which the convention was summoned and the fact that only a fraction of the voters of Pennsylvania balloted for delegates provided the Antifederalists with plenty of ammunition. The debate over ratification in this state revealed a deep sectional and even class cleavage between the pro-Constitution forces in commercial Philadelphia and their agrarian opponents in the western part of the state. The "low born" and the "six hundred well born" were accused of trying to ram this document down the throats of the rest. However, the strategy of urgency accrued to the Federalists' advantage, and the Constitution won out by a vote of forty-six to twenty-three.

The momentum seemed to be with the Federalists, who were scoring victories everywhere, but Massachusetts proved a stumbling block. There the leaderless Antifederalists poured grape and canister upon the Constitution, but were powerless to stem the tide of ratification. Farmers, often men of little learning but strong convictions, fought heroically, arguing with more passion than reason but deeply motivated by the same sense of injustice that lay behind Shays' Rebellion. "These lawyers and men of learning and money men," declared Amos Singletary, one of the Antifederalists, "that talk so finely, and gloss over matters so smoothly, to make us poor illiterate people swallow down the pill, expect to get into Congress themselves; they expect to be the managers of this Constitution, and get all the power and all the money into their own hands, and then they will swallow up all of us little folks like the great *Leviathan*. Yes," he added, "just as the whale swallowed Jonah." Hancock may have let himself be persuaded that this man and other honest rustics could feel the direction of the wind and not fight it, for he allowed himself to be won over by the pro-Constitution forces. As a result of the defection of several leaders, the Shaysites and other hardcore yeomen opponents were nosed out by a mere nineteen votes out of 355. The opposition managed to wring one concession from the victors: the convention's approval was accompanied by a recommendation for certain amendments to the Constitution.

The penultimate scene in the great drama of ratification was played out in twenty-three sweltering June days in Richmond, Virginia's New Academy on Shockoe Hill. The convention opened evenly divided, as one Antifederalist reported, "one half of her crew hoisting sail for the land of *energy*, and the other looking with a longing aspect on the shore of *liberty.*" A hall crowded with a large delegation and packed with spectators listened to the great debate dominated by Patrick Henry for the Antifederalists, and James Madison on behalf of the ratification forces. It was a repeat of David against Goliath. As for Patrick Henry, Madison was a natural antagonist, as the former made no bones about his detestation of theorists and bookworms. Brissot de Warville, the French radical reformer, who happened to be traveling in America at that time, gave us this portrait of James Madison. "This Republican appears to be about thirty-three years of age [in fact, a youngish-looking thirty-seven]. He had, when I saw him, an air of fatigue; perhaps it was the effect of the immense labors to which he has devoted himself for some time past. His look announces a censor, his conversation discovers the man of learning, and his reserve was that of a man conscious of his talents and of his duties." Madison, suffering from bouts of ill health and with so weak a voice that much of the audience often missed the sense of what he was saying, responded almost daily and sometimes five times a day to Patrick Henry, whose oratorical skills, melodious voice, and charisma managed to hold his audience spellbound regardless of the lack of substance and the demagogic cant of his speeches. His stand came as no surprise, as he had refused to go to Philadelphia because, as he put it, he "smelt a rat."

Henry and Madison each found able allies. The renowned liberal statesman George Mason took the Antifederalist side, and most delegates expected that Governor Edmund Randolph, who had declined to sign the Constitution, whose basic structure he himself had formally initiated at the Philadelphia Convention's opening session, would be an ally of Henry. Supporting Madison were such stalwarts as Edmund Pendleton, "Light Horse" Harry Lee, and John Marshall.

The Antis came mostly from the interior of the state and what soon became known as Kentucky, and polls taken at the start indicated that the Constitution would

James Madison, whose arguments carried the day at
Richmond; portrait by James Sharpless, Sr., c. 1796–97
(*Independence National Historical Park Collection*).

be in for a severe drubbing. Fortunately for the Federalist cause, the Antifederalists played right into their
hands. With the opening of the Convention on June 3,
George Mason moved that the Constitution be ana-
lyzed clause by clause before putting the whole charter
to a vote. Even though this seemed like an advantage
to Madison, who of all the delegates was the one most
capable of defending the Constitution detail by detail,
Patrick Henry proved incorrigible, running the gamut
from attacking the Constitution as a whole to picking
out at random particularly objectionable clauses.

On June 5, Henry held the floor for most of the
day. "Who had the effrontery to insert the opening
phrase 'We the People' instead of 'We the States'?
The reason for the phraseology was obvious," he continued. "It was to scrap a confederation and replace it
with a great consolidated government, destroying the
rights of the states. And other rights, too—the rights
of conscience, liberty of the press, all your communi-

ties and franchises, all pretensions to human rights and privileges, are rendered insecure, if not lost, by this change," Henry charged. Then, mingling negative analysis with threats, of which he was past master, he blustered: "It is said that eight states have adopted this plan. I declare that if twelve states and a half have adopted it, I would with manly firmness and in spite of an erring world reject it!"

Those who worried about George III, he warned, had better keep an eye on the President. "Once he gets in the field with his army, it would puzzle any American to get his neck out of the yoke. The army will salute him monarch; your militia will fight against you, and what will then become of you and your rights? I speak the language of thousands." But then, with characteristic insincerity, he added, "But, sir, I mean not to breathe the spirit nor utter the language of secession."

Then Randolph took the floor to hurl his thunderbolt. He announced that he would support the Constitution and would oppose any amendments prior to ratification. Madison, paraphrasing from *The Federalist*, and following through, gave a masterly exposition of the new government as partly consolidated, partly federal, describing its legislative powers as strictly defined and limited. "Either we grant these powers or let the Union be dissolved," he warned.

Henry, in his numerous diatribes, attacked the new taxing power in words that might have come from victims of tough IRS audits in our own day. "Stay out, stay out," Henry implored.

When Madison spoke, his hat was in his hands, his notes in his hat. Madison kept insisting that the Constitution be scrutinized in a calm and rational spirit. "If, as Mr. Henry declared the people were so content, whence was the source of the manifold complaints of national and individual distress that characterized the years of the Confederation?" Madison pointed to America's weakness in foreign relations, to the unwillingness of foreign powers to form treaties with us. He reminded his auditors that the United States had been forced to default on its debt to its generous ally, France, and called their attention to the minuscule sums the states had put up to underwrite national expenses.

For a few days Madison was missed, as a "bilious indisposition" kept him abed. Others stepped into the gap. Pendleton protested the sneering innuendoes to the effect that the Framers of the Constitution were aiming to set up a government by the "well born": "I consider every man well born who comes into the world with an intelligent mind and all his parts perfect." Not quite as sweeping or eloquent a statement as Jefferson's "all men are created equal," but it did hit a central issue constantly raised by the opposition— that this new government was elitist and was calculated to remain in elitist hands.

The indefatigable Patrick Henry was by no means finished. Over a period of several days he itemized numerous defects in the Constitution—its laws to be enforced by military coercion; the President enabled to promote his own private interests. "It is a government by force, and expresses the genius of despotism." The notion of concurrent jurisdiction was a political monstrosity, and on and on and on.

Then Mason blemished the spotless record on the evils of slavery that he had won at the Philadelphia Convention. He now offered the curious argument that the Southern states should give up the slave trade entirely, while warning them at the same time that slavery could be taxed out of existence by the national government. Which way did Mason really want it? Madison correctly pointed out that the compromise on the slave trade was prompted by a desire to prevent disunion, and that since taxation was linked with representation, no tax could be enacted that would force the South to free its slaves.

"They'll free your niggers!" Henry shouted, causing the tension to dissolve in a roar of laughter.

In the intense June heat, an ill and fatigued Madison dragged body and mind through the debates. He had to defend the federal courts, which the opponents pointed out could now collect debts due Virginians. He had to convince Tory-baiters of the unlikelihood that the confiscated property of Loyalists like Lord Fairfax would be restored. He had to persuade George Mason that he would not have to start paying quit rents all over again to a confiscated landlord. He had to reassure his fellow Virginians that a majority vote in the old Confederation Congress had been insufficient to pass a treaty forgoing for a term of years America's rights to the navigation of the Mississippi. This reminder had to be detailed without revealing how large a part he himself had played in forcing Jay to drop the proposal, since such actions of Congress were governed by the rule of secrecy. Nine states were necessary then—and now "two-thirds of the senators present . . . and the President must consent in every treaty which can be made."

Patrick Henry could never accept Madison's notion of a government partly national, partly federal. "The brain is national," he declaimed with obvious sarcasm, "the stamina federal, this limb national, that limb federal—but what it really signified was that a great consolidated government would be pressing on the necks of the people." Nor could he reconcile himself to Madison's thesis, expounded in *The Federalist*, that a republican government could exist over an extensive territory if it was judiciously organized and limited in its powers.

Henry had raised the temperature in an already steaming assembly hall. Randolph took violent offense at Henry's charges and innuendoes. "I disdain his aspersions, his insinuations. If our friendship must fall, then let it fall, like Lucifer never to rise again!"

Madison, frail and ill, still rose to the challenge and continued to keep his temper. He defended the direct tax as practicable, safe, and economical, and argued that if we did not build up our national power we could not maintain our neutral trade. "A neutral nation must be made respectable, or else it will be insulted and attacked," he insisted, sounding at that moment like John Jay, the nation's foreign secretary. Madison turned to the judiciary, showing that its jurisdiction must extend to all cases that could arise under the Constitution, including treaties. And, Mason added, *every* British creditor! "Don't worry, fellow Virginians," Madison reassured them in an unusual sardonic vein. "We well know, sir, that foreigners cannot get justice done in these courts."

The unstoppable Henry had almost finished: "The purse is gone. The sword is gone, and now the last barrier, the judiciary, is about to fall. Old as I am, I may yet have the appellation of rebel, for as this government stands I despise it and abhor it!"

Accustomed as his fellow delegates were to heavy doses of hyperbole and bombast from Patrick Henry, his latest malediction drew a gasp of disapproval. General Adam Stephen retorted: "If the gentleman does not like this government, then let him go and live among the Indians!"

The Antis were now hanging on the ropes. Their last hope was a compromise adoption of the Constitution with previous amendments. Henry and Mason proposed a bill of rights of twenty articles and some twenty other amendments. Randolph and Madison disemboweled the propositions. "The Union will be dissolved," Randolph charged, "the dogs of war will break loose, and anarchy and discord will complete the ruin of this country!"

Madison ended on a less frantic and more constructive note, stressing the example to the whole world of how a government could be cemented in the face of "such a diversity of opinions and interests." Madison's insistence on ratification without prior amendments was put forward as a proposition by Attorney General James Inness. By a vote of eighty-nine to seventy-nine, the convention ratified the Constitution unconditionally, with amendments recommended to the consideration of Congress.

If ever a victory could be attributed to one man, it

was Madison's on Shockoe Hill, and it is a tribute to *The Federalist* that Madison in his debates drew so heavily upon his own and his collaborators' contributions.

The battle was near an end.

When, in the fall of '87, the three contributors to *The Federalist* foregathered in New York and plotted out their respective contributions, they realized the depth of the opposition to the newly drafted Constitution. They identified its leaders. They recognized the obstacles to persuading the people to accept, even if with misgivings, the need for a *complete* change in the structure of the national government. They realized as well that a key battle would have to be waged in New York, still the seat of the old Congress and geographically lying athwart the nation.

In February 1788 the New York legislature, having voted to call a ratifying convention, departed from the usual suffrage requirements and resolved that every free male citizen twenty-one years or more of age was eligible to vote. An Antifederalist legislature, sensing the popular pulse statewise, calculated that the more votes, the better the likelihood that the Constitution would be defeated. The election returns for delegates revealed a formidable statewide opposition of more than two to one against the Constitution. Contrariwise, the popular vote in New York City swept the Federalists to victory by some ten to one, John Jay heading the New York City polling with 2,735 votes, followed closely by Alexander Hamilton with 2,713, and Chancellor Robert R. Livingston with 2,712, along with several other Federalist delegates.

Throughout the convention, Hamilton and Jay would provide brilliant and informed leadership comparable in depth with Madison's mastery of the Virginia debates. The opening of New York's ratifying convention took place in Poughkeepsie's old Courthouse on June 17, 1788. Quick decisions involved unanimousy electing the Constitution's formidable enemy, Governor George Clinton, as president, and ordering that the doors be kept open and that the convention start every morning with prayer. The very first speech was really an exhortation by Chancellor Robert R. Livingston to consider the advantages of union and the perils to New York State of its dissolution. Then, pursuing the Jay-Hamilton strategy, he moved "that no question, general or particular, should be put in the committee upon the proposed Constitution, or upon any clause or article thereof nor upon any amendment which should be proposed thereto, until after the said Constitution and amendments should have been considered clause by clause." The prompt adoption of this motion by the convention would ensure ultimate victory for the Federalists.

Accordingly, unlike the incoherent and often illogical steps by which the Constitution was examined in Virginia, the New York delegates, save for certain prolix and rambling members, debated the Constitution article by article. The Antifederalists, led by John Lansing and Melancton Smith, disemboweled the proposed Constitution line by line, with Livingston and Hamilton demonstrating the disputed provisions' fairness and practicability. In a flight of fancy, Smith compared the scheme proposed to "golden images, with feet part of iron and part of clay," or, on the contrary, "to a beast dreadful and terrible, and strong exceedingly, having great iron teeth—which devours, breaks in pieces, and stamps the residue with his feet." He now launched an attack on the rule of apportionment in the House of Representatives. He denounced counting slaves; he suggested that the numbers allotted each state might prove inadequate to represent so extensive a country and proposed that instead of sending one representative for every thirty thousand inhabitants, the ratio be changed to one for every twenty thousand.

Hamilton's reply on June 20 was the first of a series of masterful analyses of the Constitution to reassure the opposition that the people's liberties were not threatened. He denied that Congress had the power to reduce representation "below the number that it now stands. On the one hand," he continued, "it ought to be considered that a small number will act with more facility, system, and decision; on the other, that a large one may enhance the difficulty of corruption." He opened up a wide vista, with the likelihood that Vermont, Kentucky, and Tennessee would soon become independent states, as well as other states to be formed "from the unsettled tracts of western territory. These must be represented, and will all contribute to swell the ranks of the federal legislature." He could not leave his audience without referring to a theme that runs through *The Federalist*. He reminded Melancton Smith and the Antis that the weaknesses of the old system were not "fanciful," but "real and pregnant with destruction. Yet, however weak our country may be, I hope we shall never sacrifice our liberties. If, therefore, on a full and candid discussion, the proposed system shall appear to have that tendency, for God's sake, let us reject it! But let us not mistake words for things, nor accept doubtful surmises as the evidence of truth."

The very next day saw Melancton Smith on the floor insisting that the dubious construction by the delegates on the issue of representation in the House of Representatives be clarified. He argued that the number of representatives should be sufficiently large to admit not only "the men of the first class," but also those of "the middling class of life." Not to do so would leave the government in the hands of the "natural aristocracy."

Hamilton, in response, sought to persuade the delegates that "all governments, even the most despotic, depend, in a great degree, on opinion. In free republics, it is most peculiarly the case. In these the will of the people makes the essential principle of the government; and the laws which control the community, receive their tone and spirit from the public's wishes." To dispel the suspicions Smith had expressed, Hamilton added reassuringly, "the minds of the people are exceedingly enlightened and refined: Here we may expect the laws to be proportionably agreeable to the standard of perfect policy; and the wisdom of public measures to consist with the most intimate conformity between the views of the representative and his constituents." Again reverting to the defects of the Confederation, Hamilton closed on this note:

> I am flattered with the hope, sir, that we have now found a cure for the evils under which we have so long labored. I trust that the proposed Constitution affords a genuine specimen of representative and republican government, and that it will answer, in an eminent degree, all the beneficial purposes of society.

Hamilton was impelled to take the floor again to refute criticisms not only from Smith but from Lansing and Governor Clinton about the inadequacies of representation in the House of Representatives and the unlikelihood that it would comprehend the needs of the individual states. First, he sought to reassure the delegates that corruption by foreign nations was less likely in a government that could make war by majority vote than in one that required a mere nine votes. There would be too many more delegates to be corrupted! So far as representatives were concerned, he cited from his own experience in public affairs that members of Congress had ever demonstrated "a strong and uniform attachment to the interests of their own state." The diversity of habits of the people of the thirteen states had been raised as an argument against union, but Hamilton dismissed these diversities by pointing out that the new government could not interfere with the internal police of the state or "penetrate the recesses of domestic life. Such are not found among the general powers the Constitution gives to the new government."

John Jay made his first appearance on the floor of the convention on June 23, supporting the ratio of one representative to thirty thousand persons. He spoke with moderation and with great persuasiveness. He continually pointed out areas of agreement with his opponents, such as the need for a strong, energetic federal government. "Such declarations," he remarked, "came from all parts of the house." He distinguished between state and federal concerns. He sought to minimize the differences between himself and Melancton Smith over the question of proper representation, since Smith was willing to have the federal government possess the important power of war and peace. For the exercise of such great powers, Jay was prepared to accept a relatively modest representation in the lower house, while conceding that a much larger one for the state legislature would seem reasonable to deal with internal domestic affairs. The fact, as Jay pointed out, was that state legislatures were concerned with "innumerable things" requiring such minute and local information. The objectives of the general government were broad, comprehending "the interests of the States in relation to each other, and in relation to foreign powers. I think it best to let things stand as they are," he urged. "If I could be convinced that danger would probably result from so small a number," he added to placate the opposition, "I should certainly withhold my acquiescence." Again, a conciliatory peroration: "We did not come here to carry points. If the gentleman will convince me I am wrong, I will submit. *It is from this reciprocal interchange of ideas that the truth must come out.*"

Two days later Jay rose to reply to Samuel Jones, who opposed giving Congress the power of prescribing the time, place, and manner of holding elections. Jay regarded the Constitutional provision as vital to "prevent the dissolution of the Union" in the event that a state "by design or accident" should fail to choose senators or representatives.

By this date Jay could report to Washington that while the Antifederalist chiefs had not budged, the rank and file realized that their leaders were anchored to an extreme position and were "*averse* to a vote of

Rejection." Some would be content with recommendatory amendments; others wished for explanatory
amendments to settle points of doubtful construction.
A third group would insist on amendments precedent
to ratification. Momentum, he assured Washington,
seemed on the side of the Federalists. New Hampshire
had ratified, and the new Union was a fait accompli, a
fact that had an intangible but significant impact on
the course of the Poughkeepsie Convention.

Battles lay ahead, however. On June 26, John Wil-
liams, an upstate delegate, had proposed a resolution
denying Congress the power to impose an excise tax
on products grown or manufactured in the United
States, with strict limitations on direct taxes. Jay would
have rushed into the fray at once, save for the fact that
for a day or two Hamilton and Lansing were feuding
on the floor over a proposal that a senator be limited
to two terms of office for a total of twelve years.
Hamilton opposed the proposition on the grounds that
it would lead to an inconsistency in foreign policy,
pointing out that "a government changeable in its
policy must soon lose its sense of national character,
and forfeit the respect of foreigners." Warning that
the state legislatures should not be permitted to serve
as a "vehicle in which the evil humors may be conveyed onto the national system," and comparing the
Rhode Island legislature to "the picture of a *mob*"—
Hamilton argued that safety and permanency in government were perfectly reconcilable. The principle of
rotation, he insisted, would promote contention, and
in arguing on its behalf, its proponents carried "their
zeal beyond reasonable bounds."

In the meantime the opposition had confused issues
by raising the point of concurrent powers of the federal government and the states in areas apart from
taxation. Jay felt that these observations were "not
matured"—we would say "half-baked," but Jay was
always polite. He insisted that until more precise points
were fashioned it might be wise to go home "to cut
our Grass" rather than take matters "by halves."

Whether Jay and his supporters were bluffing or were confident that time was on their side would be anyone's educated guess. When Governor Clinton seemed to call the bluff, and asked Jay why he did not then move to adjourn, Jay responded by insisting that Clinton's side spend some time in clarifying their notions of direct taxes.

The very next day, Jay took the floor to make one of his most telling speeches. He insisted that "a government which was to accomplish national purposes should command the national resources." Would it be right, he asked, for the interest of a part to supplant that of the whole? Distinguishing between general and specific taxes, he argued that, as regards the latter, Congress would be sufficiently informed to make appropriate decisions. As he saw it, no minute knowledge was required to impose taxes on luxuries—for example, a tax on carriages (thereby anticipating Hamilton's carriage tax proposed when he was Secretary of the Treasury), or slaves, or plate. Jay was even prepared to have the obfuscations cleared up by "an explanatory amendment."

Not content with trying to curb Congress's taxing power, the Antifederalists aimed as well at curbing the power of the federal government to borrow money. Lansing would have required nine states to acquiesce. Jay swiftly rose to his feet to point out that "factions" not unknown to "republican governments" might prevent a third of Congress from allowing the other two-thirds to obtain a loan "when the exigencies of the State required it or when it would be for the public good." Even foreign nations might try to prevent Congress from borrowing money in the national interest. Jay then informed Governor Clinton that unlike the Senate, where the two-thirds rule was in force for treaties and impeachment, the lower house had nothing to do with treaties; it represented the people, whereas the Senate represented the states—for the Federalists, always a significant distinction. As for impeachment, the two-thirds rule was designed to prevent factions from removing officials for political reasons. Jay was not averse to striking a sectional note. In case of war the Western states would have power to refuse a loan to support the defense of the Atlantic states, the most likely targets and sufferers in such an eventuality. "Would you put it in the power of five men to disarm a Continent?" he asked. At this point Hamilton reinforced Jay's arguments in a powerful address, stressing national defense considerations in supporting a loan by majority vote.

To Hamilton, restrictions on borrowing could be fatal. "Limiting the resources of government to certain resources is rendering the fund precarious; and obliging the government *to ask*, instead of empowering them *to command*, is to destroy all confidence and credit. If the power of taxing is restricted, the consequence is, that on the breaking out of a war, you must divert funds, appropriated to the payment of debts, to answer immediate exigencies. Thus you violate your engagements at the very time you increase the burthen on them. Besides, sound policy condemns the practice of accumulating debts. A government to act with energy, should have the possession of all its revenues to answer present purposes."

Richard Harison, a fellow Federalist delegate, entered this comment on his record: "Bravo! As far as it went it was one of the most excellent energetic speeches that ever I heard." By now the delegates should have heard enough to reconcile themselves to the fact that an extensive republic, entrusted with ample powers, need not revert to despotism.

Differences continued, however—over textual matters, amendments compounding amendments—but nothing could spoil an Independence Day celebration in Poughkeepsie. Despite unsettled weather—it had been raining steadily for days—both factions celebrated a feast together, though not quite together. As Jay described it, "two tables, but in different Houses" were laid out for the delegates, but "the two parties mingled at each table," and toasts were announced "by sound of drum, accompanied by the discharge of cannon." We see Jay joining Melancton Smith. After a cordial exchange of greetings, Jay says, "We must find the road to compromise without gutting the Constitution."

"We must get guarantees first, though," Smith rejoins.

"At least let us try," Jay responds, as he leaves Smith with a friendly pat on the back.

How different was the July Fourth celebration in Albany, where Federalists and Antifederalists clashed bitterly, with one participant dead and eighteen wounded.

By July 8 the delegates, sitting as a committee of the whole, had completed their examination of the Constitution, allowing Jay to write Washington that "the ground of Rejection" seemed to be "entirely deserted," with the opposition reported to be divided on whether to insist on *"previous* conditional amendments" or on "subsequent ones," to which latter view Jay reported the "great number" were disposed.

By the tenth of July some fifty-five amendments had been proposed—explanatory, conditional, and recommendatory. In a fourteen-man committee to reconcile differences, Jay insisted that the word *conditional* should be erased before there could be any decision on the merits of the amendments, for, he contended, a conditional ratification amounted "to a virtual and total rejection of the Constitution."

Jay now forced the issue. On July 11 he moved that the Constitution be ratified with such explanatory amendments as were deemed useful to be recommended. His own "masterly" speech was buttressed by animated and persuasive supporting remarks from Hamilton and Livingston. The debate on adopting the Constitution stretched over four full days. Hamilton prepared a list of some thirteen recommendatory amendments, which Jay announced that he would back. Now Melancton Smith, in a last-ditch effort, moved that the Constitution be ratified on condition that a second convention be called to consider amendments seriously limiting federal power. Rejecting the motion, Jay made an eloquent plea for accommodation. A conditional ratification would have the effect of New York's remaining out of the Union, he pointed out.

It was now a race down to the wire to induce Smith and his backers to waive their insistence that the ratification be conditional upon securing amendments. "It is grown too fast to be pulled up by the roots," Jay rejoined. Others sought to withdraw New York from the Union if the Constitution was not amended at a second convention, or claimed the right to withdraw from the Union if the Constitution was not amended as a result of a circular letter addressed to the other states.

Now the sides were drawing closer, and a few of Smith's allies began to desert him. By July 23, Jay could write Washington that the convention, by a vote of thirty-one to twenty-nine, had stricken out the words "on condition" and substituted "in full confidence."

Jay knew that the deep-seated fears of the Antis were not just a figment of their imagination, but had to be assuaged. Accordingly he drafted a circular letter to Governor Clinton, supported on the subcommittee by Lansing and Smith, to be transmitted to the other states. The letter struck just the right conciliatory note and matched Jay's moderate approach throughout the convention, and his willingness to include a Bill of Rights among the amendments, reserving "expressly" to the people and the states powers not explicitly granted the federal government. Fortunately, "expressly" vanished from the final Tenth Amendment.

> We observe, that amendments have been proposed and are anxiously desired by several states as well as by this; and we think it of great importance that effectual means be immediately taken for calling a Convention to meet at a Period not far remote. . . . It cannot be necessary to observe that

> no Government, however constituted, can operate
> well, unless it possesses the Confidence and good
> will of the Body of the People.

That Jay was willing to go that far after denouncing the idea of a second convention in his *Address to the People* indicates his recognition of the realities of the situation.

The letter was agreed to unanimously, but the battle was not quite over. The convention still had to vote down a new motion by Lansing reserving the right of the state to secede if the amendments were not adopted. Lansing's motion was defeated by the perilously close vote of thirty to twenty-eight, and by almost the same slim margin of thirty to twenty-seven the convention ratified the Constitution, with Antifederalists including Gilbert Livingston, Melancton Smith, and Samuel Jones switching to the Federalist side, while seven Antis abstained.

The fact that New Hampshire and Virginia had already ratified before New York's final vote weighed heavily on the delegates at Poughkeepsie. Not only had the Union become a fait accompli before New York's final vote, but the thinly veiled threat that New York City might go it alone, isolating the rest of the state and costing it substantial revenue, along with the city's own concern that it might not be chosen as the seat of the new government should the state not ratify, seem to have constituted substantial, if intangible, factors in achieving the tight victory. Above all, however, the cause of the Constitution owed most to the brilliant oratorical efforts of Hamilton and the parts played in open convention and behind the scenes by the universally respected, conciliatory, open-minded, and persuasive Mr. Jay.

Along the coast of the American main, the ratification of the Constitution was saluted—nowhere, however, more intensely and joyfully than in New York City. There the rapid change in sentiment can be no

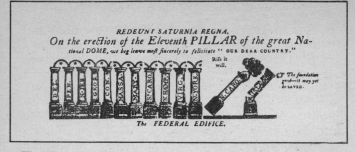

REDEUNT SATURNIA REGNA.
On the erection of the Eleventh PILLAR of the great National DOME, we beg leave most sincerely to felicitate "OUR DEAR COUNTRY."

Rise it will.

The foundation good—it may yet be SAVED.

The FEDERAL EDIFICE.

The Eleventh Pillar. By the time New York had ratified the Constitution, New Hampshire (the ninth state) and Virginia (the tenth) had preceded her. The "Federal Edifice" lacked only North Carolina and Rhode Island to make ratification unanimous.

better illustrated than by three separate spectacles. With New York's ratification still uncertain, an Antifederalist crowd in a ceremony at the Battery on the Fourth of July, 1788, gave vent to its feelings by burning the Constitution, a provocative act which led to numerous fistfights in which Federalists gave as good as they received. Then, only nineteen days later, in anticipation of New York's ratification on July 26 and in recognition of the fact that, with New Hampshire's ratification as the ninth state, a Union had been created, the Federalists staged a grand parade, colorful, stirring, imaginative, and significant in its participation by all segments of the population.

Leading the way was the Grand Marshal, wearing a blue coat and red sash, feather-tipped with black, and to his rear marched thirteen deputy marshals in white coats and blue capes. Great crowds cheered a long procession of floats. The procession was aflutter with banners held aloft by costumed marchers representing eighty-eight trades and professional artisans—mechanics, bakers, blacksmiths, cordwainers—with each group waving an appropriate slogan. The skinners, breechesmakers, and glovers carried a flag of cream-colored silk bearing their coat of arms and the motto, "Americans, Encourage Your Own Manufacturing!'' Carpenters carried the slogan "United"; hatters held up a flag in large lettering spelling out, "Success in American Manufactures"; ship captains marched under a streamer proclaiming, "Our Exports Exceed Our Imports"; sailors and ship joiners held aloft a verse:

> Our merchants may venture to ship without fear
> For pilots of skill shall the Hamilton steer
> This federal ship will our commerce revive
> And merchants and shipwrights and joiners shall thrive.

Farmers joined in, waving the banner, "God Speed the Plough!" while bakers displayed a "Federal Loaf." At the tail end was a corps of students from Columbia College (the old King's College, only recently renamed).

As the procession, to the blare of spirited bands, moved down Broadway toward Bowling Green, one might appropriately find a select company viewing the gala scene from the front drawing-room windows of the Jays' Broadway residence, one of the best views in town. Jay himself, still engrossed in winding up affairs at Poughkeepsie, would have been absent, as would Hamilton, but Sarah Livingston Jay, New York's favorite hostess, might well have invited—in addition to her own growing family—Betsey Hamilton and her eldest son, Philip, and even the bachelor James Madison, now returned to New York after his triumph at Richmond. One can well imagine the excitement inside the Jay residence as the most impressive spectacle among the multicolored floats, came rolling by—the good ship *Hamilton*, firing its cannon along the route. Built by the ship carpenters—a thirty-two-gun frigate, twenty-seven feet long, with a ten-foot beam, full-rigged as though ready to take off from the Battery where it seemed headed—it was drawn by ten white horses. The ship's figurehead bore a carved statue of Alexander Hamilton.

Sally Jay liked to make toasts, and has left us records of some that she composed, including one on the occasion of the signing of the peace with Great Britain in Paris almost a half-dozen years before. Aside from toasts to the threesome that had carried the brunt of the battle, one could imagine her holding up a glass and proposing:

"To the Constitution. *May it be perpetual.*"

Some guests might have reminded her that the Framers forgot to add that word in the text of the Constitution, although it appears in the old Articles and in the Northwest Ordinance. Had Gouverneur Morris been present, he might properly have rejoined, as draftsman of the Preamble, "If we have formed 'a more perfect union,' why should it not be a timeless one?"

Madison, still smarting from Jay's "Circular Letter" calling for a second convention, might have been heard muttering that the possibility of such a meeting could open a Pandora's box and let loose all the Patrick Henrys of the country. In Madison's troubled frame of mind, another assemblage might well undo the efforts of the Framers, among whom no one had contributed more or fought longer or harder for its adoption and ratification than he himself. Madison would never quite forgive Jay for proffering as a peace gesture the prospect of another convention, the very idea of which Jay had himself denounced both in his *Federalist* letters and in his *Address to the People of New York.*

In the euphoria of the moment, few shared Madison's fears, and in effect he himself would render them groundless when he hastened to satisfy the chief grievance of the Antifederalists—the absence in the Constitution of a Bill of Rights.

Three days had passed since the Grand Procession. On the evening of July 26, New Yorkers were intoxicated with joy over the news that their state had ratified and joined the new Union. Unfortunately, Federalist mobs got out of hand. One mob headed toward the Custom House in an effort to get their hands on John Lamb, the Antifederalist agitator. Another moved against the printing shop of Thomas Greenleaf. A perturbed Mayor Duane could not have forgotten how disorderly Patriots had smashed the Tory Rivington's printing press when the war started. Hamilton and Jay had then expressed their indignation in no uncertain terms. Had they been present, they would have felt then as they had earlier—that destroying a printing plant violated the freedom of the press. As the mayor and a small squad of constables rushed to the Custom House, they could see the attackers beating a sullen retreat, overawed by the display of bristling firearms readied by Lamb and his Antifederalist cohorts.

"Let's get Greenleaf!" was the cry. Before Duane and his constables could reach the printer's quarters, his plant had been smashed. The mob then rushed over to Governor Clinton's residence on Queen Street (soon renamed Pearl), but that worthy had shrewdly absented himself from the festivities and kept out of sight. Frustrated, the crowd gave three hisses, and then beat the "Rogue's March" around the building.

This was the ugly news that greeted Jay and Hamilton on their return from Poughkeepsie. To these Federalist leaders who had repeatedly avowed that the *people*, not the *states*, were the rulers, the lesson was worrisome. To Jay and Hamilton, the only hope for the new republic lay in the ability of the people to act in accordance with reason and due process rather than yield to the passion of the mob. After he learned the somber news, Jay might have been heard muttering to himself: "Government without liberty is a curse; but liberty without government is no blessing either."

A NEW ORDER
FOR THE AGES

One can visit the State Department in Foggy Bottom and view the Great Seal anchored to the entrance floor, or, more conveniently, one can fish out a dollar bill, where, on the left-hand reverse side, one will find imprinted a pyramid affixed in a circle, and beneath it the words NOVUS ORDO SECLORUM—"a new order for the ages." That was the way the old Congress felt about the unprecedented experiment in American republicanism when they decreed the Great Seal on June 20, 1782. America was not only a new political system but a beacon for all people and a refuge for the oppressed.

Almost immediately thereafter, questions arose. No one ventured to doubt that a new political and social system had been innovated. The troubling questions were in what form and how long it would survive. Among other Founding Fathers, John Jay, James Madison, and Alexander Hamilton had placed these questions high among the nation's priorities and had hammered away at the twin themes of structure and survival of a federal Constitution in the years of decision between the Treaty of Paris and the Philadelphia Convention.

Now the people had taken the necessary step. They had ratified a Constitution and created a Union with power to act. When it did, could it be trusted to act in the people's behalf?

The answer lay in the deepest recesses of the public mind: we must elect a President who can universally be trusted to wield power in the interest of the people of the United States. At Philadelphia, Richmond, and Poughkeepsie, and wherever delegates assembled at ratifying conventions, it was widely assumed that if General Washington could be persuaded to offer himself to occupy the highest office, many substantial fears about the new government would be dissolved. Indeed, it was the increasing likelihood of that eventuality that persuaded many Antifederalists to keep from emasculating Article II and allowing a strong Chief Executive to emerge relatively unscathed.

The leadership could not leave so vital an issue hanging in midair, to be propelled by the fickle winds of fate. All three witnesses to the creation and their partisans urged the patriarch to quit his role of Cincinnatus at Mount Vernon and make himself available for the presidency. Washington consented. When Congress counted the electoral votes for President on April 6, 1789, George Washington was the unanimous choice for the top post, while the second-choice ballots were divided among John Adams with thirty-four votes, John Jay with nine, and some scattering. Accordingly, under the unamended Constitution, John Adams was elected Vice-President.

Early 1789 saw New York, as the initial capital of the new government, in a flurry of preparations to put the City Hall (Federal Hall) in condition to accommodate the new Congress. Leading a group of New Yorkers of substance, John Jay, drawing deposits out of Hamilton's Bank of New York, advanced the sums necessary for the alterations.

The imminence of President-elect Washington's arrival in New York City sparked a flurry of renewed activity. In his triumphal, if leisurely, procession from Mount Vernon toward the Hudson, Washington spent the night at Liberty Hall, the home of John Jay's father-in-law, Governor William Livingston. There, early in the morning of April 23, he was received by a delegation from both houses, and the heads of departments under the old Confederation. All the officials crossed the bay to New York City in one of the three barges that conveyed Washington and his party. The President-elect's barge was gleaming white, and he was rowed to New York City by thirteen pilots in white uniform. Behind trailed a long procession of boats and sailing craft. As Washington disembarked in lower Manhattan, great crowds acclaimed him.

Appropriately, Jay, Madison, and Hamilton attended all the formal receptions, including the official reception of the President-elect in the Senate Chamber of Federal Hall on April 30 and the simple inaugural ceremony on noon the next day, which followed a long procession through the city's streets. There, at Federal Hall, Washington took the oath administered by Chancellor Robert R. Livingston. The leading actor in this dramatic scene stooped and kissed the Bible, adding audibly, "I swear, so help me God!" Turning to the multitude assembled in the street below, the Chancellor exclaimed: "Long live George Washington, President of the United States!" After the loud cheering had subsided, Washington delivered a brief but uplifting and conciliatory inaugural address, which Madison was known to have drafted. Therein he expressed his confidence that Congress would buttress the rights of the people, and invited constitutional amendments.

In the new government our three witnesses rose almost at once to dazzling heights. The first move was James Madison's, since Congress was the initial branch of the federal government to function. Politically he had survived the worst. Patrick Henry kept him from the senatorship from Virginia that Madison so richly merited, but despite Henry's flagrant efforts to redraw Madison's Congressional boundaries (actions that would later be called gerrymandering), Madison won a smashing victory to the House of Representatives, where he soon became its leader and, though not in the executive branch, one of Washington's intimate advisers.

Aside from framing essential revenue measures and other legislation needed to create the executive departments, Madison turned his attention to drafting a Bill of Rights. To bypass the second convention, which might well have opened the entire Constitution to reexamination, Madison used the alternative amendment procedure provided by the Constitution. That alternative required a two-thirds vote in both House and Senate and ratification by three-quarters of the states. This cumbersome but prudent procedure worked. Out of some two hundred amendments proposed in the state ratifying conventions, the Senate and House in conference reduced the number drastically. In 1791 Madison had the gratification of learning that the first ten amendments to the Constitution had been ratified. In the main they guaranteed personal liberties, but the ninth and tenth reaffirmed the reservation of rights to the states and the people—in effect, a guarantee of federalism. Of all Madison's achievements, the Bill of Rights remains his noblest heritage to the nation. Madison had sought unsuccessfully to limit the *states'* interference with civil liberties as well as Congress's, but it remained for the Fourteenth Amendment to fulfill the vision of this great civil libertarian.

At the age of forty, James Madison, still an unwilling bachelor recovering from scars not yet effaced by the Kitty Floyd affair of years before, was not too long away from his happy marriage to a young Philadelphia widow, Dolley Payne Todd. The seemingly improbable middleman in this romantic episode was Aaron Burr in the role of matchmaker.

Alexander Hamilton did not wait long to be named to an office that was commensurate with his genius. In the post of Secretary of the Treasury, Hamilton demonstrated administrative talents, perhaps the greatest America has yet produced. A believer in a strong executive, as he had made clear in *The Federalist*, he guarded the presidency from encroachments upon its power by the legislative branch, and assumed an influence in Washington's cabinet that is unmatched in the annals of the American cabinet system.

Hamilton's inventive mind grasped an extraordinary range of governmental problems—constitutional, economic, diplomatic, and military. His fiscal program

Alexander Hamilton in maturity. Oil portrait by Charles Willson Peale, c. 1791 (*Independence National Historical Park Collection*).

was bold, original, and constructive, and he firmly established American credit at home and abroad. To do so he created a national debt and made effective use of the government's taxing power—not without challenge. Truly, one may say that Hamilton constantly seized the initiative and kept ahead of events. Talleyrand said of him, "He has anticipated Europe." It may be asserted, with just as much accuracy, that he anticipated America. Hamilton envisioned America as a great industrial giant whose manufacturing output would raise the general standard of living and stimulate both commerce and agriculture. He believed that the nation must be put into a strong posture of defense, that it could not rely upon the long-range peaceful intentions of foreign governments or count upon permanent alliances.

As a constitutional thinker, Hamilton anticipated the later assumption by the Supreme Court of powers for the federal government on the basis of three clauses of the Constitution—the necessary-and-proper clause, the general welfare clause, and the commerce clause. These three clauses, as Hamilton interpreted them, have provided the constitutional foundation for much of the activity of our modern federal government in the fields of taxation, finance, business regulation, and social welfare, activities undreamed of when the nation was in its infancy.

Hamilton's failures as a statesman are attributable more to personality and tactics than to basic principles. He carried courage in politics to the point of self-immolation. If there was any attacking to be done, he did not assign the task to someone else, but took it on himself. Opinionated and self-assured, he lacked understanding of the art of compromise, the mastery of which is so essential to the aspiring politician. Thus he was inflexible when a little yielding would have made all the difference. Hamilton was candid, but he was also indiscreet. He wrote brilliantly, but he wrote too much and too often. Feeling it "a religious duty" to oppose Aaron Burr's political ambitions, he would have been a better actuarial risk had he shown more literary restraint.

Reviewing those early years as an impoverished West Indian half-orphan, burning for fame, he confessed to Gouverneur Morris not too long before fate overtook him at the heights of Weehawken:

> Mine is an odd destiny. Perhaps no man in the United States has sacrificed or done more for the present Constitution than myself; and contrary to all my anticipations of its fate, as you know from the very beginning, I am still laboring to prop the frail and worthless fabric.

Disappointed and disillusioned as he was, Hamilton's "sacred honor" had been most distinctively vindicated in his heroic fight for national union, in his polemics in support of the Constitution, and in his unparalleled efforts to give it substance.

Last of the three witnesses, Jay had an opportunity as first Chief Justice of the United States to put his legal imprimatur on the writings of *The Federalist*, to which, as "Publius," he, along with Hamilton and Madison, had made signal contributions. While his service to the nation in foreign affairs was of longer duration and has perhaps left a stamp more durable, he utilized the High Court to provide an audaciously nationalistic exposition of the Constitution, one that has been reaffirmed and applied in areas beyond the purview of the Founding Fathers. By character, training, and experience he was peculiarly fitted to occupy the posts of responsibility and decision-making that he filled during a period when the national government cried out for energetic and bold direction and an outlook that was continental rather than provincial.

Rather than as a technician of the law, Jay is remembered as a creative statesman and activist Chief Justice whose concepts of the broad purpose and powers of the Constitution were to be upheld and spelled out with boldness and vigor by John Marshall. In bringing the states into subordination to the federal government, in securing from both the states and the people reluctant recognition of the supremacy of treaties, and in laying the foundation for the later exercise by the Supreme Court of the power to declare acts of Congress unconstitutional, Jay gave bold direction to the new constitutional regime. His tireless efforts to endow the national government with energy, capacity, and scope, and to assert the authority of the people over that of the states, attest to his vision, courage, and tenacity. It remained for others to spell out the safeguards for individual liberties and the limitations on national power which are so essential to the maintenance of a democratic society, and which Jay himself had been prepared to define at the Poughkeepsie convention. As a humanitarian and a civil libertarian, John Jay, the patrician, could take pardonable pride in the result.

*　　　*　　　*

For all too short a time, all three Nationalists were united under the administration of President Washington, without parties to divide them. But the time of unity was fated to be brief. The French Revolution and the European war that ensued forced the President to adopt a policy of strict neutrality, advocated by Jay and Hamilton, and opposed by Madison and Jefferson. The overseas tension prompted the President to dispatch Chief Justice Jay to England to make a commercial treaty, but aside from leading to the removal of British troops from American soil, the treaty left many issues unsettled and further divided the country. It thrust Hamilton, the sound money man and nationalist, against Thomas Jefferson, earlier Secretary of State, and Madison, the latter's protégé and political partner. Out of the conflict over issues both foreign and domestic emerged the party system. Ironically, parties were not recognized in the Constitution. None of the Founding Fathers had professed affection for them, but in the long run it was the party system that seemed to make the Constitution more workable and more responsive to the American people. An opposition party in its modern form might well have been viewed with dismay by the Founding Fathers, who, depending on their point of view, would have disapproved of them as antigovernment or antirepublican. Today political parties are accepted as the touchstone of a democratic society, and the repression of opposition parties as one of the most visible symptoms of a totalitarian state.

Hamilton, who returned to private life and his law practice, was fatally wounded in 1804. Jay retired from public life in 1801 after serving two successive terms as governor of New York State and turning down a second appointment as United States Chief Justice. The home he had built at Bedford for himself and Sally was occupied by her for less than a year, and the death of his dearest companion cast a profound shadow over Jay's long years in retirement. James Madison lived the longest, becoming Secretary of State under Jefferson and President in 1809.

These three witnesses had lived to see the rise of parties, which they had once deplored and which would divide them just as the challenge of a stronger union had united them. All three, however, had at the critical moment placed union ahead of partisanship. The last survivor of the trio, Madison echoed the sentiments of all three on his deathbed: *"The advice nearest to my heart and deepest in my conviction is, that the Union of the States be cherished and perpetuated."*

Notes on the Sources

The Federalist

Save for the four drafts by John Jay available in original or photocopy at the Rare Book and Manuscript Library of Columbia University, no original drafts of the remaining eighty-one letters of "Publius" are known to be extant. For the best newspaper texts of *The Federalist*, the reader should use the edition of Jacob E. Cooke (Middletown, Conn., 1961). Therein the texts of Essays 1–77 have been taken from the newspapers in which they first appeared; the texts of Essays 78–85 are from volume II of the first edition in book form, printed by J. and A. McLean and corrected by Hamilton (New York, 1788). Hamilton may also have approved revisions found in the 1802 edition published by G. F. Hopkins. An edition published by Jacob Gideon (Washington, 1818) included Madison's own authorized corrections. A useful listing of numerous editions of *The Federalist* published here and abroad is provided by Roy P. Fairfield, ed., *The Federalist Papers* (2d ed., Baltimore, 1981), 308–14, 321–22.

The question of the disputed authorship of certain *Federalist* letters has been substantially resolved as a result of the efforts of Douglass Adair, "The Authorship of the Disputed Federalist Papers," *William and Mary Quarterly*, 3d ser., I (1944), 97–122, 235–64. Applying statistical analysis to the text to determine authorship, Frederick Mosteller and David L. Wallace, *Inference and Disputed Authorship: The Federalist* (Reading, Mass., 1964), arrived at Adair's principal conclusions.

Of the innumerable monographs that *The Federalist* has spawned, one will find a helpful bibliographic guide in Fairfield, cited above. Among the most recent should be mentioned Garry Wills, *Explaining America: The Federalist* (New York, 1981), with its emphasis upon the influence of the Scottish Enlightenment on "Publius," Albert Furtwangler, *The Authority of Publius* (Ithaca, 1984), which tends to minimize the impact of *The Federalist* on the voting behavior of delegates to the ratifying conventions, and David F. Epstein, *The Political Theory of The Federalist* (Chicago, 1984), which argues that the authors favored a "strictly republican" system.

Hamilton, Madison, and Jay

The author has gone directly to the recent or current scholarly published editions of the writings and correspondence of the trio:

For Hamilton: Harold C. Syrett et al., eds., *The Papers of Alexander Hamilton* (26 vols., New York, 1961–79); Julius Goebel, Jr., Joseph B. Smith, et al., eds., *The Law Practice of Alexander Hamilton: Documents and Commentary* (5 vols., New York, 1964–81).

For Madison: William T. Hutchinson, William M. E. Rachal, Robert A. Rutland, et al., eds., *The Papers of James Madison* (14 vols. to date; Chicago, 1962–76; Charlottesville, 1977–).

For Jay: Richard B. Morris et al., eds., *John Jay: The Making of a Revolutionary, 1745–80: Unpublished Papers* (New York, 1975); *John Jay: The Winning of the Peace, 1780–1784: Unpublished Papers* (New York, 1980); "John Jay: Confederation and Union, 1784–1789: State Papers and Private Correspondence" (forthcoming).

The author has considered and evaluated the array of interpretations offered by the biographical literature. For Hamilton: Henry Cabot Lodge, *Alexander Hamilton* (Boston, 1882); Nathan Schachner, *Alexander Hamilton* (New York, 1946); Broadus Mitchell,

Alexander Hamilton (2 vols., New York, 1957–62); Jacob E. Cooke, ed., *Alexander Hamilton: A Profile* (New York, 1967), and his biography of Hamilton (New York, 1982); James Thomas Flexner, *The Young Hamilton: A Biography* (Boston, 1978); Robert Hendrickson, *Hamilton* (2 vols., New York, 1976); and Gerald Stourzh, *Alexander Hamilton and the Idea of Republican Government* (Stanford, 1970).

For Madison: William C. Rives and Philip R. Fendall, eds., *Letters and Other Writings of James Madison* (4 vols., Philadelphia, 1865); the monumental achievement of Irving Brant, James *Madison* (6 vols., New York and Indianapolis. 1941–61); and more recently Ralph Ketcham's *James Madison* (New York, 1971). Some acute observations about both Madison and Hamilton are to be found in Trevor Colbourn, ed., *Douglass Adair: Fame and the Founding Fathers: Essays* (New York, 1974).

A rich ore may be mined from the published papers of the trio's major correspondents, notably from: John C. Fitzpatrick, ed., *The Writings of George Washington from the Original Manuscript Sources, 1745–1799* (39 vols., Washington, 1931–44); Julian P. Boyd et al., eds., *The Papers of Thomas Jefferson* (20 vols. to date, Princeton, 1956–); Charles Francis Adams, ed., *The Works of John Adams* (10 vols., Boston, 1850–56); Lyman H. Butterfield et al., eds., *Diary and Autobiography of John Adams* (4 vols., Cambridge, Mass., 1961); Robert Rutland, ed., *The Papers of George Mason, 1725–92* (3 vols., Chapel Hill, 1970); Albert Henry Smyth, ed., *The Writings of Benjamin Franklin* (10 vols., New York, 1905–07).

The Confederation Years

The sources moist frequently consulted by the writer for this period are the *Journals of the Continental Congress, 1774–1789* (Washington, 1904–37), Worthington C. Ford et al., eds., along with the Papers of the Continental Congress, 1774–1789 (Record Group

360, National Archives—on microfilm). In addition, the happenings of Congress are often acutely reported in Edmund C. Burnett, ed., *Letters of Members of the Continental Congress* (8 vols., Washington, 1921–36); and in a new and enlarged edition currently edited by Paul H. Smith et al., *Letters of Delegates to Congress, 1774–1789* (10 vols. to date, Washington, 1976–).

The monographic literature on the Congress is enriched by Edmund C. Burnett, *The Continental Congress* (New York, 1941); by H. James Henderson, *Party Politics in the Continental Congress* (New York, 1974); by Jack N. Rakove, *The Beginnings of National Politics: An Interpretive History of the Continental Congress* (New York, 1979); and by Peter S. Onuf, *The Origins of the Federal Republic* (Philadelphia, 1983).

The Confederation years generally, and a variety of topics considered in this book, have been examined, and with variety of interpretations, by Andrew C. McLaughlin, *The Confederation and the Constitution* (New York, 1905); Allan Nevins, *American States During and After the Revolution* (New York, 1927); Merrill Jensen, *The New Nation: A History of the United States During the Confederation, 1781–1789* (New York, 1950); E. James Ferguson, *The Power of the Purse: A History of American Public Finance, 1776–1790* (Chapel Hill, 1961); Jackson Turner Main, *Political Parties Before the Constitution* (Chapel Hill, 1973), and *The Social Structure of Revolutionary America* (Princeton, 1965); and W. W. Crosskey and W. Jeffrey, *Politics and the Constitution in the History of the United States* (3 vols., Chicago, 1953–80).

For the Newburgh Affair see especially Richard H. Kohn, *Eagle and Sword: The Federalists and the Creation of the Military Establishment in America, 1783–1802* (New York, 1975).

The economy and the depression are concisely but expertly treated in Curtis P. Nettels, *The Emergence of a National Economy, 1775–1815* (New York, 1961). Among a variety of treatments of foreign trade, and most definitive for its subject is Jacob M. Price, *France and the Chesapeake: A History of the French Tobacco Monopoly, 1674–1791, and of Its Relationship to the British and American Trade* (2 vols., Ann Arbor, 1973).

For the issues of foreign affairs in these years, see particularly Richard B. Morris, *The Peacemakers: The Great Powers and American Independence* (New York, 1965; reprint Boston, 1983) and his "John Jay: Confederation and Union," cited above. See also Samuel Flagg Bemis, *Pinckney's Treaty: America's Advantage from Europe's Distress, 1783–1800* (rev. ed., New Haven, 1960); and Frederick W. Marks III, *Independence on Trial: Foreign Affairs and the Making of the Constitution* (Baton Rouge, La., 1973).

For Shays' Rebellion the author has examined the Massachusetts county court records of Berkshire, Hampshire, and Worcester, as well as the Hawley Papers in the New York Public Library. The interview of Daniel Shays with General Rufus Putnam is recorded in C. O. Parmenter, *History of Pelham, Massachusetts* (Boston, 1898), 395–98. See also David P. Szatmary, *Shays' Rebellion: The Making of an Agrarian Insurrection* (Amherst, 1980); Neville Meaney, Studies in the American Revolution (North Sydney, 1976); Van Beck Hall, *Politics Without Parties: Massachusetts, 1780–1791* (Pittsburgh, 1972); and Richard B. Morris, "Insurrection in Massachusetts," in Daniel Aaron, ed., *America in Crisis* (New York, 1952), 21–49.

The Ideological Battle

The political issues of the Revolutionary era have been reexamined with discernment in Bernard Bailyn's *Ideological Origins of the American Revolution* (Cambridge, Mass., 1967), with special emphasis on the heavy debt of some American pamphleteers to English radical Whig thought; and in Gordon Wood's magisterial *The Creation of the American Republic* (Chapel Hill, 1969), with its extensive and sympathetic treatment of the Whig republican arguments. For a critique of the Populist-Progressive interpretation of the Confederation years, see Richard B. Morris, *The American Revolution Reconsidered* (New York, 1967), 127–62. Parallels between the Federalist-Republican controversy of the 1790s and the much earlier contest between the Country and Court parties in England are underscored in J. G. A. Pocock, *The Machiavellian Movement: Florentine Political Thought and the Atlantic Republican Tradition* (Princeton, N.J., 1978). On both sides of the ocean it was the fear of corruption and the abuse of power which moved discordant factions to accept the notion of balanced government. James H. Hutson, "Country, Court and Constitution: Antifederalism and the Historians," *William and Mary Quarterly,* 3d ser. (1981), XXXVIII, 337–68, finds in Pocock a model to reconcile historiographic issues of the previous decade. Contrariwise, John Patrick Diggins, *The Lost Soul of American Politics* (New York, 1985), sees self-interest and property as the driving forces in the drafting of the Constitution and would discount virtue, community, and benevolence as so much rhetoric.

The pamphlet war between Federalists and Antifederalists is covered in a number of monographs and editions, including Jackson Turner Main, *The Antifederalists: Critics of the Constitution, 1781–88* (New York, 1974); Paul Leicester Ford, ed., *Pamphlets on the Constitution of the United States* (Brooklyn, N.Y., 1888), and Herbert J. Storing, ed., *The Complete Anti-Federalist* (7 vols., Chicago, 1981).

The Constitutional Convention

The standard source is Max Farrand, ed., *The Records of the Federal Convention of 1787* (3d ed., 3 vols., New Haven, 1927), for which a supplement is currently being compiled by James H. Hutson. The Convention records can be found in compact one-volume format in the selection and arrangement of Charles C. Tansill, *Documents Illustrative of the Formation of the Union* (Washington, 1927).

Ratification

For coverage of the ratification debates throughout the country, see Jonathan Elliot, ed., *The Debates in the Several State Conventions on the Adoption of the Federal Constitution . . .* (reprint ed., 5 vols., Philadelphia and Washington, 1866)—an edition that is being superseded by the current series in progress by John F. Kaminski and Gaspare J. Saladino et al., eds., *The Documentary History of the Ratification of the Constitution* (4 vols. to date, Madison, 1981–).

In this book special attention has been paid to the ratification in Virginia and New York. For the former, see David Robertson, *Debates and Proceedings of the Convention of Virginia* (2nd ed. Richmond, Va., 1805), and Hugh Blair Grigsby, *History of the Virginia Convention of 1788* (2 vols., Richmond, 1890–91). Narrative accounts drawn upon Grigsby are provided in Albert J. Beveridge, *The Life of John Marshall* (2 vols., Boston, 1916), especially vol. I, chaps. IX–XII, and in Brant's *Madison,* cited above.

The debates in the New York Ratifying Convention are covered in a variety of discrete sources. Jay's protégé, Francis Child, published *The Debates and Proceedings* (New York, 1788), but unfortunately discontinued a stenographic record beyond June 28, thereafter merely summarizing motions introduced. The significant gap can be filled by examining the "Journal" of the Convention's secretary, John McKesson, in the New York State Library, and his "Notes" in the New-York Historical Society. Other missing gaps were captured by Melancton Smith's Notes in the State Library, and the notes of Gilbert Livingston, a delegate from Dutchess County, which provide the most complete coverage for the period beginning July 14 (New York Public Library). There are fragmentary bits by Robert R. Livingston in the New-York Historical Society, and by Robert Lansing, covering June 27–28, in the Genêt Papers at the Library of Congress. Finally, contemporary newspaper coverage and the correspondence of Jay and Hamilton during those weeks in Poughkeepsie help round out the record. A useful monograph is Linda Grant De Pauw's *The Eleventh Pillar: New York State and the Federal Constitution* (Ithaca, 1966).

Acknowledgments

Like James Madison, I feel that one must settle one's debts, and a considerable number have been incurred in the course of this project. From its inception I have been sustained by the encouragement of a great history buff, Lou Reda of Easton, Pennsylvania, and by my wife, Berenice Robinson Morris, whose literary assessments, as in past undertakings, have saved me from a number of wrong turnings. At every stage of writing, research, and production of copy I have levied heavily on the special skills of Ene Sirvet, Associate Editor of the Papers of John Jay. She has proved indefatigable in running down leads, resolving ambiguities, and verifying the facts. On numerous occasions I have drawn upon the constitutional scholarship of my associates in Project '87, and have exploited the learning of Richard B. Bernstein of the New York Bar and my son Jeffrey B. Morris of the University of Pennsylvania. Cynthia Harrison, the editor of *this Constitution*, has been most helpful in locating illustrations, as have Hobart G. Cawood, Superintendent, Independence National Historical Park, and Margaret C. M. Christman and Monroe H. Fabian, Curator, Department of Painting and Sculpture of the National Portrait Gallery, Smithsonian Institution. This book has immensely profited by the advice of John Macrae III, editor-in-chief of Holt, Rinehart and Winston, whose scrupulous reading of my manuscript and literary judgments, both critical and constructive, are deeply appreciated, along with the valued editorial burdens assumed by Meta Brophy, and others on the firm's staff.

I am, perhaps, less fortunate than the "three witnesses" who, by writing pseudonymously, managed to avoid individual responsibility for any imperfections in their incomparable essays. The debts I have incurred need be gratefully acknowledged, but the responsibility cannot be shared.

—Richard B. Morris

Index